COOL CACTI AND SUCCULENTS FOR HOT GARDENS

Greg Sta—
12/3/2024

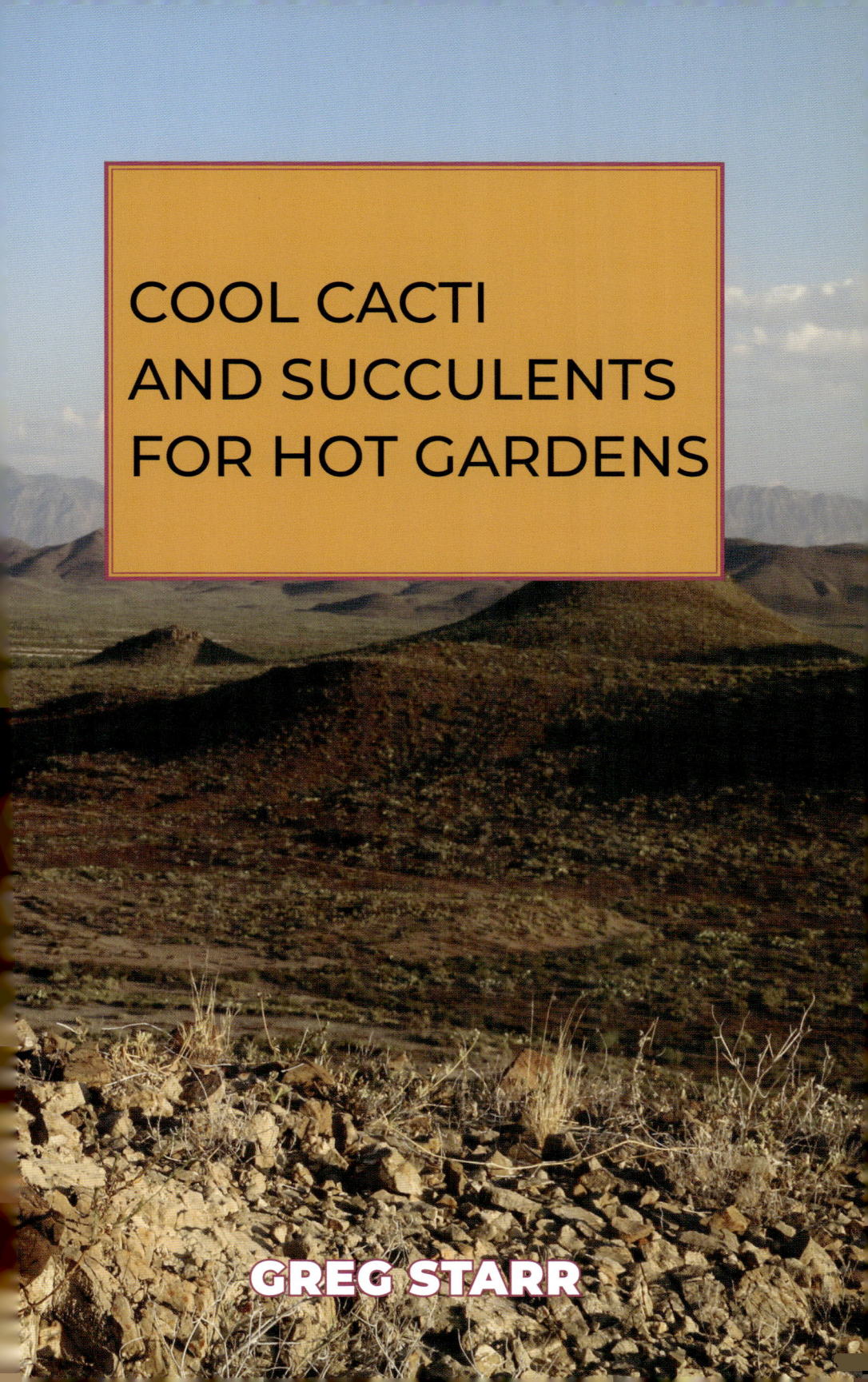

COOL CACTI AND SUCCULENTS FOR HOT GARDENS

GREG STARR

To Carol, the guiding light in my life – without her love and support, this hobby gone wild would never have found its direction and focus.

To Brian, the steadying hand and voice of reason – without your tireless efforts and willingness to learn new skills this book would not have become a reality.

© 2024 Greg Starr
All rights reserved

No part of this publication may be reproduced, stored in or introduced into a retrieval system or transmitted, in any form by any means (electronic, mechanical, photocopy, recording, or otherwise), without the prior written permission of the copyright owner, except by a reviewer who may quote brief passages in reviews or citations.

This book is sold subject to the condition that it shall not, by way of trade or other means, be lent, re-sold, hired out, or otherwise circulated without the author's prior consent in any form of binding or cover other that in which it is published and without a similar condition including this condition being imposed on the subsequent purchaser.

All photographs are copyrighted by the author and photographers.
Published in 2021 by Greg Starr

Printed in Tucson, Arizona at Arizona Lithographers
All photos by the author, except where noted
Cover: clockwise from top left: *Agave parryi, Astrophytum capricorne, Yucca carnerosana, Ferocactus pilosus, Opuntia santa-rita* Pages 2-3: *Echinocereus stramineus*; page 5: *Thelocactus heterochromus*; page 6: *Agave ovatifolia*; page 7: *Neolloydia conoidea*; page 8: *Nolina nelsonii*; page 19: *Echinocactus platyacanthus*; page 20: *Yucca rigida*; page 332: *Dasylirion quadrangulatum*; page 336: *Carnegiea gigantea*; page 343 *Ferocactus acanthodes*: page 344: *Dasylirion miquihuanense*; page 349: *Ariocarpus retusus* (lower left) *Agave victoriae-reginae* (lower right); page 352 *Fouquieria columnaris*.

Proofing and editing by Tristan Davis
Design: Brian Starr, Phoenix, Arizona

Library of Congress Cataloging-in-Publication Data

Starr,Greg, 1957-
Cool Cacti and Succulents for Hot Gardens / Greg Starr p. cm.
Includes index.
ISBN: 979-8-218-49354-7
1. Drought-tolerant plant--Southwest, New. 2. Landscape gardening--Water conservation—Southwest, New. 3. Xeriscaping—Southwest, New. 4. Cactus, New. 5. Succulent, New.

http://www.starr-nursery.com

TABLE OF CONTENTS

Preface 7
Introduction 9
    Categorization and Terminology 10
    How to use This Book 11
    Etymology 12
    Field Notes 12
    Description 12
    Culture 13
    Identification 15
    Landscape Application 15
    Precautions 15
    Landscape Design in the West 17
    Digging in the Dirt 17
The Plant Encyclopedia 21
Glossary 327
References 330
Plant Database 333
Plant Index 341
    By Common Name 341
    By Botanical Name 343
Acknowledgements 346

PREFACE

When the first version of Cool Plants for Hot Gardens sold out, the decision was made to not reprint, so I took the opportunity to put together a revised edition. The format was changed drastically and each species was given two facing pages allowing for larger pictures and for all the information to be more easily seen. However, to keep the size manageable, I had to reduce the number of species from 200 to 150. To achieve this number I removed all the cacti and succulents with the intent to produce a companion book devoted solely to those magnificent plants. This decision allowed me to increase the number of cacti and succulents from about 50 to 150.

For Cool Cacti and Succulents for Hot Gardens, I have followed the same format as used in Cool Plants, so each species has two facing pages, at least two large photos, generally one of the plant and one of the flowers or another distinctive feature.

INTRODUCTION

Many residents in urban areas of the southwestern United States are transplants from regions where cacti and succulents are misunderstood. They are viewed as prickly plants that hurt if you touch them. While this may be true, many have large showy flowers that attract a variety of pollinators including birds, bees, butterflies, moths, and even bats. Some cacti and succulents have a long blooming season so the splashy flowers can be enjoyed for an extended period. Some cacti are large and have a bold form drawing attention when planted in the landscape while others are small and best viewed close-up in decorative pots. Many of the non-cactus succulents included are large statement plants that can be used as an accent in a xeric landscape much the same way large cacti are used.

This book is designed to help the homeowner, gardener, and landscape professional not only understand, select, install, and maintain cool cacti and succulents that can be used in the southwestern United States but also to generate interest in the field of cacti and succulents by including some plants that you must view up close. While selecting the plants for this book I took a hard look at which cacti and succulents to include. There were more than 150 plants that I would like to have included here but I had to draw the line at some point. Forgive me if I left out one or more of your favorite plants but know that I had to leave out some of my favorites as well. For example, *Aztekium* species and *Geohintonia mexicana* are exciting to see in habitat, but they are very small and difficult to find in the trade. However, plants such as ***Astrophytum asterias*** and ***Ariocarpus fissuratus*** may be on the small side, but they are more easily found in the trade and can be showcased in a potted collection.

While the term **cactus** is straightforward and unambiguous, referring to members of the family Cactaceae, the term "**succulent**" is fraught with controversy within the cactus and succulent community. Exactly what the term succulent means has been debated for many years and will not be resolved here. Rather, I use succulent as a loose concept incorporating plants that may not necessarily store water but are xeric and have a "cool factor" whether in a landscape or container. I chose not to include many traditional succulent plants such as *Crassula*, *Echeveria*, and *Kalanchoe* because of their limited use as landscape plants outside of frost-free regions. Other succulents like *Conophytum* and *Lithops* are well covered in other books and can be somewhat touchy to grow for many gardeners. I wrestled with including palms, cycads, and bulbs, finally deciding against including those because they have been thoroughly covered in other books.

My personal interest has been in those plants that are native to North America, and I have included some of my personal experiences with them in their natural habitat. I talked to other cactus fanciers who have more experience with plants from South America.

Many of the plants included here are staples in the cactus and succulent trade while others are relative newcomers. Many cacti have large showy flowers, but some have small flowers that are best viewed up close making those plants ideal for container culture.

Categorization and Terminology

In Cool Plants for Hot Gardens, I used standard categories such as groundcover, shrub, tree, or vine for the plants but cacti and succulents are their own distinct categories. Here, I use the following categories and subcategories:

- **Accent Plant** - This is not a biological term but a design concept and is reserved for plants used as focal points that catch the eye. Many accent

BOTANICAL NAMES

Recently, there has been an explosion of botanical reclassification resulting in many of our favorite cacti and succulents being burdened with new, difficult to learn names that can be next to impossible to remember, and seemingly make no sense to the casual gardener. For instance, many plants in the genus *Mammillaria* have been moved to the genus *Cochemia* based on DNA analysis. I have decided to retain the more well-known names while also listing the current name.

Much of this taxonomic reclassification is the result of DNA studies and the biological classification system known as **cladistics** in which plants and other organisms are grouped together based on whether they are derived from a common ancestor. The goal of cladistics is to have **monophyletic** groups, plants or other organisms, that are all descendants of an inferred common ancestor. If this is all too much for you, you are not alone, my eyes sometimes glaze over when reading about this also.

plants are cactus and succulents such as *Agave* species, *Aloe* species, *Dasylirion* species, *Nolina* species, *Fouquieria* species, and *Yucca* species. These have bold or dramatic forms and catch the eye drawing admiring glances. They are frequently long-lived plants that, along with trees, can be used as the backbone of a landscape.

- **Cactus** - These plants are all in the family Cactaceae, and as such are generally succulent and spiny with large colorful flowers. They can be used in just about any xeriscape in the southwestern U.S.. Some are large and some are small and I have further refined the category to quickly identify the general form:
  - **Barrel Cactus**
  - **Clustering Cactus**
  - **Columnar Cactus**
  - **Small Barrel Cactus**
  - **Small Cactus**
  - **Small Columnar Cactus**
  - **Sprawling Cactus**

- **Succulent** - A loosely defined category generally used for plants that have some type of succulence whether in the leaves, roots, or trunks.
  - **Succulent Rosette**
  - **Shrub-like Succulent**
  - **Tree-like Succulent**
  - **Columnar Succulent**

HOW TO USE THIS BOOK

Each of the 150 species accounts in the plant encyclopedia is designed to provide both a narrative description of the plant as well as a reference source for quickly looking up pertinent information. An "at a glance" summary table provides a quick reference on the plant's size, flower color and season, sun exposure, water usage, relative growth rate, pruning requirements, and hardiness. There will also be one or more of the following icons at the top of each species accounts indicating:

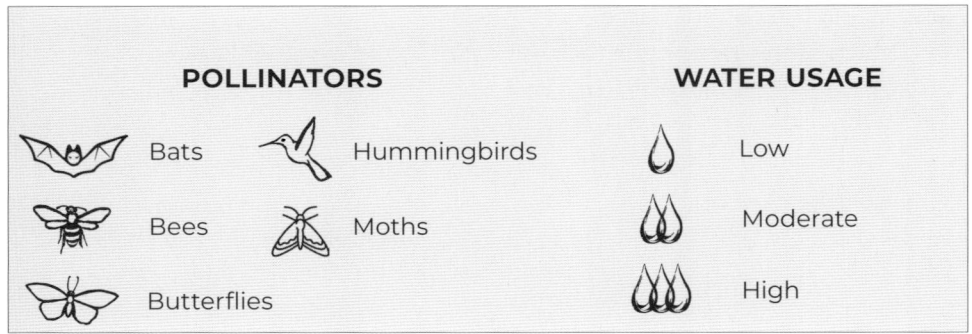

Introduction

ETYMOLOGY
When possible, I give the name of the person who described the plant and the meaning of the species name.

FIELD NOTES
Many of the featured plants grow in arid North America, and I offer personal accounts when possible and information relating to native distribution, soil type, exposure, and elevation that will assist the intrepid explorer to spot these plants when out hiking the desert. To plant nerds or natural history buffs, these details are inherently interesting, while to the non-traveler, the accounts might just be fun reading. Knowing these things may also help you select plants that are compatible with each other or those that will give a consistent look or feel to your landscape.

DESCRIPTION
A full description of the plant is included, detailing the usual height and width, the leaves (if present), flowers, flowering season, and any significant fruit characteristics. The focus is on striking features of the plant, which might be the overall form, the spines, or the flowers.

CULTURE
In this section I discuss the following topics for growing the particular plant.

FROST DAMAGE FACTORS
Several factors influence the severity of damage to frost sensitive plants:

 Overnight low - The lower the temperature, the more likely that damage will occur.

 Duration - The longer a plant is exposed to subfreezing temperatures, the more likely it is to be damaged.

 Daytime temperatures - The colder the next day, the more likely the plant will be damaged.

 Consecutive nights below freezing - Some plants can withstand one night of extreme cold, but not a second night.

 Winter precipitation - Plants that are normally cold hardy when dry are generally not as hardy when subject to both cold and wet conditions.

However, cacti and succulents grown in an area that receives snow might actually benefit from the insulation provided by that snow layer.

Hardiness

Some plants are inherently more frost-tolerant than others. Typically, plants that have evolved in cold climates can tolerate lower temperatures than those from tropical areas. Those plants from cold climates undergo winter acclimation, which is a process of shutting down in preparation for the cold weather to come. This physiological hardening off process can begin as early as late summer and might be triggered by decreasing day length, in which case the plant will begin to shut down regardless of temperature, going into winter dormancy even if the fall temperatures are abnormally high. Decreasing temperature could also trigger the process, and plants that start going dormant based on temperature are more susceptible to frost damage if the fall temperatures stay abnormally high and then are hit with a sudden, dramatic drop in temperature.

Although I use USDA plant hardiness zones for cold hardiness, that does not tell the whole story of a plant's ability to survive long term in a southwestern U.S. landscape. Some low elevation southwestern cities experience brutally hot and long summers, and some plants that can make it through their winter temperatures, might have trouble acclimating to the heat, especially when overnight summer temperatures might not drop below 90°F. Still, if a plant strikes your fancy, it might be worth a try to see if you can find the right conditions for it to grow.

Drinking Habits

All plants, including those that are drought tolerant, will require supplemental watering when planted in the ground, especially after being pampered while growing in the nursery. The key is to provide enough water to get the plants established, but not so much that they put on abnormal growth and become dependent on receiving supplemental water for the rest of their lives. Many plants that are considered drought tolerant in the southwestern United States will be able to survive on rainfall or minimal supplemental water in the hottest part of the year but will grow better if given some extra water in times of no rainfall. Obviously, water needs will vary depending on soil type, sun exposure, type of plant, time of year, and age of the plant. Most cacti and succulents have CAM metabolism in which stomates are closed when temperatures are very hot. This can be a problem in cities where overnight lows in summer stay above 80–90°F. If you live in Phoenix, AZ try giving your plants sips of water on a regular basis in summer rather than large gulps infrequently. The idea is to prevent the soil from becoming too wet and drowning the roots, and inhibiting the plants' ability to take up water. Misting the plants and lightly wetting the top layer of soil should keep the roots healthy without drowning them.

Growth Rates are Relative

In general, the terms "fast," "moderate," and "slow" are used to describe the growth rate of a plant relative to its form (i.e., groundcover, shrub, tree, succulent) and its eventual size. You will notice in this book that I could not fit some plants into "fast," "moderate," or "slow," so I used fuzzy, overlapping terms "moderately fast" or "moderately slow."

Growth rate will vary dependant on several factors, including but not limited to climate of the city they are grown in, length of growing season, and amount of supplemental water supplied during the growing season.

Exposure

Every plant looks and grows best when planted in the proper exposure, and finding that perfect spot will sometimes take trial and error. Some plants prefer full sun, while others like to hang out in some shade. Many plants that need some afternoon shade in the desert cities like Tucson and Phoenix, where summer temperatures routinely climb above 100° F during the day, will grow fine in full sun in the more moderate climate of coastal cities like San Diego and Santa Barbara or even cities with summer temperatures in the low 90's F.

I make a distinction between partial shade and filtered light. Partial shade means the plant can be in full shade for part of the day, such as when planted on the east or west side of a building. Filtered light means the plant can be placed under the shade of a tree or shrub that provides a mix of shade and sun all day long. Many desert and desert-adapted plants will require less maintenance and look more natural if they are "grown hard." This refers to placing the plant in as much sun as it will tolerate and applying as little water as it will tolerate.

Agaves pruned into manicured pineapple tops and shrubs into cylinders create high-maintenance and unnatural landscapes

Avoid Pruning Atrocities

Very few cacti or succulents require any pruning although the occasional tree-like succulent might need minimal trimming to enhance its shape. However, as with landscape trees and shrubs too much pruning or indiscriminate shearing can be unhealthy and weaken the plant. A plant that has been damaged by frost will need some careful selective pruning to remove the damaged growth.

IDENTIFICATION

In this section I give tips on how to distinguish the species from similar looking plants or related species that are covered in the book.

LANDSCAPE APPLICATION

Here, I give suggestions for how the plants can be used in a southwestern U.S. landscape and recommend some plants that pair well and have similar cultural requirements. Species names that appear in ***purple bold italics*** indicate those can be found in this book, while those that are not in the book are simply italicized. For a detailed description of most Agaves, check out my other publication, *Agaves: Living Sculptures for Landscapes and Containers.* Many of the recommended companion plants are covered in Cool Plants for Hot Gardens.

PRECAUTIONS

Although I have picked plants for this book that can succeed in xeric landscapes in many southwestern U.S. cities, every gardener runs into challenges, and I have tried to give you a heads up on some of the more common ones. Sometimes it may be that rabbits will munch on your new plantings or that packrats have set up shop in your yard and nibble on your favorite plants overnight. I mention likely insect pests and other diseases that affect the plants, but by no means do I cover every problem encountered in every situation. If you and your plants are struggling, contact your local agricultural extension service for more specialized help.

There are two simple criteria to consider when picking plants for your landscape. First, choose the plant that will fit in the available space and not outgrow the spot. Second, make sure the plant will grow in the sun exposure offered by that spot. A plant that is adapted to full sun performs better when placed in full sun than when planted in deep shade, and a plant that needs shade will burn when planted in full sun. Be aware that many cacti and succulents are frequently grown under shade cloth in nurseries and will need to be slowly acclimated to full sun. The south side of plants grown in full sun in the nursery should be marked so they can be oriented the same way in the landscape to prevent sunburning.

Geographic Scope and Climate Zones

Geography is one key to a good fit between your landscape and what thrives in it. The geographic range covered here includes the arid areas in the southwestern United States extending from southern California east through southern Nevada, Arizona, New Mexico, and into central Texas. The area encompasses Chihuahuan, Sonoran, and Mohave Desert climates plus parts of coastal southern California that receive similar amounts of annual rainfall as some places in the Sonoran Desert. Each plant described in this book is suitable for cultivation in some of the following metropolitan areas of Los Angeles, San Diego, and Palm Springs in California; Las Vegas, Nevada; Phoenix, Tucson, Sierra Vista, Green Valley, and Yuma in Arizona; Albuquerque, Lordsburg, and Las Cruces in New Mexico; El Paso, Austin, and San Antonio in Texas. If you live in a city or town between these places, use the one most like your neighborhood to guide your selections.

There are obsessed growers around the country who frequently experiment with new plants. One of my favorite sayings comes from Tony Avent at Plant Delights Nursery in Raleigh, North Carolina. He says, "I consider every plant hardy until I've killed it myself, at least three times." Sometimes it might take even more than three trials to find the right spot for that special plant, so do not give up; try it again.

Although I use USDA plant zones for cold hardiness, that is not the only climatic factor that affects the health of your plants. Summer highs and rainfall should also be considered when selecting plants for your landscape. I have included an abbreviated USDA Plant Hardiness Zone table starting with zone 7a. Microclimates should be considered when contemplating which plants to put where in your landscape. A south or west-facing wall will give a couple degrees of heat in the winter allowing the use of marginally hardy plants, but will also radiate heat in summer making it more difficult for plants to survive the heat.

Landscape Design in the West

This book is a plant encyclopedia, not a design manual, but a few tips on design can help you pick the right plants. The first is to find healthy gardens you like in your area and shamelessly copy favorite elements. Second, dream up ideas as you peruse beautiful books, letting your imagination run wild. Third, check plantings in the street medians and along sidewalks for tough plants that perform well in your immediate

Typical Lowest Annual Temperature (F)	USDA Hardiness Zone
0 to 5	7a
5 to 10	7b
10 to 15	8a
15 to 20	8b
20 to 25	9a
25 to 30	9b
30 to 35	10a

area and use those in the outer zone of your xeriscape.

You will probably agree that many commercial landscapes throughout the southwestern United States lack flair. You can avoid this uninspiring effect in your space by growing a wonderful garden if you unlock your imagination, lose your inhibitions, and let go of your need to control. Key building blocks are hardscape features like patios and walkways. These elements provide structure yet allow the flexibility of working with all manner of plants. Place trees where you will want shade and work in cactus and succulents in concert with flowering shrubs and perennials for a complete well-rounded landscape.

People frequently comment to me that they just need another plant or two and their landscape will be finished, but some plants are naturally short-lived while others die out for one reason or another. You might be cruising one of the many local plant sales and find a plant new to you that you just have to try. Try to think of your landscape garden as a living, dynamic project that is always growing and changing. You should be having fun by now and ready to get creative as you choose and place long-lived cacti and succulents including bold and beautiful *Agave*, *Aloe*, *Dasylirion*, *Hesperaloe*, and *Yucca*. Along with your trees, these accents will make up the backbone of your garden and allow you to play around with other perennials, bulbs, and seasonal flowers.

DIGGING IN THE DIRT

Admit it, you have only skimmed the "soils" section of those other gardening books on your shelf and gone straight to the pretty pictures of plants. You are forgiven if you do that with this book, but there are some things that would not hurt you to know about the primary source of nutrients, water, and oxygen for all land plants.

Soils 101

Soil is a mixture of organic and inorganic components, and many large cities in the southwestern United States are in dry climates where there is very little opportunity for organic matter to accumulate in the soil. Therefore, the native plants are adapted to these soils and do not need large amounts of organic material to grow.

Inorganic materials are sand, silt, or clay, and these materials affect the rate of water movement in the soil, its availability to plants, and the subsequent watering schedule. Sand particles are relatively large, allowing for fast penetration and good drainage. Sandy soils generally mean more frequent watering. Clay particles are the smallest, which translates into slow water penetration and poor drainage, greater water holding, and less frequent watering. For example, you might need to thoroughly soak the root zone of an established low water use plant in a sandy soil 1–2 times a week during the summer, while that same plant in a clay soil might need soakings only 2–3 times a month.

To a point, soil depth and consistency can make or break a root system. In general, the deeper the soil, the deeper the roots can go, which gives the plant a larger base from which to draw water and nutrients. Because cacti and succulents have shallow root systems, the soil depth is not too critical unless there is an underlying layer of **caliche**.

Caliche is composed of calcium carbonate and acts like a layer of cement. At times you may feel that your landscape sits on the largest caliche deposit ever discovered, but it is found widely across arid and semi-arid parts of the world. **Hardpan** is a general term for a dense layer of fused soil that is impervious to water. Alter **hardpan** by working in sand and compost to improve drainage and create more air pockets for the roots. Another work-around is to create large flowing mounds with soil more conducive to growing cacti and succulents. A third method is to experiment with creating a crevice garden that uses porous soil and narrow planting slots. This could be especially useful for small cacti and succulents that grow well when crowded by rocks such as ***Ariocarpus***, ***Astrophytum***, and smaller ***Mammillaria*** species.

Planting

Cacti and succulents generally prefer being in soil with excellent drainage but will adapt to heavy soil if supplemental watering is adjusted to prevent roots from rotting. Dig the planting hole to about the depth of the rootball and up to twice the width. Fill the hole with water to check the drainage. If the water drains out at the rate of about 1-inch per hour, the soil is fine. If the water remains, it might be necessary to amend the soil to increase the drainage. After you dig the hole, remove the plant from the pot and, if the roots are packed into the soil, roughen and loosen the soil and existing roots. This promotes vigorous rooting that gives the plant a much larger nutrient and water base to draw from, resulting in a healthy plant. Place the plant at the "Goldilocks" level (not too high and not too low) then backfill with the native soil that was removed when digging the hole.

Sit back and watch your plants grow!

THE PLANT ENCYCLOPEDIA

150+
COOL CACTI AND SUCCULENTS

Agave bovicornuta
Cow's Horn Agave
SUCCULENT ROSETTE

SIZE (H x W)	2–3 feet x 2–4 feet
FLOWER COLOR	Yellow
FLOWER SEASON	Spring
EXPOSURE	Filtered sun, part shade
WATER	Low to moderate
GROWTH RATE	Moderate to fast
PRUNING	None
HARDINESS	Low 20's F, zones 9a–11

Etymology When naming this species, Howard Gentry used the Latin *bovi-* for cow and the Latin *cornutus-* for horned, a reference to the marginal teeth that resemble the horns on a cow.

Field Notes Plants occur along Mexico Highway 16, a twisting turning road that snakes its way between Hermosillo and Ciudad Chihuahua. In June of 2006, I was traveling west along Highway 16 from the logging town of Yecora to Hermosillo and rounded a bend only to see the bright green dots of these agaves as they stood out against the barren landscape beneath leafless oak trees waiting on the summer rains before bursting into life. Plants grow on rocky open slopes in the oak woodland and pine-oak forest zones between about 3,000–6,000 feet elevation.

Description The **rosettes** are medium-size and solitary, growing 2–3 feet tall and 2–4 feet wide, rarely larger if in the right climate. Leaves are bright green to dark green, broadly **lanceolate**, 18–24 inches long by 6 inches wide, and narrowing to a sharp terminal point. Yellowish, reddish, or dark brown **teeth** decorate the **crenate** leaf edges and curve both away from and back toward the center of the plant. The flower stalk is 15–22 feet tall that has short side branches with bright yellow and green flowers clustered at the ends.

Culture Plants are generally hardy to the low-20's F and can be used in USDA zones 9a–11, but might need protection on the really cold nights. Keep the soil dry in winter and they will have a better chance of surviving winter low temperatures in the low 20's F. Established plants are low-water-using but will grow faster if you provide supplemental water during the growing season, but make sure the soil has very good drainage so roots can dry out. These do best when placed in some shade in cities with very hot summers such as Phoenix, Tucson, and Yuma. They can tolerate full sun in zones that do not experience extreme summer temperatures.

Identification *Agave bovicornuta* plants are smaller than those of *Agave inaequidens* and *Agave maximiliana*.

Landscape Application In cities with hot summers, plants are best placed under the canopy of a deciduous or semi-deciduous desert tree such as *Acacia constricta*, or *Eysenhardtia orthocarpa*. Plant one near a patio or other visible spot to best appreciate the marvelous bud prints created by the highly decorative teeth. Mix this agave with other green leaved plants to create a lush, subtropical effect. Plant among lush green shade-loving accent plants, perennials, and small shrubs including *Ageratum corymbosum*, *Aquilegia chrysantha*, *Conoclinium dissectum*, *Dioon edule*, *Heuchera sanguinea*, and *Poliomintha maderensis*.

Precautions Be on the lookout for any one of the following pests that can impact agaves; Agave weevil, Agave mites, **running bugs**, and **mealybugs**. Rabbits and packrats might chew on leaves and javelina like to uproot plants.

Agave bracteosa
Squid Agave, Green Spider Agave
SUCCULENT ROSETTE

Etymology   The species name is based on the Latin *bracteosus* – referring to the many bracts on the inflorescence as noted by the 19th Century American botanist Sereno Watson.

SIZE (H x W)	1–2 feet x 1–2 feet, clusters 3–6 feet across
FLOWER COLOR	White
FLOWER SEASON	Summer
EXPOSURE	Filtered sun, full sun
WATER	Low to moderate
GROWTH RATE	Moderately slow
PRUNING	None
HARDINESS	10° F, zones 8a–11

Field Notes   Plants of this attractive species are fond of desperately clinging to vertical limestone rock where they look like huge green spiders climbing along the cliff faces. One of my favorite stops along Mexico Highway 57 is San Lazaro Pass. One can generally find a safe spot to park along the side of the road and walk to the limestone cliff face. The plants are tucked in small cracks and fissures on the north and northeast-facing cliffs, so arrive early on a crisp summer morning for maximum ambient light for your photos. *Agave bracteosa* is restricted to limestone cliffs in Coahuila and Nuevo León in northeastern Mexico from about 3,000–5,500 feet elevation.

Description   In their native habitat, plants grow to about 1–2 feet tall by 1–2 feet across with clusters reaching about 3 feet in diameter. Individual **rosettes** have a graceful urn-like shape formed by the narrow

Cool Cacti and Succulents for Hot Gardens

leaves that grow up and curve out and down, resembling the drooping handlebar mustache seen on cowboys of the Old West. In cultivation, plants will produce numerous offsets and form a 3–6-foot diameter mass of **rosettes**. Leaves are narrow, medium green, and toothless measuring 18–24 inches long by 1-inch-wide. Although the overall shape resembles an urn, the plants do not make a good water jug. The flower stalk is 4–8 feet tall and densely packed with white 1-inch-long flowers.

Culture Keep plants dry in winter, and they will tolerate winter lows to at least 10° F, meaning they are fine for use in USDA zones 8a–11. The growth rate is moderately slow but can be bumped up with supplemental watering once every 10–14 days in summer. Plants develop their most interesting forms when grown in filtered light in cities that experience temperatures above 100° F for much of the summer. They can tolerate full sun in cities with mild summers where the temperature rarely goes above 90° F. Grow in a fast-draining soil whether in pots or in the ground.

Identification With their soft toothless and spineless recurving leaves, *Agave bracteosa* is unlike any other species.

Landscape Application Plant these beneath the shade of a small desert tree with an open canopy such as *Acacia constricta* or *Eysenhardtia orthocarpa*. Use other Chihuahuan Desert cacti and succulents like **Echinocactus platyacanthus**, **Echinocereus enneacanthus**, **Ferocactus pilosus**, **Hesperaloe campanulata**, and **Yucca rostrata**. Mix in colorful perennials and small shrubs such as *Amoreuxia palmatifida, Conoclinium dissectum, Dalea capitata, Hibiscus martianus,* and *Zinnia grandiflora*. Get up close and personal with plants in a large decorative container that is placed near the front door or on a patio.

Precautions Young or newly planted specimens will most likely be taste-tested by packrats, rabbits, and javelina, so either plant them inside a secure yard or screen them for the first two or three years.

Agave cerulata
Baja Wax Agave
SUCCULENT ROSETTE

SIZE (H x W)	1–2 feet x 1½–3½ feet
FLOWER COLOR	Yellow
FLOWER SEASON	Spring to summer
EXPOSURE	Full sun
WATER	Drought tolerant to low
GROWTH RATE	Moderately slow
PRUNING	None
HARDINESS	20° F, zones 9a–11

Etymology American botanist William Trelease chose the Latin *cera-*, meaning wax and indicated the **glaucous** inflorescence was "touched with wax."

Field Notes I have seen the three subspecies of *Agave cerulata* in Baja California and the fourth on Isla San Esteban in the Gulf of California. Some of the most attractive plants to be seen are on a hill near the dry lakebed of Laguna Chapala, which is just off Mexico Federal Highway 1. *Agave cerulata* subspecies *subcerulata* is common in the Sierra San Francisco in the northern part of Baja California Sur. There are beautiful plants of *Agave cerulata* subspecies *nelsonii* at the southern end of the Sierra San Pedro Mártir. These attractive plants primarily grow on rocky granitic hillsides and sandy flats from about 300–2,400 feet.

Description There is a large amount of variation in the plants, and they can form small to medium size **rosettes** and **offset** prolifically to eventually form clusters up to 6 feet in diameter. Rosettes are 1–2 feet tall by 1½–3½ feet across. Leaves are thick and rigid 8–15 inches long by 2–3½ inches wide and **acuminate** to the sharp tip. Color varies from yellowish green, green, **glaucous** green, or **glaucous** blue. Leaf margin is straight or rarely **crenate** with small **teats** topped by small white, brown, or gray **teeth** with a brown ring encircling the base. An 8–15-foot tall stalk has short side branches in the upper one-third, each with small clusters of 2-inch-long yellow flowers at the tips.

Culture Plants are generally hardy to at least 20° F and can be used in USDA zones 9a–11 although they might need some protection on the coldest nights. Keep the soil dry in winter to maximize the cold hardiness. Plants have a moderately slow growth rate that speeds up slightly when given supplemental water once every 2–3 weeks during the growing season. Established plants are low-water-using, but do not grow much unless watered. These will tolerate full sun in most any zone 9a–11 city in the desert southwest. Place them in a soil type that has very good drainage and allow roots to dry between water applications.

Identification Typically, *Agave cerulata* plants have a brown "ringlet" at the base of the teeth that separates them from *Agave deserti* and *Agave sobria*.

Landscape Application These are perfect for the hot summer cities in the desert southwest and thrive in harsh conditions. They are equally at home in a hardcore cactus and succulent garden or mixed with tough, low-water-use desert trees, shrubs, and perennials. Use plants such *Baileya multiradiata*, *Calliandra eriophylla*, *Glandularia gooddingii*, and *Tetraneuris acaulis* for color, and cacti and succulents such as *Agave gentryi*, *Echinocereus enneacanthus*, *Ferocactus gracilis*, and *Fouquieria splendens*.

Precautions Watch for Agave snout weevil, mites, and **running bugs**. Packrats and rabbits might taste-test the leaves and javelina might dig them up for fun.

Agave colorata
Mescal Ceniza
SUCCULENT ROSETTE

SIZE (H x W)	1–2 feet x 1–2 feet
FLOWER COLOR	Greenish yellow
FLOWER SEASON	Spring
EXPOSURE	Full sun
WATER	Drought tolerant to low
GROWTH RATE	Moderately fast
PRUNING	None
HARDINESS	Low 20's F, zones 9a–11

Etymology Howard Scott Gentry used the Latin *color-* referring to the leaf color.

Field Notes The common form of *Agave colorata* seen in cultivation most likely originated from near Aquibiquichi in southern Sonora. Brian Kemble and I made the trip to see them on our way back from eastern Mexico in April 2010. We were too late to see plants in flower, but we did find several with very prominent cross-banding. *Agave colorata* is uncommon on volcanic hills along the coast and foothills in thorn forest in southern Sonora and northern Sinaloa from near sea level to about 1,300 feet elevation.

Description These are medium-sized **rosettes** growing to 1–2 feet tall and 1–2 feet wide. The commonly grown form produces many small **offsets** that can be removed and planted elsewhere. Powdery blue-gray leaves are broadly **obovate**, about 12–20 inches long by 6 inches wide at the widest point, narrowing to a sharp 2-inch-long terminal **spine**. Small gray **teeth** are

perched atop large teats on the coarsely **mammillate** leaf margin. The 10–12-foot tall flower stalks have short side branches with numerous greenish yellow flowers and reddish filaments.

Culture Plants are hardy to the low-20's F and can be used in USDA zones 9a–11. Keep the soil dry in winter, and they will have a better chance of surviving winter low temperatures in the high teens F. They have a moderately fast growth rate if given supplemental water during the growing season. Established plants are low-water-using, even drought tolerant, but grow very slowly unless watered in spring and summer. Plants tolerate full sun and are best grown in a fast draining soil.

Identification *Agave colorata* plants are very distinctive and not easily confused with any other species.

Landscape Application These tough sun-loving plants are perfect for just about any low-water-use landscape in the desert climes of Arizona and southern California. Find a spot where the plants will be highly visible to take advantage of the marvelous bud prints pressed deeply into the blue-gray leaves. Plant several among perennials and small shrubs that provide seasonal color. Some great combinations would include *Berlandiera lyrata*, *Chrysactinia mexicana*, *Ericameria laricifolia*, *Penstemon parryi*, *Salvia greggii*, and *Tetraneuris acaulis*. Use several in a cactus and succulent garden alongside plants such as ***Bursera microphylla***, ***Cleistocactus strausii***, ***Echinocereus enneacanthus***, ***Ferocactus gracilis***, ***Fouquieria macdougalii***, ***Mammillaria geminispina***, and ***Yucca rostrata***.

Precautions Agave snout weevil, mites, **running bugs**, and the occasional **mealybug** infestation in the leaf cone can be problems. All these are treatable if caught early, but you might want to throw away plants with weevils or mites.

Agave deserti
Desert Agave
SUCCULENT ROSETTE

Etymology German-born, American-trained botanist George Engelmann used the word *desert-* to note this species was of the desert in southern California.

SIZE (H x W)	1–2 feet x 1½–2½ feet
FLOWER COLOR	Yellow
FLOWER SEASON	Spring
EXPOSURE	Full sun
WATER	Drought tolerant to low
GROWTH RATE	Moderate
PRUNING	None
HARDINESS	15° F, zones 8b–11

Field Notes This hardcore desert native is easily seen in the hills along Interstate 8 as you drive east from San Diego. I went to Anza-Borrego Desert State Park in April 2010 and hiked along the California Riding and Hiking Trail where there were many clusters of these plants in bloom: some in sandy soil on flat ground others nestled among the well-weathered boulders. I have seen them growing in the sandy flats and the rocky foothills of the Sierra Juárez along Mexico Federal Highway 3 in the state of Baja California. *Agave deserti* is common in sandy soil and among boulders in the desert and mountains of southern California and northern Baja California from about 1,800–3,000 feet elevation.

Description These are **offsetting** types with small- to medium-sized **rosettes** that get 1–2 feet tall by 1½–2½ feet wide with clusters to 5–6 feet

across. Thick and rigid leaves are usually blue-gray and sometimes decorated by darker cross-banding. They are about 10–16 inches long by 2–3 inches wide and shaped like a bayonet afixed to the rifle carried by foot soldiers in World Wars I & II. Margins are armed with small slender **teeth** and the stout 1–2- inch-long terminal **spine** is brown to gray. The 8–14-foot-tall flower stalk has 6–15 side branches with many bright yellow flowers at the ends.

Culture Plants are hardy to 15–20° F and can be used in USDA zones 8b–11. Keep the soil dry in winter, and they will have a better chance of surviving winter low temperatures in the high teens F. The growth rate is moderate, and it will take many years to form large clusters. Established plants are drought tolerant, but growth will speed slightly if given supplemental water in spring and summer. They are best grown in full sun and a fast draining soil.

Identification *Agave deserti* produces offsets which distinguishes it from the solitary *Agave simplex*.

Landscape Application These tough sun-loving plants are perfect for low-water-use landscapes in the desert cities of Arizona and southern California. They take many years to fully develop but still allow ample room. Place a couple among perennials and small shrubs to add color to the landscape. Some suggestions would include *Baileya multiradiata*, *Calliandra eriophylla*, *Glandularia gooddingii*, *Penstemon superbus*, and *Telosiphonia brachysiphon*. Mix with cacti and other succulents such as *Cleistocactus strausii*, *Echinocactus grusonii*, *Echinocereus engelmannii*, *Ferocactus acanthodes*, *Fouquieria splendens*, and *Yucca rostrata*.

Precautions Watch for Agave snout weevil, mites, **running bugs**, and the occasional **mealybug** infestation in the leaf cone.

Agave geminiflora
Twin-flowered Agave
SUCCULENT ROSETTE

SIZE (H x W)	2–3 feet x 2–3 feet
FLOWER COLOR	Reddish-purple with yellowish green inside
FLOWER SEASON	Late winter to spring
EXPOSURE	Full sun
WATER	Low to moderate
GROWTH RATE	Moderate
PRUNING	None
HARDINESS	18° F, zones 8b–11

Etymology Giuseppe Tagliabue named this using the Latin *gemin-* meaning twin and the Latin *flor-* meaning flower to denote the paired flowers on the stalk. Apparently in 1813, this was unusual for agaves.

Field Notes I have yet to see *Agave geminiflora* in habitat, but it is on my radar. Plants have been documented from near the town of Ocotillo in Nayarit, Mexico. Recently, plants have been found near Tequila in Jalisco, Mexico. They grow along shallow washes and gentle slopes in oak and pine-oak vegetation from about 3,000–7,000 feet elevation.

Description Plants are solitary, or rarely **offsetting**, with the **rosettes** growing to about 2–3 feet tall and 2–3 feet across. Numerous, thin, flexible, straight to slightly arching leaves are 15–24 inches long by about ¼-inch-wide and lack teeth along the edge, instead having numerous thin curly threads or rarely lacking threads. There is a short, yet sharp, brown or white terminal **spine** that is about 1-inch-long. The **spike-like** flower stalk is about 12–20 feet

Cool Cacti and Succulents for Hot Gardens

tall with numerous 2-inch-long flowers densely packed in the upper ½–⅔ of the stalk. Individual flowers are dark red to reddish-purple on the outside and yellowish green on the inside. Flowering generally occurs in late winter to spring.

Culture Plants grown in Tucson, have experienced winter low temperatures of 18° F without damage and are hardy in USDA zones 8b–11. They grow well in full sun in nearly all southwestern U.S. cities, even in the hot summer cities of Phoenix, Tucson, and Palm Springs. Place them in a fast draining soil and keep the roots evenly moist or slightly dry when summer nighttime temperatures stay above 80° F. Although low-water-using, they like occasional supplemental water during the growing season.

Identification *Agave geminiflora* has floppy and flexible leaves while the superficially similar ***Agave multifilifera*** has stiff leaves.

Landscape Application *Agave geminiflora* is a great choice for a **xeriscape** throughout the warmer winter cities in the southwest. These get along well with cacti and other succulents such as ***Astrophytum ornatum***, ***Cephalocereus senilis***, ***Echinocereus stramineus***, ***Ferocactus wislizenii***, ***Mammillaria petterssonii***, and ***Oreocereus celsianus***. Group several together for a mass display and mix with low-growing plants and seasonally flowering perennials. Some ideal companion plants are *Calliandra eriophylla*, *Chrysactinia mexicana*, *Dalea frutescens*, *Glandularia gooddingii*, *Haplophyton crooksii*, and *Penstemon* species.

Precautions Plants are susceptible to Agave snout weevil, mites, **running bugs**, and the occasional **mealybug** infestation in the leaf cone. Protect from damage by rabbits, packrats, and javelina.

Agave gentryi
Gentry's Agave, Maguey Verde
SUCCULENT ROSETTE

SIZE (H x W)	3–5 feet x 3–6 feet
FLOWER COLOR	Yellow
FLOWER SEASON	Spring to summer
EXPOSURE	Full sun, part shade
WATER	Moderate
GROWTH RATE	Moderately slow
PRUNING	None
HARDINESS	10° F, zones 8a–11

Etymology Agave expert Bernd Ullrich named this one in honor of renowned Agave researcher, Dr. Howard Scott Gentry.

Field Notes One of my favorite drives is the long cobblestone road up Cerro Potosí in Nuevo León where there are large plants with stout wide leaves. A beautiful drive is along the spine of the Sierra Madre Oriental where the plants grow among pine trees and tend to have a more open rosette with long-triangular darker green leaves. When this species starts to flower, the leaves will frequently turn brilliant yellow, orange-red, or even reddish purple. *Agave gentryi* is common in pine and pine-oak forests and open treeless slopes of high mountains in northeastern Mexico from about 7,000–9,200 feet elevation.

Description These large plants will have individual **rosettes** 3–5 feet tall and 3–6 feet wide. They may or may not produce **offsets**, but if they do, clusters may reach 6–8 feet or more across. Medium green to deep green leaves are 2–4 feet long and 6–10 inches wide, and either broadest at the base to above the middle or long triangular and **acuminate** to the sharp 2–3-inch-long terminal **spine**. Small to large marginal **teeth** create exceptional bud prints on the leaves. At flowering time, the plants produce a very thick stalk that grows to about 15–18 feet tall with short to long side branches with clusters of yellow flowers.

Culture These are from high elevation, are hardy to at least 10° F, and can be used in USDA zones 8a–11. Established plants are low-water-using but grow slowly unless they are given supplemental water during the growing season. Plants grown in the hot southwestern cities prefer some mid-day or afternoon shade in summer, but will tolerate full sun in cities that rarely experience summer temperatures above 100° F. They are best grown in a soil type that has very good drainage.

Identification *Agave gentryi* leaves tend to be straight throughout while those of *Agave salmiana* tend to have an S-shape near the tip.

Landscape Application These plants can be a bit finicky if placed in too much sun in cities with hot summers. Try growing under the shade of a tree with an open canopy like *Acacia berlandieri* or *Eysenhardtia orthocarpa*. These make great specimens when full grown and will display nicely when planted among low growing perennials and small shrubs. For seasonal color, try using *Conoclinium dissectum*, *Menodora longiflora*, and *Telosiphonia brachysiphon*. Grow with cacti and succulents such as ***Echinocereus enneacanthus***, ***Fouquieria splendens***, and ***Mammillaria petterssonii***.

Precautions Give these plants shade in the desert and consistent water in the summer. Packrats and rabbits might taste-test the leaves.

Agave nickelsiae
Synonym: *Agave ferdinandi-regis*
Nickels' Agave, King Ferdinand Agave
SUCCULENT ROSETTE

SIZE (H x W)	2 feet x 2½–3 feet
FLOWER COLOR	Yellowish green
FLOWER SEASON	Summer
EXPOSURE	Full sun
WATER	Drought tolerant to low
GROWTH RATE	Very slow
PRUNING	None
HARDINESS	10° F, zones 7b–11

Etymology Frenchman Robert Roland-Gosselin named this in 1895 for Texas nurserywoman Anna B. Nickels who found this plant outside of Saltillo.

Field Notes There is a small population of plants growing on a limestone hill to the northeast of Saltillo. In June of 2006, I went to this hill with a big group of plant fanatics and saw these growing with *Agave asperrima*, *Agave lechuguilla*, and ***Agave striata***. While walking around on the limestone ridge, we saw hybrids between *Agave nickelsiae* and *Agave asperrima* resulting in some plants reminiscent of *Agave* 'Sharkskin'. They grow with typical Chihuahuan Desert vegetation consisting of *Acacia*, *Larrea*, *Thelocactus*, *Ariocarpus*, and several grass species. They occur on rocky slopes of limestone origin not far from the city of Saltillo, Coahuila generally between about 4,500–6,500 feet elevation.

Description Plants are usually solitary in habitat but may produce a few **offsets** in cultivation, sometimes over 12 inches from the parent plant.

Rosettes can get about 2 feet tall and 2½–3 feet wide. Dark green leaves are about 10–15 inches long by 2–3 inches wide marked with decorative white bud prints lacking **teeth** along the margin but with a deep black terminal **spine** that usually has two smaller spines, one on either side. The **spike-like** flower stalk is 10–20 feet tall, and densely packed with 1½–2-inch-long yellowish-green flowers. The flower stalk signals the end of the line for that plant.

Culture Plants have been known to withstand winter lows into high single digits F and can be used in USDA zones 7b–11. You might want to protect them from excess winter moisture though. Established plants are low-water-using but will appreciate some supplemental water during the growing season. Plants will tolerate a variety of soil types if watering is adjusted accordingly. These grow well in full sun even in cities with very hot summers such as Phoenix, Tucson, and Yuma. They are very slow growing so look for plants in larger containers.

Identification *Agave nickelsiae* is a larger plant with darker green leaves and a more open rosette than *Agave victoriae-reginae*.

Landscape Application With their dark green leaves and bold white markings, these are excellent plants for any **xeriscape** or cactus and succulent garden. They are low-water-using, can take full sun, and get along well with other xeric plants. These are not overly large and fit in limited size landscapes that seem to be more prevalent these days. Use with other Chihuahuan Desert cacti such as *Ariocarpus fissuratus*, *Astrophytum capricorne*, *Echinocereus stramineus*, *Neolloydia conoidea*, and *Thelocactus rinconensis*. Plant a few small shrubs and perennials for a complete landscape. Try using *Calliandra eriophylla*, *Chrysactinia mexicana*, and *Zinnia acerosa*.

Precautions Make sure the soil has perfect drainage and keep the plants dry in winter. Protect young plants from packrats and rabbits.

Agave ocahui
Ocahui
SUCCULENT ROSETTE

SIZE (H x W)	1½–2½ feet by 2–3 feet
FLOWER COLOR	Bright yellow
FLOWER SEASON	Late spring
EXPOSURE	Full sun
WATER	Low
GROWTH RATE	Moderate
PRUNING	None
HARDINESS	15° F, zones 8b–11

Etymology   Dr. Howard Scott Gentry used the indigenous name "ocahui", which means fiber, when describing this species.

Field Notes   In May of 2007, I went to the famous Palm Canyon 17 miles southeast of Magdalena de Kino to see these plants in bloom, and they were spectacular. My friends and I saw the bright yellow flames of flowers reaching high above the **rosettes**. Plants occur on cliffs, rocky volcanic hills, and occasionally limestone soil in harsh desert to oak-woodland in northeastern Sonora from 1,500–4,500 feet elevation.

Description   The beautifully symmetrical rounded **rosettes** are solitary and grow to about 1½–2½ feet tall and 2–3 feet across. The numerous **linear-lanceolate** dark green leaves are 1–2 feet long by ½–1-inch-wide, toothless along the margin, instead having a thin white border, and a short but sharp terminal spine. The **spike-like** inflorescence reaches about 10–12 feet tall and is densely covered with bright yellow flowers in the upper ⅔ of the stalk. Flowering is primarily in May but can stretch into June.

Culture These spectacular plants are hardy to at least 15°F and make excellent landscape plants in zones 8b–11. Plants grow well in full sun even in the hottest cities of the desert southwest such as Palm Springs, Phoenix, and Tucson. They grow best in a rocky fast-draining soil and are low-water-using, surviving and even growing with twice monthly supplemental water once established. Do not even think about trimming the leaves as that would destroy the attractive symmetry of these plants.

Identification The yellow flowered *Agave ocahui* has a shorter terminal **spine** than the red flowered *Agave pelona* with nearly 2-inch-long terminal **spines**.

Landscape Application Plant these in full sun in groups of odd numbers in a southwestern U.S. **xeriscape** complete with large boulders and low-water-use perennials, small shrubs, cacti, and other succulents. Because these are smaller-sized plants, they are perfect for both residential and commercial landscapes and have been used equally effectively in street medians as in front yards. Some great companion plants could include *Baileya multiradiata*, *Calliandra eriophylla*, *Chrysactinia mexicana*, *Dalea capitata*, *Glandularia gooddingii*, *Haplophyton crooksii*, *Penstemon superbus*, *Salvia greggii*, and *Zinnia acerosa*. Grow with cacti and succulents such as ***Astrophytum ornatum***, ***Coryphantha poselgeriana***, ***Echinocereus engelmannii***, ***Ferocactus gracilis***, ***Fouquieria splendens***, ***Mammillaria petterssonii***, and ***Yucca rostrata***.

Precautions These are relatively care-free plants once established, but young ones or newly planted ones should be protected from damage by packrats, rabbits, and javelina. They are moderately susceptible to agave mites.

Agave ovatifolia
Whale's Tongue Agave
SUCCULENT ROSETTE

SIZE (H x W)	3–4 feet x 4–6 feet
FLOWER COLOR	Yellow
FLOWER SEASON	Summer
EXPOSURE	Full sun, filtered sun
WATER	Moderate
GROWTH RATE	Moderately fast
PRUNING	None
HARDINESS	10° F, zones 8a–11

Etymology I teamed up with Mexican botanist José Angel Villarreal-Quintana and we used the Latin *ovat-* for egg-shaped, and the Latin *foli-* meaning leaf, to describe the leaf shape of this species.

Field Notes In 1999, I was sent a picture of an unidentified *Agave* species by my friend George who was working at Mountain States Wholesale Nursery and had to learn more about it. I was told that plantsman Lynn Lowrey brought this back from a ranch in the Sierra Lampazos of Nuevo León. I contacted botanist Dr. José Angel Villarreal-Quintana, and in April of 2000, we retraced Mr. Lowrey's route. We received permission to visit the ranch to study and eventually describe this species. I have returned several times, and at one point the owner talked of turning the ranch into an ecotourist destination. Unfortunately, he passed away before he could get the project started, and his children showed little interest in transforming the property, and the last time I visited the buildings had fallen into a state of disrepair. So far,

Cool Cacti and Succulents for Hot Gardens

Agave ovatifolia is confirmed from the Sierra Lampazos in Nuevo León of northeastern Mexico at elevations between about 3,000–4,000 feet.

Description These are very attractive plants growing to 3–4 feet tall and 4–6 feet wide. Plants in the ground are normally solitary rosettes but some plants will occasionally **offset**. They sometimes **offset** when grown in containers. Broadly **ovate** to **obovate**, silvery blue to blue-gray leaves are 18–24 inches long and 9–11 inches wide near the middle of the blade. Small to large **teeth** are widely spaced along the leaf margin. The thick flowering stalk can appear in 10–15 years and will grow to about 10–15 feet tall with 15–20 side branches, each terminating in a cluster of numerous greenish yellow flowers. Flowering time is primarily in early summer.

Culture Plants have been through winter lows of 10° F without being killed and should be good for USDA zones 8a–11. Keep plants and soil dry through winter to minimize potential frost damage. Grow in a soil with good drainage and provide supplemental water in spring and summer. They prefer some shade in cities with very hot summers like Palm Springs, Phoenix, and Tucson, but will grow best in full sun in cities where summer temperatures top out in the 90's F.

Identification Full size plants are easily identified by their distinctive leaves.

Landscape Application Plants make spectacular specimens in the landscape, but do relish some shade in hot desert cities. Try growing under the shade of a tree with an open canopy like *Acacia berlandieri* and *Acacia constricta*. These look great when planted among perennials and small shrubs such as *Acourtia wrightii*, *Hibiscus martianus*, and *Salvia greggii*. Grow them with **Ferocactus pilosus** and **Fouquieria splendens**.

Precautions Packrats and/or rabbits will munch on the leaves. Treat for mites, **running bugs**, or **mealybugs** if there are signs of damage.

Agave palmeri
Palmer's Agave
SUCCULENT ROSETTE

SIZE (H x W)	2–5 feet x 3–7 feet
FLOWER COLOR	Yellow
FLOWER SEASON	Spring to summer
EXPOSURE	Full sun
WATER	Low to moderate
GROWTH RATE	Moderately fast
PRUNING	None
HARDINESS	10° F, zones 8a–11

Etymology This species was named by German-American botanist George Engelmann to honor Dr. Edward Palmer, one of the early collectors of the plant in southern Arizona.

Field Notes As currently defined, *Agave palmeri* is easy to see in habitat. I have seen them while visiting Kartchner Caverns State Park just off Arizona State Highway 90: also, farther along the dirt road to Dry Canyon in the Whetstone Mountains while looking for *Dermatophyllum arizonicum*. If you are feeling more adventurous, drive the Box Canyon Road in the Santa Rita Mountains where the plants are very numerous. These are common in the mountains of southeastern Arizona, southwestern New Mexico, and adjacent Sonora and Chihuahua. Plants usually inhabit the flats in open grasslands and rocky slopes of oak woodland at elevations between about 2,300–6,700 feet.

Description These vary in size ranging from 2–5 feet tall and 3–7 feet wide, depending on where they are growing. They have a single **rosette** but rarely produce an **offset** or two. Leaves are pale blue, yellowish green, light green,

or dark green, 14–30 inches long and 2½–4 inches wide near mid-blade. Leaf margins have mostly evenly-spaced small to medium size **teeth**. The flowering stalk emerges in late spring with flowers opening in summer. The stalk is about 10–16 feet tall with 15–20 side branches, each terminating in a cluster of numerous greenish and white flowers. The flower color is starkly contrasted by the very distinctive deep red or reddish-purple filaments. Flowers are an important source of nectar for bats as they migrate.

Culture These occur in areas that experience winter low temperatures of about 10° F so can be considered hardy in USDA zones 8a–11. They grow best in full sun, even in hot summer cities like Phoenix and Tucson, and do very well in mid-elevation cities such as Sierra Vista and Las Cruces. They prefer a fast draining soil and will respond well to supplemental water from late spring through summer but should be kept dry in fall and winter.

Identification *Agave palmeri* leaves have relatively straight margins which distinguish the plants from *Agave chrysantha* with their undulate margins.

Landscape Application These plants are perfect for most any **xeriscape** in southwestern U.S. cities such as Phoenix, Tucson, Sierra Vista, and Las Cruces. Use the plants singly as a focal point or group several together if there is ample room to let them spread. Plant with perennials and small or medium size shrubs that will add seasonal color. Try using *Anisacanthus thurberi*, *Calliandra eriophylla*, *Chrysactinia mexicana*, *Dalea pulchra*, *Glandularia gooddingii*, *Justicia xylosteoides*, *Penstemon* species, and *Telosiphonia brachysiphon*. Grow with cacti and succulents such as ***Dasylirion wheeleri***, ***Echinocereus engelmannii***, ***Ferocactus wislizeni***, ***Fouquieria splendens***, and ***Hesperaloe funifera***.

Precautions Packrats and/or rabbits will likely munch on the leaves, while Agave weevil, **running bugs**, mites, and **mealybugs** could also be a problem.

Agave palmeri

Agave parrasana
Cabbage Head Agave
SUCCULENT ROSETTE

SIZE (H x W)	1–2 feet x 1½–2½ feet
FLOWER COLOR	Yellow
FLOWER SEASON	Spring to summer
EXPOSURE	Full sun
WATER	Low to moderate
GROWTH RATE	Moderately slow
PRUNING	None
HARDINESS	10° F, zones 8a–11

Etymology Alwin Berger named this species for its occurrence in the Sierra de Parras in Coahuila, Mexico.

Field Notes In 2006, I saw these in the Sierra Patagalana where they grow in Pinyon-Juniper vegetation at about 7,500 feet elevation. In June 2021, I hiked into the Sierra la Gloria east of Monclova where there were a few *Agave parrasana* growing at about 5,400–6,000 feet elevation. *Agave parrasana* is not very widespread, being found in only a handful of mountain ranges in southern Coahuila. Plants are frequently found on north-facing exposures and prefer limestone based rocky soil from about 5,000–7,500 feet elevation.

Description In habitat, **rosettes** are not large, generally growing to about 1–2 feet tall and 1½–2½ feet wide, but in cultivation they can sometimes reach up to 3 feet across. Normally they have a single **rosette** but cultivated plants might produce **offsets**. Thick and rigid leaves are blue-gray to gray-green, about 8–14 inches long by 4–5 inches wide broadest from the base to the middle and tapering abruptly to the tip. Leaf margins are straight to undulate with medium size **teeth** that make deep bud prints on the leaves. The long terminal **spine** is dark chestnut brown aging to gray. Flower stalk is 10–13 feet tall with 12–15 side branches all in the upper one-third of the stalk. Two-inch-long flowers are reddish or purplish in bud and open yellow to create a colorful appearance.

Culture   Plants can tolerate winter low temperatures of 10° F without flinching and are hardy in USDA zones 8a–11. There are reports of plants surviving 5° F, so if you live in a zone 7b city, live dangerously, and push the plants to their limit, but be prepared to protect them if you have winter moisture. These grow best in fast draining soil that is kept evenly moist from late spring through summer and dry in winter. Plants grow well in full sun in most southwestern U.S. cities, even those with extremely hot summers.

Identification   *Agave parrasana* is a distinctive species with its "cabbage head-like" form and is not easily confused with any other *Agave* species.

Landscape Application   These are ideal for use in full sun in southern California, San Francisco Bay area, Tucson, Sierra Vista, and Las Cruces. Group several together and plant perennials and small shrubs that will cool the surroundings and add seasonal color. Try using *Chrysactinia mexicana*, *Justicia xylosteoides*, and *Leucophyllum candidum*. Grow with cacti and succulents such as ***Coryphantha poselgeriana***, ***Echinocereus stramineus***, ***Ferocactus pilosus***, and ***Fouquieria splendens***.

Precautions   Make sure soil has excellent drainage to keep plants from rotting due to excess water not allowing the roots to breathe. Be on the lookout for Agave weevil, **running bugs**, mites, and **mealybugs**.

Agave parryi
Parry's Agave, Mescal
SUCCULENT ROSETTE

Etymology German-born, American-trained botanist George Engelmann named this species for Dr. Charles Parry who was the first to collect this plant.

SIZE (H x W)	1½–3 feet x 2–3 feet
FLOWER COLOR	Yellow
FLOWER SEASON	Summer
EXPOSURE	Full sun, filtered sun
WATER	Low to moderate
GROWTH RATE	Moderate
PRUNING	None
HARDINESS	10° F, zones 8a–11

Field Notes There are some easy to get to spots where *Agave parryi* can be seen in Arizona and in New Mexico. An interesting spot is northeast of Bagdad, Arizona where plants dot the open slopes among grasses and mesquites. At the end of May 2020, several plants were quite colorful with red buds and yellow flowers decorating the tall stalks. *Agave parryi* has a very wide-spread distribution ranging from north-central Arizona southeast into southern New Mexico and south to Aguascalientes in Mexico. These grow on mountain slopes in rocky soil from about 5,000–9,000 feet elevation.

Description These vary in size with **rosettes** growing to about 1½–3 feet tall and 2–3 feet across. Some plants produce few **offsets** while others pump out many **offsets**. Leaves are blue-gray to gray-green, generally 8–15 inches long by 3–5 inches wide. Leaf margins are straight with evenly spaced, black **teeth**, and a black terminal **spine** to about 1-inch-long. Flower stalk is about 15–20 feet tall with 20–30 side branches, each with 2-inch-long yellow flowers. Flowering occurs primarily in early summer.

Culture The most hardy plants are from northern Arizona and subspecies *neomexicana*. These are able to tolerate winter low temperatures down to at least 10° F (USDA zones 8a–11) while variety *truncata* can be damaged when winter lows dip to the high teens F (USDA zones 8b–11). These prefer full sun in cities with high temperatures below 100° F for most of the summer, but will thank you for a bit of afternoon shade in hotter cities. Place them in a soil type that has very good drainage and keep the roots evenly moist or slightly dry in summer.

Identification *Agave parryi* is generally identified by the distinctive shape, straight leaf margin, and small black teeth.

Landscape Application Any form is ideal for use in cities with moderate summer temperatures such as San Diego, Los Angeles, Santa Barbara, and the Bay area, and Sierra Vista in Arizona, and Las Cruces in New Mexico. They will do okay in hot summer cities if supplemental water is monitored to prevent soggy soil. Use with perennials and small shrubs to cool the surroundings and add seasonal color. Try using *Calliandra eriophylla*, *Dalea versicolor*, *Justicia xylosteoides*, *Leucophyllum candidum*, *Penstemon* species, and *Thymophylla pentachaeta*. Grow with cacti and succulents such as **Coryphantha recurvata, Echinocereus parkeri, Ferocactus histrix, Fouquieria splendens, Hesperaloe funifera**, and **Yucca madrensis**.

Precautions Inspect for Agave weevil, mites, **running bugs**, and **mealybugs**.

Agave parryi

Agave schidigera
Splinter Agave, Durango Delight
SUCCULENT ROSETTE

SIZE (H x W)	1½–2 feet x 2–3 feet
FLOWER COLOR	Reddish purple
FLOWER SEASON	Spring to summer
EXPOSURE	Full sun, filtered sun
WATER	Moderate
GROWTH RATE	Moderately fast
PRUNING	None
HARDINESS	18–20° F, zones 8b–11

Etymology Charles Lemaire was creative when he named this species, using the Greek *schidi-* meaning split or divide and the Greek *gera-* meaning carrying, a reference to the leaf margins splitting away and dividing into fibers as the leaves age.

Field Notes I first saw *Agave schidigera* plants in August 1983 growing on cliffs high above the road in the Sierra Madre Occidental along Mexico Federal Highway 40 between Mazatlán and Ciudad Durango. Subsequently, I have seen specimens with thick marginal fibers in several spots in Jalisco. In June 2021, Tristan Davis and I saw several plants with their spectacular flower display in the Sierra Gorda in Guanajuato. Plants prefer growing on rocky ledges and outcrops or on gentle slopes in pine-oak vegetation at about 1,500–8,000 feet elevation.

Description The symmetry of a solitary **rosette** is outstanding; each one grows to about 1½–2 feet tall and 2–3 feet across. Numerous narrow leaves are medium green to dark green, 12–18 inches long and ½–1-inch-wide, adorned

with faint to prominent white markings, and marginal fibers instead of **teeth**. The short, yet sharp, brown or white terminal **spine** is about ½-inch-long. A **spike-like** flower stalk is about 12–15 feet tall and densely packed with 1½-inch-long deep wine red or purplish red flowers crowded in the upper ⅔ of the stalk. The flower stalk usually starts to emerge in late spring with flowers appearing in summer.

Culture Plants have been through overnight winter lows of 18°–20° F, indicating they should be fine in USDA zones 8b–11. These grow well in full sun in nearly all southwestern U.S. cities, even Phoenix, Tucson, and Palm Springs where triple digit temperatures are a daily occurrence in summer. Place them in a soil with very good drainage and keep the roots evenly moist or slightly dry when summer nighttime temperatures stay above 80° F. Keep the soil dry in winter to help plants withstand winter temperatures.

Identification *Agave schidigera* has solitary symmetrical rosettes while *Agave filifera* has more asymmetrical rosettes that produce several offsets.

Landscape Application Use plants singly or in groups in a cactus and succulent garden or a southwestern **xeriscape**. They look great when placed among large boulders and mixed with a field of perennials and small shrubs with colorful flowers such as *Baileya multiradiata*, *Calliandra eriophylla*, *Dalea frutescens*, *Ericameria laricifolia*, *Glandularia gooddingii*, *Haplophyton crooksii*, *Isocoma tenuisecta*, *Penstemon superbus*, *Salvia greggii*, and *Zinnia acerosa*. Grow with cacti and succulents such as ***Astrophytum ornatum***, ***Coryphantha erecta***, ***Echinocereus pentalophus***, ***Ferocactus gracilis***, ***Fouquieria splendens***, ***Mammillaria petterssonii***, ***Neolloydia conoidea***, and ***Yucca rostrata***.

Precautions These are easy to grow, but be on the lookout for damage from Agave snout weevil, mites, **running bugs**, **mealybugs**, packrats, or rabbits.

Agave striata
Espadin, Needle-leaf Agave
SUCCULENT ROSETTE

SIZE (H x W)	1½–2 feet x 2–3 feet
FLOWER COLOR	Reddish purple
FLOWER SEASON	Spring to summer
EXPOSURE	Full sun, filtered sun
WATER	Moderate
GROWTH RATE	Moderately fast
PRUNING	None
HARDINESS	15° F, zones 8b–11

Etymology German botanist Joseph Zuccarini based the species name on the Latin *striatus*- meaning furrowed or streaked to denote the furrows or striations in the leaves.

Field Notes This is widely distributed throughout the Chihuahuan Desert Region. The desert forms, seen near Guadalcázar in San Luis Potosí and northeast of Doctor Arroyo in Nuevo León, have much tighter more symmetrical rosettes than the ones found at higher elevations near Rayones in Nuevo León. Plants can be found in a variety of situations from rocky outcrops to gentle slopes in desert scrub or pine-oak vegetation at about 3,200–6,000 feet elevation.

Description A single **rosette** of the desert form can be a beautiful ball of leaves, while a cluster of them looks a bit like a group of porcupines huddled together. An individual rosette will grow to about 1½–2 feet tall and 2–3 feet across, and an ancient cluster of these gorgeous rosettes can reach 5–8 feet across. Numerous needle-like leaves vary in color from silver-blue, yellowish

green, blue-green, or medium green, sometimes tinged with red or purplish red for much of their length. Leaves measure 12–18 inches long and about ½-inch-wide. They lack prominent **teeth**, instead having **serrated** margins and a sharp terminal **spine** about ½-inch-long. The narrow **spike-like** flower stalk is 5–8 feet tall with 1½-inch-long greenish yellow or reddish purplish flowers.

Culture Plants have skated through lows of 15° F without suffering any damage, so they are fine in USDA zones 8b–11. Find a sunny spot with ample room for the clustering nature that will eventually result in masses of **rosettes** up to 8 feet across. They can tolerate the sun and heat of southwestern U.S. cities like Phoenix, Tucson, and Palm Springs. Place them in a soil that has good drainage and keep roots evenly moist in summer and dry out in winter.

Identification *Agave striata* leaves are more varied in color than *Agave stricta* leaves which tend to be yellow-green on young plants. Leaves on *Agave striata* var. *falcata* are noticeably curved or sickle shaped.

Landscape Application Give *Agave striata* ample room to spread, and plant with cactus and succulent or perennials and shrubs in nearly any southwestern landscape. They look great when placed among large boulders and in a field of plants such as *Baileya multiradiata, Calliandra californica, Dalea bicolor* var. *argyrea, Ericameria laricifolia, Glandularia gooddingii, Haplophyton crooksii, Isocoma tenuisecta, Penstemon eatonii, Senna covesii,* and *Zinnia acerosa*. Grow with cacti and succulents such as ***Astrophytum ornatum**, **Echinocereus enneacanthus**, **Ferocactus pilosus**, **Fouquieria splendens**, **Jatropha dioica**,* and ***Yucca rostrata***.

Precautions These are easy to grow, but be on the lookout for damage from Agave snout weevil, mites, **running bugs**, packrats, or rabbits.

Agave victoriae-reginae
Queen Victoria Agave
SUCCULENT ROSETTE

SIZE (H x W)	1–1½ feet x 1–2 feet
FLOWER COLOR	Greenish yellow
FLOWER SEASON	Spring to summer
EXPOSURE	Full sun, filtered sun
WATER	Low to moderate
GROWTH RATE	Moderately fast
PRUNING	None
HARDINESS	10° F, zones 8a–11

Etymology Thomas Moore named this species in honor of England's Queen Victoria.

Field Notes A visit to the famous Huasteca Canyon south of the bustling and ever expanding city of Monterrey in Nuevo León is a must for any agavephile. You will see countless plants inhabiting the steep limestone walls making them virtually unreachable by people and even goats. Plants are known from about a half-dozen localities scattered about in the central Chihuahuan Desert Region. They mostly are found growing on cliffs and vertical walls composed of limestone from about 3,000–5,500 feet elevation.

Description Plants can be a single dense and compact **rosette** to about 1–1½ feet tall and 1–2 feet across, or they can produce few to numerous **offsets**. Medium green to dark green leaves are short and stout broadest at the base and tapering to the tip. They have decorative white markings making this a desirable species in any collection. Leaves lack marginal **teeth**, but the short sharp terminal **spine** does pack a punch if hit just right. The narrow 10–15-foot tall

stalk loaded with numerous yellow flowers, appears in summer.

Culture Plants have been reliably hardy to 10°F and are ideal in USDA zones 8a–11 and make excellent container plants anywhere. Established landscape specimens can generally tolerate full sun throughout much of the southwestern U.S., although they do best with filtered sun in blazing hot cities of Las Vegas, Phoenix, and Tucson. Even though they are considered drought tolerant, smaller plants not well established in a landscape or those in pots will benefit from receiving supplemental water from spring until fall. They grow best in a soil that has very good drainage. Keep soil dry in winter while the plants are dormant.

Identification *Agave victoriae-reginae* has greener leaves and more of them than the dark olive-green, fewer-leaved *Agave nickelsiae*. *Agave pintilla* tends to have darker green leaves with more white markings.

Landscape Application Mass several of these together in a cactus and succulent garden and mix in some small shrubs and perennials with colorful flowers to provide seasonal interest. Use cacti and succulents such as *Agave parrasana*, *Astrophytum coahuilense*, *Echinocereus stramineus*, and *Yucca rostrata*. Plant alongside low-water-using plants like *Baileya multiradiata*, *Chrysactinia mexicana*, *Glandularia gooddingii*, and *Penstemon superbus*. Collect as many forms as you can, grow them in decorative pots, and create an impressive display.

Precautions These are sometimes favored by mites, **running bugs**, and **mealybugs**, while leaves are sometimes munched on by packrats.

Aloe comosa
Clanwilliam Aloe
SUCCULENT ROSETTE

SIZE (H x W)	4–10 feet x 3–5 feet
FLOWER COLOR	Pink or white white
FLOWER SEASON	Summer
EXPOSURE	Full sun
WATER	Low
GROWTH RATE	Moderately slow
PRUNING	None
HARDINESS	25° F, zones 9b–11

Etymology   Herman Marloth and Alwin Berger described this species using the Latin *comos-* meaning long hairs, a nod to the brush-like appearance of the inflorescence due to the long-tapering bracts.

Field Notes   In 2023, Carol and I were in South Africa with our friends Thomas and Maria. We stayed at Hartnekskloof near the Groenfontein Private Nature Reserve where we saw majestic specimens of these plants occupying the rocky north slopes. This is at the southern end of the distribution, and they are more common in the region around Clanwilliam, which is north and west of Hartnekskloof. Plants grow on rocky slopes among large boulders from about 1,100–2,600 feet elevation.

Description   These striking single-stemmed plants grow to 4–10 feet tall with a leaf crown to 3–5 feet across. Pale blue-gray leaves can turn pinkish when dry. They are thick and succulent and nearly 2 feet long. Pinkish margins are armed

with small reddish-brown **teeth**. Old leaves dry and hang down to protect the trunk from sun and cold. The flower stalk is tall, narrow, **spike-like**, and covered with dull pink or whitish flowers in summer.

Culture Plants are hardy to at least the upper 20's F and can be used in USDA zones 9b–11. They are low-water-using with leaves taking on a pinkish tinge when dry in summer. Plants can be grown in full sun in cities such as Las Vegas, Palm Springs, Phoenix, and Yuma. Soil should have excellent drainage to keep roots from becoming waterlogged.

Identification *Aloe comosa* plants have tall **spike-like** flower stalks while *Aloe ferox* and *Aloe marlothii* have branched flower stalks.

Landscape Application These can be used singly or grouped together in a low-water-use landscape in cities where frost is rare. Place them in an open exposure or against a south or west-facing wall in cities that experience low 20's F for several nights in winter. They make great additions to a cactus and succulent garden with a variety of perennials and small to medium shrubs planted throughout. A few great companion plants would be *Anisacanthus quadrifidus*, *Eremophila hygrophana*, *Leucophyllum candidum*, *Psilostrophe cooperi*, and *Ruellia peninsularis*. *Aloe comosa* is compatible with other succulents and cacti such as *Cephalocereus senilis*, *Echinocactus grusonii*, *Euphorbia resinifera*, and *Mammillaria sonorensis*.

Precautions Protect plants, especially flower stalks, from frost and discard any plants infected with Aloe mite.

Aloe ferox
Fierce Aloe
SUCCULENT ROSETTE

SIZE (H x W)	4–10 feet x 3–4 feet
FLOWER COLOR	Red-orange, red, yellow, rarely white
FLOWER SEASON	Late winter to spring
EXPOSURE	Full sun, reflected heat, filtered light
WATER	Low to moderate
GROWTH RATE	Moderately slow
PRUNING	None
HARDINESS	25° F, zones 9b–11

Etymology Phillip Miller was an English botanist who used the Latin *fero-* meaning fierce, in recognition of the sharp prickles on the leaves.

Field Notes I have been to South Africa three times and have been fortunate enough to see these plants in a few different spots. In 2002, the group I was with saw a fine stand of these tall plants in the Groot-Swartberge Mountains in the Little Karroo. In 2016, I saw them along route 341 north of the Kammanassie Nature Reserve. These are very common and wide-spread mostly in southern and south-eastern South Africa. They grow on flat ground or on mountain slopes among large boulders from about 50–4,500 feet elevation.

Description These are robust single-trunked plants growing to 4–10 feet tall with a leaf crown to 3–4 feet across. Leaves are thick and succulent dull green to dark green and nearly 2 feet long by 4–6 inches across near the base. They generally have sharp **teeth** along the margin and may or may not be covered with sharp **prickles** on one or both surfaces. Old leaves dry and hang down to protect the trunk from sun and cold. The flower stalk is a branched **panicle** with 5–8 upright **racemes** giving the plant a candelabra appearance. Orangish red, bright red, yellowish, or even white, tubular, 2-inch-long flowers attract a plethora of hummingbirds. Prime flowering time is usually late winter to spring.

Culture Plants are hardy to about 25° F and can be used in USDA zones 9b–11. They are low- to moderate-water-users, but will grow a little faster if given supplemental water from late spring until early fall. They can be grown in full sun or even reflected heat, but like filtered light in cities such as Las Vegas, Palm Springs, Phoenix, Tucson, and Yuma. Soil should have excellent drainage to keep roots from becoming waterlogged.

Identification *Aloe ferox* has upright flower stalks while those on *Aloe marlothii* grow at about a 45 degree angle.

Landscape Application Plants can be used singly or grouped to create an eye-catching display in a southwestern **xeriscape** in cities where frost is infrequent. Place these against a south or west-facing wall in cities that experience low 20's F for several nights in winter. They are great additions to a cactus and succulent garden and fit in with plants like *Agave parryi*, *Cephalocereus senilis*, *Echinocactus grusonii*, *Euphorbia resinifera*, *Mammillaria geminispina*, and *Trichocereus terscheckii*. Plants are also compatible with a variety of perennials and shrubs such as *Abutilon palmeri, Anisacanthus quadrifidus, Conoclinium dissectum, Dalea frutescens, Leucophyllum candidum, Psilostrophe cooperi,* and *Ruellia peninsularis*. In really hot summer cities use *Acacia berlandieri, Acacia constricta,* or *Eysenhardtia orthocarpa* to provide summer shade.

Precautions Protect plants, especially flower stalks, from frost and discard any plants infected with Aloe mite.

Aloe marlothii
Marloth's Aloe, Mountain Aloe
SUCCULENT ROSETTE

SIZE (H x W)	4–10 feet x 4–5 feet
FLOWER COLOR	Red-orange, red, yellow
FLOWER SEASON	Winter to spring
EXPOSURE	Full sun, reflected heat, filtered light
WATER	Low to moderate
GROWTH RATE	Moderately slow
PRUNING	None
HARDINESS	25° F, zones 9b–11

Etymology Alwin Berger, a German botanist, named this for fellow German botanist Hermann Rudolf Marloth.

Field Notes I have not seen *Aloe marlothii* in habitat but have it on my to do list. I will need to travel to the northeastern part of South Africa or farther north in Eastern Africa as the species ranges from KwaZulu-Natal to Mozambique and Zimbabwe. They are found in a variety of habitats, from open bushveld to exposed rocky areas. Although there are records of plants being found at low elevation, mostly they are spotted in the mountains from about 3,000–6,500 feet elevation.

Description Plants are large and single-trunked growing to 4–10 feet tall with a leaf crown to 4–5 feet across. Leaves are thickly succulent, dull green to grayish-green, and nearly 2 feet long by 4–6 inches across near the base. Leaf margins and both surfaces are adorned with dark brown **prickles**. The flower

stalk is a much-branched **panicle** with 20–30 horizontal, slanted, or nearly erect **racemes**. Bright red, orange-red, yellowish, or sometimes bicolored flowers are tubular, about 2 inches long, and attract scores of hummingbirds. Prime flowering time is usually late winter to spring.

Culture These are hardy to about 25° F and can be used in USDA zones 9b–11. They are low- to moderate-water-users, but will grow a little faster if given supplemental water from late spring until early fall. Grow them in full sun or even reflected heat in southwestern cities that stay below 100° F during summer, but give them some mid-day shade in summer in cities such as Las Vegas, Palm Springs, Phoenix, Tucson, and Yuma.

Identification Flower stalks on *Aloe marlothii* are generally slanted to horizontal while those on *Aloe ferox* are more vertical.

Landscape Application Use these singly or in groupings to create an eye-catching display in a southwestern **xeriscape** in cities where frost is an infrequent occurrence. Place them against a south or west-facing wall in cities that experience low 20's F for several nights in winter. They are great additions to a cactus and succulent garden and fit in with *Aloe striata*, *Agave gentryi*, *Euphorbia resinifera*, and *Yucca rigida*. Plants are also compatible with a variety of perennials and shrubs such as *Anisacanthus quadrifidus*, *Justicia candicans*, and *Ruellia peninsularis*. In really hot summer cities use *Acacia constricta* or *Parkinsonia microphylla* to provide summer shade.

Precautions Aloe mite will cause a mass of gall-like growth on the leaves and recommended treatment is to physically remove infected leaves. Protect developing inflorescences if night-time lows dip into the 20's F.

Aloe striata
Coral Aloe
SUCCULENT ROSETTE

SIZE (H x W)	1–2 feet x 2–3 feet
FLOWER COLOR	Coral red or pinkish red
FLOWER SEASON	Winter to spring
EXPOSURE	Full sun, filtered sun
WATER	Low to moderate
GROWTH RATE	Moderately fast
PRUNING	None
HARDINESS	20° F, zones 9a–11

Etymology Englishman Adrian Haworth used the Latin *striatus-* meaning streaked, for the striations on the leaves.

Field Notes I got to see *Aloe striata* in habitat on my first trip to South Africa in September 2002. I was with a group of plant nerds traveling on Route 323 through the Witberge Mountains from Laingsburg toward Oudtshoorn. We stopped at a rocky outcrop where some of these plants were tucked among large rocks. *Aloe striata* is widespread in the southern part of South Africa and occurs from about 100–7,000 feet elevation.

Description True *Aloe striata* plants are solitary stemless rosettes to about 1–2 feet tall and 2–3 feet across. Light blue-green leaves are thickly succulent, flat and long-triangular, and about 1–1½ feet long by 4–6 inches across near the base. Leaf margins are toothless, instead having a continuous reddish edge. The flower stalk is a much-branched 2-foot-tall **panicle** loaded with numerous coral red or pinkish red 2-inch-long tubular flowers that attract hummingbirds

from around the neighborhood. Peak flowering usually occurs in late winter to spring. There are hybrids between this and a spotted *Aloe* species in cultivation that has spots and produces offsets.

Culture These are hardy to the low 20's F and can be used in USDA zones 9a–11. They are low- to moderate-water-users, but will grow a little faster and flower more profusely when given supplemental water from late spring until early fall. Grow these in full sun in southwestern

cities that stay below 100° F during summer, but give them some filtered sun in summer in cities such as Las Vegas, Palm Springs, Phoenix, and Yuma.

Identification True *Aloe striata* plants are solitary rosettes and have a narrow pale reddish margin on the leaves which make these very distinctive.

Landscape Application Group several of these for their late winter to early spring flower color in cities where frost is not frequent. Place them against a south-facing wall or under the protection of a tree in cities that experience low 20's F for several nights in winter. Try a group of these in front of a purple-colored south-facing wall for the color contrast plus the extra heat in winter. Grow these with other *Aloe* species including *Aloe buhrii*, **Aloe ferox**, **Aloe marlothii**, and *Aloe reynoldsii*. Plants are also compatible with a variety of perennials and shrubs with white, yellow, or purple flowers. Try using *Conoclinium dissectum*, *Justicia longii*, and *Ruellia peninsularis*. In hot summer cities use *Acacia berlandieri* or *Acacia constricta* for shade.

Precautions Aloe mite will cause a mass of gall-like growth on the leaves and recommended treatment is to physically remove infected leaves. Protect developing inflorescences if night-time lows dip into the 20's F.

Aloe striatula

Synonym: *Aloiampelos striatula*
Hardy Aloe, Striped-stemmed Aloe
SHRUB-LIKE SUCCULENT

SIZE (H x W)	4–6 feet x 6–8 feet
FLOWER COLOR	Yellow
FLOWER SEASON	Spring to summer
EXPOSURE	Full sun, filtered sun
WATER	Low to moderate
GROWTH RATE	Moderately fast
PRUNING	Trim to keep tidy
HARDINESS	15° F, zones 8b–11

Etymology Englishman Adrian Haworth used the Latin *striatus*- meaning streaked, for the striations on the leaf sheaths.

Field Notes I have missed out on seeing these the two times I was in eastern South Africa, so will have to go back! *Aloe striatula* occurs in several localities in the mountains of the eastern Cape and in southern Lesotho at about 4,000–5,000 feet elevation.

Description These plants branch profusely from near ground level or low down on the stems to form large robust shrubs to about 4–6 feet tall and 6–8 feet across. Dark glossy-green leaves are long and narrow, deeply channeled, and have distinct striations on the leaf back and extending to the stem. Leaf margins have a narrow cartilaginous border with small teeth. The flower stalk is unbranched and **spike-like** growing to 6–8 inches long. In spring and summer, the stalk is loaded with reddish-yellow flower buds that open to yellow or orange-yellow flowers that sometimes attract hummingbirds and bees.

Cool Cacti and Succulents for Hot Gardens

Culture Plants will tolerate winter lows to about 15° F with minimal damage and can be used in USDA zones 8b–11. They are low- to moderate-water-users, but will grow a little faster and flower more profusely when given supplemental water from late spring until early fall. Grow these in full sun in southwestern cities that stay below 100° F during summer, but give them some filtered sun in summer in cities such as Las Vegas, Palm Springs, Phoenix, Tucson, and Yuma.

Identification *Aloe striatula* is one of the scrambling type aloes and is distinguished by the dark glossy-green leaves, yellow flowers, and distinct striations on the leaf sheath.

Landscape Application Grow these singly in a cactus and succulent garden, and allow ample room for them to develop because they can get large. Place them against a south-facing wall or under the protection of a tree in cities that experience winter lows into the teens F for several nights in winter. Try placing in front of a purple-colored south-facing wall for the color contrast plus the extra heat in winter. Plant with other *Aloe* species including *Aloe buhrii*, **Aloe ferox**, **Aloe marlothii**, and **Aloe striata**. Plants are also compatible with a variety of perennials and shrubs with purple flowers, and a couple suggestions include *Conoclinium dissectum*, *Justicia longii*, and *Ruellia peninsularis*.

Precautions Aloe mite will cause a mass of gall-like growth on the leaves; the recommended treatment is to remove infected portions.

Aloe striatula

Aloe variegata

Synonym: *Gonialoe variegata*
Partridge-Breast Aloe, Tiger Aloe
SUCCULENT ROSETTE

SIZE (H x W)	6–12 inches x 6–8 inches
FLOWER COLOR	Orange-red or pinkish-red
FLOWER SEASON	Late winter to spring
EXPOSURE	Filtered sun to full sun
WATER	Drought tolerant to low
GROWTH RATE	Moderate
PRUNING	None
HARDINESS	20° F, zones 9a–11

Etymology   Carl Linnaeus used the Latin *variegat-* to describe the white marked leaves.

Field Notes   In September 2002, I was with a group of plant nerds being shown around South Africa by the late couple, Rod and Rachel of Silverhill Seeds. One of our target plants was *Aloe variegata*, which we did find buried in shrubbery. More recently, Carol and I were in South Africa with our friends Thomas Staudt and Maria Voris looking at plants, birds, reptiles, and rocks, and we came across blooming plants of *Aloe variegata* out in the open. *Aloe variegata* is widespread in the western part of South Africa and occurs from about 600–2,000 feet elevation.

Description   These are small plants with one or more leaf clusters, each one grows to about 6–12 inches tall and 6–8 inches across. Clusters can get as big as 20–24 inches across. Each rosette consists of several thickly succulent, deeply folded, tiger-striped, triangluar leaves stacked in three vertical columns. Deep pinkish-red to orange-red, nearly 2-inch-long flowers appear on 10–15-inch tall stalks in late winter and early spring, and will draw in hummingbirds.

Cool Cacti and Succulents for Hot Gardens

Culture These are hardy to about 20° F and can be left unprotected in winter in USDA zones 9a–11. Plants can tolerate full sun in cities with summer temperatures topping out in the high 80's or low 90's F, but they should be grown in some shade in cities where temperatures routinely climb above 100° F for much of the summer. Although drought tolerant, the plants will respond to receiving supplemental water on a weekly basis from spring until fall. They prefer to be in soil with excellent drainage to keep excess moisture away from the roots.

Identification With their deeply folded and **keeled**, three-ranked, triangular leaves, Aloe variegata are very distinctive plants.

Landscape Application These small plants are best used in a small residential landscape along with other *Aloe* species, small cacti, and flowering perennial plants. Use *Aloe karasbergensis* and *Aloe striata*, *Ariocarpus* species, *Astrophytum* species, *Coryphantha* species, and *Echinocereus* species in a succulent garden. Plant perennials and small shrubs such as *Conoclinium dissectum*, *Dalea capitata*, *Euphorbia rigida*, *Salvia greggii*, *Tetraneuris acaulis*, and *Zinnia acerosa* to help cool the soil and provide seasonal color. *Aloe variegata* plants are ideal for growing in decorative containers and fit in with other succulents and cacti in a collection.

Precautions Plants in the ground might be taste tested by packrats and rabbits, while those in pots should be kept in a spot that packrats cannot access.

Ariocarpus fissuratus
Living Rock
SMALL CACTUS

SIZE (H x W)	1–4 inches x 4–6 inches
FLOWER COLOR	Pink to magenta
FLOWER SEASON	Fall
EXPOSURE	Full sun, filtered sun
WATER	Drought tolerant to low
GROWTH RATE	Moderately slow
PRUNING	None
HARDINESS	15° F, zones 8b–11

Etymology German-born, American-trained botanist George Engelmann chose the Latin *fissur-* for the **fissures** in the **tubercles**.

Field Notes I feel like it's an Easter Egg hunt whenever I go searching for plants of *Ariocarpus fissuratus* in the field. They tend to hide among the limestone rubble and blend in by mimicking the surrounding rock. However, if they are in flower, the bright pinkish flowers stand out from a mile away, well, maybe not a mile, but they are certainly much easier to spot. I have seen them growing on slopes and ledges of low limestone hills throughout much of its range which is from western Texas south into Coahuila, Durango, and northern Zacatecas from near sea level up to about 4,000 feet elevation.

Description Plants have a low flattened or sometimes rounded dark green or gray-green body that is usually less than 4 inches tall by 4–6 inches in diameter. Triangular **tubercles** that occur in a spiral around the central

Cool Cacti and Succulents for Hot Gardens

growing point have numerous **fissures** making the plants look old and wrinkly. Large pink to magenta flowers are up to 2 inches in diameter and appear near the center of the plant, attracting bees and the occasional hummingbird. Blooming season is fall at which time the plants are easier to spot in habitat.

Culture Plants are generally easy to grow once they are situated in their forever home. They are hardy to at least 15° F and can be used in USDA zones 8b–11. Keep dry in winter but some supplemental water from late spring until early fall is fine. If the soil is kept too wet, plants can rot and die. Given a fast draining soil and supplemental water in summer, these can be grown in full sun throughout much of the southwest, but they prefer to have some afternoon shade in hot summer cities such as Las Vegas, Palm Springs, Phoenix, and Tucson. Plants can be showcased when grown in decorative pots, but if grown in the ground, they are likely to be overlooked until they flower.

Identification *Ariocarpus fissuratus* has short, dark green or gray-green, triangular **tubercles** with prominent fissures, while **tubercles** are blue-gray on *Ariocarpus retusus* and elongated on *Ariocarpus trigonus*.

Landscape Application Plants can be mixed into a cactus and succulent garden, but because they are small they tend to get overlooked until they flower in the fall. The pinkish to magenta flowers are vibrant and colorful and even the casual observer will sit up and take notice. Mix these with small perennials such as *Baileya multiradiata*, *Hymenoxys acaulis*, *Penstemon triflorus*, or *Thymophylla pentachaeta*. Display your prized specimens in decorative pots and enjoy them all year.

Precautions Watch for **mealybugs** that might be hiding out in the **fissures** or under the flowers and flower remnants. Do not keep soil too wet.

Ariocarpus fissuratus

Ariocarpus retusus
Living Rock
SMALL CACTUS

SIZE (H x W)	1–5 inches x 4–10 inches
FLOWER COLOR	White
FLOWER SEASON	Fall
EXPOSURE	Full sun, filtered sun
WATER	Drought tolerant to low
GROWTH RATE	Moderately slow
PRUNING	None
HARDINESS	15° F, zones 8b–11

Etymology Botanist Michel Scheidweiler used the Latin *retus*- meaning blunt to describe the bluntly triangular **tubercles**.

Field Notes I have had a long-time fascination with the Chihuahuan Desert Region where these plants grow and have made many trips to look for interesting plants. I have seen these awesome little plants in southern Nuevo León not far from Doctor Arroyo and in San Luis Potosí. In one spot we stumbled upon a very curious crested form that was both grotesque and beautiful at the same time. Plants are usually found among limestone pebbles and rocks, tucked in beside large boulders, or partially hidden by grasses. Distribution is from north of Saltillo in Coahuila south into San Luis Potosí at elevations from about 4,200–6,600 feet elevation.

Description In their habitat, the blue-gray or blue-green body is generally slightly above ground level and rounded on top, about 1–5 inches tall by 4–10 inches in diameter. Plants will occasionally offset and produce 2 or more **rosettes** with the cluster growing to nearly 15–18 inches across. Sometimes one will see specimens in cultivation that look to have been watered and

Cool Cacti and Succulents for Hot Gardens

fertilized too much resulting in short columns to 6–8 inches or more tall. Bluntly triangular **tubercles** are attenuate at the tip and diverge from the central growing point. Large white flowers are up to 2 inches in diameter and appear near the center of the plant. Blooming season is fall, and plants stand out among the gray limestone rock.

Culture Plants are easy to grow once they are settled into their permanent home. They are hardy to at least 15° F and can be used in USDA zones 8b–11. Keep soil dry during the cool months but provide some supplemental water from late spring until early fall. However, too much water combined with poorly draining soil can cause plants to rot and die. They can be grown in full sun in southwestern cities that stay below 100° F during summer, but should be grown in filtered light in hot summer cities such as Las Vegas, Palm Springs, Phoenix, and Tucson. These can also be planted in decorative pots.

Identification *Ariocarpus retusus* has bluntly triangular **tubercles** lacking fissures as on the short-triangular **tubercles** of *Ariocarpus fissuratus*. *Ariocarpus trigonus* is a larger plant with a brownish green body.

Landscape Application These can be grown in a cactus and succulent garden, but because plants are relatively small they tend to get overlooked until they flower in the fall. The white flower is large and very prominent drawing in bees and the occasional hummingbird along with the seasoned cactus grower. These can be mixed with small perennials such as *Baileya multiradiata*, *Hymenoxys acaulis*, *Penstemon triflorus*, or *Thymophylla pentachaeta*. However, display your prized specimens in decorative pots and put them on raised shelves so you can enjoy the cool bodies anytime of the year.

Precautions Watch for mealy bugs that like to live under the flowers and flower remnants near the apex, or in any small cracks or crevices in the plant body. **Mealybugs** can be physically removed with a pair of sharp tweezers.

Ariocarpus trigonus
Living Rock
SMALL CACTUS

SIZE (H x W)	2–4 inches x 4–8 inches
FLOWER COLOR	Pale yellow or cream
FLOWER SEASON	Fall
EXPOSURE	Full sun, filtered sun
WATER	Low to moderate
GROWTH RATE	Moderately slow
PRUNING	None
HARDINESS	15° F, zones 8b–11

Etymology Frenchman Frederic Albert Constantin Weber used the Greek *trigon-* for the long-triangular **tubercles** seen on these plants.

Field Notes In 1986, Ron Gass and I traveled to southern Tamaulipas searching for intriguing plants that could be used for landscaping in the desert southwest. We camped among tall yuccas and lush shrubs and trees northwest of Palmillas one night, and the next day awoke to a smorgasbord of awesome plants with *Ariocarpus trigonus* being one of the coolest finds. In 2014, I was traveling with Jeff

Chemnick and Brian Kemble in northeastern Mexico, where we visited a hill laden with these plants. Most of the plants were nearly hidden, but the long-triangular tubercles were visible above the crumbly rock. Plants are usually found among limestone pebbles and rocks on the eastern slopes of the Sierra Madre Oriental from Nuevo León south to southern Tamaulipas at about 1,600–4,000 feet elevation.

Description Plants usually have a slight yellowish or brownish cast over the green body, which is generally flat

Cool Cacti and Succulents for Hot Gardens

to the ground or slightly elevated above ground level. The bodies can be 2–4 inches tall by 4–8 inches in diameter. They occasionally offset, producing 2 or more additional rosettes with the cluster growing to nearly 15–18 inches across. Some plants in cultivation grow into short columns to 6–8 inches tall. Long-triangular **tubercles** are acute or attenuate at the tip and curve up. Pale yellow or cream-colored flowers are up to 2 inches in diameter and appear near the center of the plant. Blooming season is fall at which time the plants scream "look at me."

Culture Plants are low care and easy to grow once they are acclimated to a permanent spot. They are hardy to at least 15° F and can be used in USDA zones 8b–11. These do not require any supplemental water from late fall until the weather warms in spring, but they will grow fine with some supplemental water from late spring until early fall. Plants can be grown in full sun in southwestern cities that stay below 100° F during summer, but prefer filtered light in hot summer cities such as Las Vegas, Palm Springs, Phoenix, and Tucson.

Identification *Ariocarpus trigonus* has yellowish flowers and fewer **tubercles** that are more of an olive brown-green than those seen on the white flowered ***Ariocarpus retusus***.

Landscape Application Plants will grow well in the ground with other cactus and succulents but are likely to be overlooked until they flower in the fall. The yellowish flower is large and very prominent drawing in bees along with the curious cactus grower. These can be mixed with small plants such as *Berlandiera lyrata*, *Dalea capitata*, *Justicia longii*, *Penstemon triflorus*, or *Thymophylla pentachaeta*. However, it is best to grow them in decorative containers in a spot where you will be able to enjoy them every day.

Precautions **Mealybugs** will sometimes inhabit the areas under flowers and flower remnants and can be physically removed using a pair of sharp tweezers.

Astrophytum asterias

Sand Dollar Cactus, Sea Urchin Cactus, Star Cactus
SMALL CACTUS

SIZE (H x W)	1–3 inches x 3–6 inches
FLOWER COLOR	Yellow with red in the center, rarely pink or red
FLOWER SEASON	Summer to fall
EXPOSURE	Filtered sun, part shade
WATER	Low
GROWTH RATE	Moderate
PRUNING	None
HARDINESS	High teens F, zones 9a–11

Etymology Joseph Zuccarini was an early 19th century German botanist, and he used the Greek *aster-*, meaning star, as the inspiration for the species.

Field Notes This is one of those plants that has eluded me in habitat. I have not been near where they grow in south Texas and have never looked for them in the flats to the east of the Sierra Madre Oriental in Tamaulipas, Mexico. Guess I will have to spend some quality time in the low desert of Tamaulipas! Plants tend to hang out under shrubs and trees in south Texas and on the flats of the Sierra Madre Oriental in Tamaulipas at elevations below about 1,000 feet.

Description These plants have an unusual body shape in that they are flat and round, only reaching 1–3 inches high and 3–6 inches across. They are solitary with eight ribs and woolly **areoles** down the center of each rib. Plants may or may not have small or large patches of white **trichomes**, sometimes referred to as flecks, resulting in some very intriguing patterns. Large yellow flowers are red at the base of the **tepals** and are up to 2 inches in diameter. There are forms that have pink to dark red flowers, which are in high demand in the cactus and succulent trade. Plants in cultivation will bloom several times from late spring through summer with individual flowers usually lasting only one or two days.

Culture Plants are hardy to the high teens F and can be used in USDA zones 9a–11. I have found these to be the most difficult *Astrophytum* species to grow. They seem to be finicky about sun exposure; too much sun and they burn, too little and they stretch out. I grow them under 50–60 percent shade, and that seems to be about right. Plants are also touchy about watering: too much and they rot, too little and the roots die off. They should be grown in a gritty soil mix that has perfect drainage. Keep plants and soil dry when the weather is cold.

Astrophytum asterias 'Super Kabuto'

Identification There are many cultivars coming out of Asia, and it is difficult to keep up with all the names, but two of the most popular are 'Super Kabuto' with many large **trichomes** and 'nudum' that lacks **trichomes** completely. I have found the website: www.cactus-art.biz to be a good source on which to spend hours looking at all they have to offer.

Landscape Application Although hardy enough to grow in the landscape, these small plants look great in decorative pots where they can be displayed alongside other cool looking cactus. Collect several different forms with various amounts of flecking. These hybridize with *Astrophytum capricorne* and *Astrophytum coahuilense*, resulting in interesting forms.

Precautions **Mealybugs** like to live in the grooves between the ribs, in any wrinkles in the body, and under the flowers or flower remnants near the apex. Plants will sometimes up and die when summer temperatures go over 100° F for multiple days, and sometimes the bodies split open along the ribs.

A. asterias - rare red flowered form

Astrophytum asterias

Astrophytum capricorne
Goat's Horn Cactus
SMALL CACTUS

SIZE (H x W)	6–12 inches x 5–6 inches
FLOWER COLOR	Yellow with red in the center, rarely pink or red
FLOWER SEASON	Summer to fall
EXPOSURE	Full sun or filtered light
WATER	Low
GROWTH RATE	Moderately slow
PRUNING	None
HARDINESS	15° F, zones 8b–11

Etymology German botanist Albert Gottfried Dietrich noticed the spines resembled the horns on a goat and selected the Latin *capri-* meaning goat and the Latin *corne-* meaning horn to reflect that characteristic.

Field Notes There are several named varieties; variety *aureum*, a form with new spines being yellow then aging to gray, which I have come across near Estación Marte in southern Coahuila, variety *niveum*, a heavily flecked form with large woody spines, which I have seen nestled in the limestone rocks near Parras de la Fuente and near Cuatrociénegas in central Coahuila, variety *crassispinum*, a form without flecks and heavy woody spines that is supposed to be near Cuatrociénegas. Plants favor limestone soil and grow near large rocks or under the edge of low shrubs in the states of Coahuila and Nuevo León from about 3,000–5,000 feet.

Description These eventually reach 6–12 inches tall (rarely more) and 5–6 inches across. The bodies have 7–8 ribs and may be densely covered or have no white flecks. **Spines** are quite variable and can be yellow as in var. *aureum*, brown, black, or white and thick as in var. *niveum* or thin and very curly as in var. *senile*. Large yellow flowers are red or orange-red at the base and are up to 2 inches in diameter.

Culture Plants are easy to cultivate and tolerate full sun nearly throughout the desert southwest, but prefer filtered afternoon sun in the hottest and driest cities such as Las Vegas, Palm Springs, and Phoenix. I grow my young plants under 40 percent shade, and that seems to be about right for them in Tucson, but larger plants can tolerate full sun if acclimated properly. They are hardy to about 15° F and can be used in USDA zones 8b–11, and prefer a gritty soil with excellent drainage.

Identification *Astrophytum capricorne* is a distinctive plant.

Landscape Application Plants are easily grown in the landscape and work well near large boulders or in combination with a variety of cactus and succulents. A tall **Yucca rostrata** can be used effectively and not overpower these smaller plants, but smaller agaves such as **Agave parviflora** and **Agave victoriae-reginae** are a perfect size. These combine well with other Chihuahuan Desert species such as **Ariocarpus fissuratus**, **Coryphantha poselgeriana**, **Mammillaria candida**, and **Thelocactus rinconensis**.

Precautions Check for **mealybugs** in any wrinkles in the body and under the flowers. Occasionally **spine mealies** will be attached to the spines, but these can be scraped off with sharp tweezers.

Astrophytum capricorne

Astrophytum coahuilense
Coahuila Star Plant
SMALL CACTUS

SIZE (H x W)	6–8 inches x 4–6 inches
FLOWER COLOR	Yellow with red in the center
FLOWER SEASON	Summer to fall
EXPOSURE	Full sun or filtered light
WATER	Low
GROWTH RATE	Moderately slow
PRUNING	None
HARDINESS	15° F, zones 8b–11

Etymology Heinrich Moeller was a German botanist who used the occurrence of this plant in the state of Coahuila as the basis for the species name.

Field Notes I first saw *Astrophytum coahuilense* in June 2007 while climbing around Cerro Bola, a dry limestone hill along Mexico Federal Highway 40 east of Torreón, Coahuila. This particular hill is full of cool cacti and succulents along with a host of interesting shrubs and perennials. Plants favor limestone soil and grow in the cracks and fissures or near large rocks in the southwestern corner of Coahuila and adjacent Durango from about 3,000–4,000 feet elevation.

Description Plants have a single five-ribbed body that becomes short columnar with age, eventually reaching 6–8 inches tall (rarely more) and 4–6 inches across. The bodies are spineless and densely covered with large soft fuzzy flecks. Large yellow flowers have red at the base of the **tepals** and are up to 2 inches in diameter. Fruits open at the base.

Culture Plants are hardy to at least 15° F and can be used in USDA zones 9a–11. They are easy to cultivate and can be grown either in the ground or in decorative

Cool Cacti and Succulents for Hot Gardens

pots. These can tolerate full sun throughout much of the desert southwest, however they prefer filtered afternoon sun in the hottest and driest cities such as Las Vegas, Phoenix, and Tucson. They grow best in a gritty soil with excellent drainage that should be allowed to dry between waterings. Reduce watering when night-time temperatures drop to the low 40's F and colder.

Identification These have large fuzzy flecks, yellow flowers with red at the base of the **tepals**, and fruit that opens at the base while *Astrophytum myriostigma* plants have smaller flecks with more well-defined edges, pure yellow flowers, and fruits that split open at the top.

Landscape Application Plants are easily grown in the landscape and look natural when placed near large boulders or in combination with a variety of cactus and succulents. *Agave parrasana* and other Chihuahuan Desert cacti such as *Coryphantha poselgeriana*, *Echinocactus horizontha-lonius*, *Echinocereus enneacanthus*, and *Thelocactus bicolor* make great companion plants. Plant flowering perennials to give some color in the landscape.

Precautions Carefully check for **mealybugs** hiding in any wrinkles in the body and under the flowers and physically remove them.

Astrophytum coahuilense

Astrophytum myriostigma
Bishop's Cap
SMALL CACTUS

SIZE (H x W)	6–15 (rarely 24) inches x 4–10 inches
FLOWER COLOR	Yellow
FLOWER SEASON	Summer to fall
EXPOSURE	Full sun or filtered light
WATER	Low
GROWTH RATE	Moderately slow
PRUNING	None
HARDINESS	15° F, zones 8b–11

Etymology Charles Lemaire used the Greek *myriad-* for numberless and the Greek *stigm-* for point and refers to the countless white dots on the body.

Field Notes I first saw plants of *Astrophytum myriostigma* near Cerritos, San Luis Potosí in 1983 while on a trip with then PhD candidate Russ Buhrow who was studying the genus *Phaseolus*. We spotted a couple plants growing out of cracks in limestone slabs along the side of the road. Thirty-one years later while exploring cactus localities for an upcoming tour, Jeff Chemnick, Brian Kemble, and I stopped at a limestone hillside in central San Luis Potosí and spotted several small plants tucked in between the rocks. These grow in the cracks and fissures of limestone rocks in San Luis Potosí and southern Tamaulipas from about 2,500–5,300 feet elevation.

Description The single body has five ribs, although there can be as few as three or as many as eight. These become a short column with age, reaching 6–15 (rarely 24) inches tall (rarely more) and 4–10 inches across. The bodies are spineless and densely covered with white flecks, or rarely without flecks in the form called "nudum". Clear yellow flowers are 1–2 inches wide and appear several times in late spring and summer. Fruits are dry and split open at the top with a distinctive five-pointed star-shape.

Culture   This is possibly the easiest species to grow and does well either in the ground or in decorative pots. Plants are hardy to at least 15° F and can be used in USDA zones 8b–11. When planted in the ground, these are nearly bullet-proof and can tolerate full sun throughout much of the desert southwest. However, they appreciate afternoon filtered light in the hottest and driest cities such as Las Vegas, Phoenix, and Tucson. In containers, they prefer a gritty soil mix with excellent drainage, but in the ground they will tolerate a heavy native soil laden with rocks. Stop applying any supplemental water for winter.

Astrophytum myriostigma 'Onzuka'

Identification   Compared to *Astrophytum coahuilense*, *Astrophytum myriostigma* has smaller flecks with more well-defined edges, pure yellow flowers, and fruits that split open at the top.

Landscape Application   Plants are easily grown in the landscape and are right at home in a cactus and succulent garden. Try using medium-sized agaves such as *Agave parrasana* and small to medium-sized cacti such as *Coryphantha poselgeriana*, *Echinocactus horizonthalonius*, *Echinocereus stramineus*, and *Thelocactus rinconensis*. They get along well with perennials and small shrubs such as Chrysactinia mexicana and Glandularia gooddingii.

Precautions   Carefully check for **mealybugs** beneath old flower remnants and fruits. Old plants are susceptible to splitting longitudinally.

A. myriostigma var. *columnare*

Astrophytum myriostigma   **79**

Astrophytum ornatum
Star Cactus, Monk's Hood
SMALL CACTUS, SHORT COLUMNAR CACTUS

Etymology Augustin de Candolle used the Latin *ornat-* for adorned to describe the various flecking patterns seen on the underlying green body.

SIZE (H x W)	6–24 (sometimes 36) inches x 6–10 inches
FLOWER COLOR	Yellow
FLOWER SEASON	Summer to fall
EXPOSURE	Full sun or filtered light
WATER	Drought tolerant to low
GROWTH RATE	Moderately slow
PRUNING	None
HARDINESS	15° F, zones 8b–11

Field Notes In April 2010, I came face-to-face with tall specimens of *Astrophytum ornatum* while climbing around the rocky cliffs at the bottom of Toliman Canyon in Hidalgo, Mexico with good friend and frequent traveling partner Brian Kemble. I was able to revisit Toliman Canyon in May 2014 while on a trip with Jeff Chemnick and Brian Kemble and made it a point to find more of these growing out of the cracks in the rocks. The next day while exploring another canyon, I found small plants of *Astrophytum ornatum* var. *mirabelii* growing among rocks. *Astrophytum ornatum* occurs in the states of Hidalgo and Querétaro from about 3,000–5,600 feet elevation.

Description Plants have a single short columnar body 6–24 (sometimes 36) inches tall and 6–10 inches across generally with 8 ribs, each lined with clusters of golden-yellow **spines**. The bodies are green and sparsely to densely covered with white flecks. Yellow flowers are 2–3 inches across and occur repeatedly in summer into early fall. Fruits are dry and covered with sharp spinescent scales.

Culture   These are easy to grow and are suited for either planting in the ground or growing in decorative pots. When planted in the ground, they can tolerate full sun in all but the hottest and driest cities such as Las Vegas, Palm Springs, and Phoenix. Plants are hardy to at least 15° F and can be used in USDA zones 8b–11. They prefer a rocky or gritty soil with excellent drainage and supplemental water every 2–3 weeks in summer. Stop watering from fall through winter.

Identification   With their green bodies decorated with white flecks, golden yellow **spines**, and large yellow flowers, *Astrophytum ornatum* are not readily confused with any other species.

Landscape Application   These can become sizable plants when grown in the landscape and make a statement in any cactus and succulent garden. Try planting alongside small or medium sized agaves such as ***Agave colorata*** and ***Agave parrasana***, and mix in with Chihuahuan Desert cacti such as ***Coryphantha poselgeriana***, ***Echinocactus horizonthalonius***, ***Mammillaria candida***, and ***Thelocactus bicolor***. They look great when placed near large boulders and mix well with a variety of perennials and small shrubs. Some perfect companion plants would include *Glandularia gooddingii*, *Justicia longii*, *Penstemon triflorus*, *Thymophylla pentachaeta*, and *Zinnia acerosa*.

Precautions   Inspect under the flowers and fruits for **mealybugs**. These are easily controlled by physically removing them from the plant.

Beaucarnea gracilis
Mexican Ponytail Palm, Slim-leaf Ponytail Palm
SHRUB-LIKE SUCCULENT, TREE-LIKE SUCCULENT

SIZE (H x W)	4–10 (20) feet x 2–6 feet
FLOWER COLOR	Creamy white
FLOWER SEASON	Summer
EXPOSURE	Full sun, part shade, reflected heat
WATER	Low to moderate
GROWTH RATE	Slow
PRUNING	None
HARDINESS	25° F, zones 9b–11

Etymology French botanist Charles Lemaire used the Latin *gracil-* meaning slender to indicate the narrow leaves.

Field Notes I first saw these majestic beasts with their swollen trunks in 1985 on a trip to southern Puebla and northern Oaxaca. Now every time I travel to Puebla and Oaxaca it is an unwritten rule that we must stop to see some spectacular specimens. These massive monsters grow on hills and flat ground in open desert scrub in southern Puebla and northern Oaxaca from 5,000–7,900 feet.

Description Mature plants have a massive swollen base that can get 4–8 feet in diameter at ground level tapering to the branches. Individual stems are thin, 2–6 feet long, and topped by a **rosette** of upright to spreading leaves. Plants in cultivation are usually grown in containers and are much smaller and can only aspire to attain super large trunks. However, those in cultivation still show the enlarged base that can become the size of a softball or even cantaloupe inside of a decade. The light gray-green leaves are about 1-foot-long by less than ½-inch-wide and edged with minute razor-sharp **teeth**.

Cool Cacti and Succulents for Hot Gardens

Culture Young plants can tolerate temperatures down to the high 20's F while older plants are hardy to about 25° F if the low is not too prolonged. They can be grown as landscape plants in USDA zones of 9b–11 if protected from frost when young. Grow as a potted plant in nearly any southwestern U.S. city if you can bring it inside for the winter. These are low-water-using when in the ground but potted plants prefer to have supplemental water in summer. They can survive all winter without supplemental water, especially if moved inside.

The slow growth rate means these will require many years to develop the extremely large base, so be prepared to pass these on to great-grandchildren.

Identification *Beaucarnea gracilis* has erect to spreading light gray-green leaves, and **Beaucarnea recurvata** has long dark green leaves that droop down over the skinny stem.

Landscape Application For the most part, these will be grown as potted plants because the growth rate is very slow. However, you might be able to find the occasional large plant that was grown in a ground bed in a frost-free area. If you do manage to find a large one, and can afford to buy it, plant with colorfully spined cacti such as **Echinocactus grusonii**, **Ferocactus pilosus**, **Mammillaria geminispina**, and stout **rosette**-forming **Agave bovicornuta** and **Agave gentryi**. Add seasonal color by including shrubs such as *Anisacanthus quadrifidus, Calliandra californica, Dalea frutescens,* and *Salvia greggii*. For those in cities that regularly receive frost, grow these in large clay pots but not so large you cannot move them around. If you are young enough, start with small plants and watch them grow over your lifetime, otherwise find a plant with a significantly-sized base and put it in the perfect spot so you will not have to move it when winter comes around.

Precautions These are mostly bullet-proof plants when grown in frost-free climates, but keep an eye out for **mealybugs** on leaves at the top of the plant.

Beaucarnea recurvata
Ponytail Palm
SHRUB-LIKE SUCCULENT, TREE-LIKE SUCCULENT

Etymology French botanist Charles Lemaire used the Latin *recurv-* to signify the drooping leaves of this species.

Field Notes July 2007 found me traveling with three other plant fiends in southern Tamaulipas when we spotted a huge *Beaucarnea recurvata* announcing its presence by poking its many flowering stems above the surrounding vegetation. These stunning plants are known to occur in dense forests in southern Tamaulipas and Veracruz from 300–3,000 feet elevation.

SIZE (H x W)	4–10 (20) feet x 2–6 feet
FLOWER COLOR	Creamy white
FLOWER SEASON	Summer
EXPOSURE	Full sun, part shade, reflected heat
WATER	Low to moderate
GROWTH RATE	Slow
PRUNING	None
HARDINESS	28°–30° F, zones 10a–11

Description These have a large swollen base that can get 1–3 feet or more in diameter and tall stems to 4–10 feet. Very old specimens growing in frost-free climates can reach up to 20 feet tall with a spread of 6–12 feet. The distinctive drooping leaves are rich green to dark green, 1–3 feet long by ¾-inch-wide, and edged with minute razor-sharp **teeth**. Old plants will produce creamy white flowers in summer and are **dioecious** with the female plants producing seed.

Culture Young plants are not hardy and can be damaged when temperatures dip into the high 20's F. They can be grown as landscape plants in the frost-free or nearly frost-free USDA zones of 10a–11 and in warm micro-climates in 9b with some winter protection. Grow as a potted plant in nearly any southwestern U.S. city if you can bring it inside for the winter. These are low-water-using when in the ground but potted plants prefer to have supplemental water in summer. They can survive all winter without supplemental water, especially if moved inside.

Identification *Beaucarnea recurvata* has long dark green leaves that droop down over the skinny stem while *Beaucarnea gracilis* has erect to spreading light green leaves.

Landscape Application There are some very large plants at the Huntington Botanical Gardens in the Los Angeles area and are the center of attention among various cacti and other succulents. For those in frost-free zones surround these with colorfully spined cacti such as *Echinocactus grusonii*, *Ferocactus pilosus*, *Mammillaria geminispina*, and stout **rosette**-forming *Agave bovicornuta* and *Agave gentryi*. Add seasonal color by including shrubs such as *Ageratum corymbosum*, *Anisacanthus quadrifidus*, *Caesalpinia mexicana*, *Galphimia glauca*, and *Poliomintha maderensis*. For those in cities that regularly receive frost, grow these in large clay pots but not so large you cannot move them around. If you are young enough, start with small plants and watch them grow over your lifetime, otherwise find a plant with a significantly sized base and put it in the perfect spot so you will not have to move it when winter comes around.

Precautions These are care free plants when grown in frost-free climates but keep an eye out for **mealybugs** on leaves at the top of the plant. Protect young plants from freeze damage.

Bulbine frutescens
Shrubby Bulbine
SHRUB-LIKE SUCCULENT

SIZE (H x W)	1½–2 feet x 3–4 feet
FLOWER COLOR	Yellow or orange
FLOWER SEASON	Winter to spring
EXPOSURE	Full sun to reflected heat
WATER	Low to moderate
GROWTH RATE	Fast
PRUNING	Occasional thinning
HARDINESS	16–18° F, zones 8b–11

Etymology Botanist Carl Ludwig von Willdenow used the Latin *frut-*, meaning shrubby, which describes this plant perfectly.

Field Notes In September of 2000, springtime in the southern Hemisphere, I was in the Groot-Swartberg Mountains of South Africa with the now deceased Rod and Rachel Saunders of Silverhill Seeds and a dozen other plant fanatics. We stopped to photograph an intriguing bulb called *Boophone disticha* on a dry rocky slope when we happened to spot a lonely *Bulbine frutescens* in flower. Plants are wide-spread in southern Africa growing in dry grassland, dwarf Karoo shrub land, woodland, and on rocky slopes.

Description These are shrubby plants growing to 1½–2 feet tall and spreading to 3–4 feet across. The rounded leaves are green, thick, succulent, and 3–6 inches long. In late winter and spring, plants are topped by 12–18-inch-long flower **spikes** with yellow flowers, or orange flowers in the case of the cultivars 'Hallmark' and 'Tiny Tangerine'.

Culture Plants can be grown in USDA zones 8b–11 and in warm microclimates in zone 8a. These grow great in full sun or against a south or west-facing wall for the reflected heat in winter. Plants are fast growing and will recover quickly if they sustain any frost damage. They are low-water-using when established but will look their best when given periodic supplemental water from spring through summer provided they are in soil that drains quickly. Because of the fast growth, you might need to prune judiciously if the plants grow too quickly or develop an open form.

Identification *Bulbine frutescens* normally has all yellow flowers, but the cultivars 'Hallmark' and 'Tiny Tangerine' have orange petals and yellow anthers.

Landscape Application Use Shrubby Bulbine for its seasonal color in hot low elevation cities like Phoenix, Palm Springs, and Yuma. They are perfect for coastal California cities and do well in cities like Tucson, Sierra Vista, and Las Cruces. Plants look great in any small scale residential or large scale commercial **xeriscape** and are compatible with many other low-water-use plants. These combine well with the likes of **Agave palmeri**, **Cleistocactus strausii**, **Dasylirion acrotrichum**, **Ferocactus rectispinus**, and **Yucca rostrata**, as well as small trees and shrubs like *Acacia willardiana*, *Eysenhardtia orthocarpa*, *Calliandra eriophylla*, and *Justicia spicigera*.

Precautions Although these will tolerate supplemental water in summer, do not water too much in fall and winter.

Bulbine frutescens

Bursera fagaroides
Elephant Tree, Torote
SHRUB-LIKE SUCCULENT, TREE-LIKE SUCCULENT

SIZE (H x W)	6–12 (18) feet x 6–10 (15) feet
FLOWER COLOR	Pale yellow-green
FLOWER SEASON	Summer
EXPOSURE	Full sun, reflected heat, part shade
WATER	Low to moderate
GROWTH RATE	Moderately slow
PRUNING	Occasional thinning
HARDINESS	28°–30° F, zones 10a–11

Etymology The species name is from the Latin *faga-* and refers to the resemblance to plants in the genus *Fagus* or Beech.

Field Notes Large plants of *Bursera fagaroides* are some of my favorites to see while traveling in Mexico. I rarely see a solitary specimen that is screaming "look at me", so photos in the field are uncommon for me. I have mostly photographed small plants or close ups of the peeling bark on the trunks. The opportunity to photograph a stand-alone plant presented itself in 2008 while traveling along Mexico

Highway 16 in Sonora on the way to see *Agave multifilifera* at the Basaseachic Falls in Chihuahua. These are wide-spread throughout Mexico and occur from near sea-level to 4,400 feet elevation.

Description These can be large shrub-like plants branching down low or tree-like with one or two well-defined trunks and branching up high. Old plants in nature can grow to about 18 feet tall and 15 feet across, while in cultivation a reasonable size to expect is about 6–12 feet tall and spreading to 6–10 feet across. Medium green to dark green leaves are winter **deciduous** and once **pinnate** with 5–13 **leaflets**, each ¾–2 inches long. Bark on trunks and branches is coppery-green and peels off in papery sheets.

Culture Plants are a little frost sensitive, suffering tip damage when temperatures drop into the mid-20's F. They can be grown in the ground in USDA zones 10a–11 and possibly in zone 9b if planted where they receive reflected heat in winter. These are perfect for large clay pots in colder zones. They can be grown in partial shade, full sun, or reflected heat. The growth rate is moderately slow so be patient for them to achieve small tree size. In the ground, they are low-water-using but will grow slightly faster when given supplemental water from spring through summer. A small tree shape can be achieved by judicious pruning.

Identification *Bursera fagaroides* has peeling bark and narrow elongated **leaflets** usually with some **teeth** along the margins while *Bursera hindsiana* lacks peeling bark and has shorter almost rounded **leaflets**, and *Bursera microphylla* has peeling bark but smaller more numerous **leaflets**.

Landscape Application *Bursera fagaroides* can be used as a landscape plant in coastal southern California cities and hot low elevation cities like Phoenix, Palm Springs, and Yuma. They will grow well in reflected heat of south and west facing walls in cities like Tucson and Sierra Vista. These combine well with a variety of plants ranging from cacti and other succulents like *Agave parryi*, *Dasylirion acrotrichum*, *Fouquieria splendens*, *Yucca elata*, and *Yucca torreyi*, and shrubs with showy flower displays like *Calliandra eriophylla, Chrysactinia mexicana, Dalea pulchra, Justicia xylosteoides*, and *Leucophyllum laevigatum*.

Precautions Be aware that plants might suffer some twig damage when winter lows drop into the mid- to high 20's F and freeze severely if exposed to low 20's F.

Bursera hindsiana
Copal, Red Elephant Tree, Torote Prieto
SHRUB-LIKE SUCCULENT, TREE-LIKE SUCCULENT

SIZE (H x W)	5–15 (20) feet x 5–15 (20) feet
FLOWER COLOR	White
FLOWER SEASON	Late summer to fall
EXPOSURE	Full sun, part shade, reflected heat
WATER	Drought tolerant to low
GROWTH RATE	Moderate
PRUNING	Occasional thinning
HARDINESS	28°–30° F, zones 10a–11

Etymology George Bentham was a 19th Century English botanist who described this in honor of British naval surgeon Richard Hinds.

Field Notes These are readily seen on sandy flats in the hyper-arid climate north of San Felipe in Baja California. This area is home to cacti and succulent shrub-like trees. Plants are also commonly seen near San Carlos just north of Guaymas in Sonora. *Bursera hindsiana* is wide-spread throughout the Baja California peninsula and along the coast in Sonora. Plants can be seen growing in arroyos and washes, on gentle slopes, and even rocky hillsides from about sea-level to about 2,300 feet elevation.

Description These can be either large, wide-spreading, and shrub-like with red to reddish-gray bark on multiple trunks branching from down low, or tree-like with a wide-spreading canopy. In habitat, they will grow anywhere from 5–20 feet tall by 5–20 feet across, while in cultivation one can reasonably expect a size of 5–8 feet tall and 5–8 feet across. Leaves can be simple or **odd-pinnate** with 3–5 **ovate**, **obovate**, or broadly **lanceolate leaflets**. These leaves are drought and winter **deciduous** and appear in response to warmth and water. Bark is red or reddish brown and does not peel.

Culture Plants are slightly frost sensitive, suffering tip damage when temperatures drop into the high-20's F with severe damage when exposed to low 20's F. They can be grown in the ground in USDA zones 9b–11 and possibly zone 9a if they receive reflected heat and the trunks are wrapped for protection. These are ideal for large clay pots in colder zones if they can be moved indoors or under cover during winter. Grow in partial shade, full sun, or against a wall. Plants have a moderate growth rate and will take several years to achieve small tree size. They  are drought tolerant, but will benefit from supplemental water in summer. A small tree shape can be achieved with selective pruning.

Identification *Bursera hindsiana* has dark red or reddish-gray bark that does not peel - a characteristic that distinguishes the plants from both *Bursera fagaroides* and *Bursera microphylla*.

Landscape Application *Bursera hindsiana* can be used as a landscape plant in coastal southern California cities and hot low elevation cities like Phoenix, Palm Springs, and Yuma. They should be tried in reflected heat of south and west facing walls in cities like Tucson and Sierra Vista. In coastal southern California cities, these look great when planted with cacti and other succulents like *Agave cerulata*, *Ferocactus acanthodes*, *Fouquieria splendens*, and *Yucca thompsoniana*, as well as drought tolerant shrubs like *Asclepias subulata*, *Calliandra californica*, *Encelia farinosa*, *Justicia californica*, *Penstemon parryi*, and *Trixis californica*.

Precautions Plants might suffer some twig damage when winter lows drop to the high 20's F.

Bursera microphylla

Elephant Tree, Copal, Torote Blanco

SHRUB-LIKE SUCCULENT, TREE-LIKE SUCCULENT

SIZE (H x W)	6–10 (20) feet x 6–10 feet
FLOWER COLOR	Cream-white or pale greenish yellow
FLOWER SEASON	Summer
EXPOSURE	Full sun, part shade, reflected heat
WATER	Drought tolerant to low
GROWTH RATE	Moderately slow
PRUNING	Occasional thinning
HARDINESS	25° F, zones 9b–11

Etymology   American botanist Dr. Asa Gray used the Greek *micro-* for small and the Greek *phyll-* for leaf to describe the small **leaflets** of this species.

Field Notes   These are commonly seen growing on sandy flats and among large boulders north of San Felipe in the northeastern part of the state of Baja California, while plants are more tree-like farther south on the peninsula. *Bursera microphylla* is native to the Sonoran Desert and can be found throughout the Baja California peninsula, Sonora, and southern Arizona from near sea-level to about 3,300 feet elevation.

Description   These can be low and wide-spreading shrub-like plants or more upright and tree-like with a single trunk and branching up high. They are generally about equal in height and width growing between 6–10 high and wide, while tree-like plants can reach 20 feet tall and 10 feet across. **Odd-pinnate** medium green to dark green leaves have up to 35 small and narrow **leaflets**. Leaves are drought and winter **deciduous**. Bark on trunks and branches is whitish and papery, peeling in large flakes; the bark of smaller branches and twigs is reddish brown.

Culture Being moderately frost sensitive, these will suffer some stem damage when overnight lows drop below 25° F. They can be grown in the ground in USDA zones 9b–11 and possibly zone 9a if situated against a south or west-facing wall in winter. These are ideal for large clay pots in colder zones if they can be protected during winter. They can be grown in partial shade, full sun, or reflected heat in winter. Plants have a moderate growth rate and will take several years to achieve small tree size. They are drought tolerant but will thank you for supplying occasional supplemental water in summer. Selectively trim out extraneous side branches to shape as a small tree.

Identification *Bursera microphylla* has up to 35 small narrow **leaflets** that are linear in outline. *Bursera hindsiana* has shorter almost rounded **leaflets**, and *Bursera fagaroides* has fewer **leaflets**.

Landscape Application *Bursera microphylla* can be used as a landscape plant in coastal southern California cities and hot cities like Phoenix. Grow them next to south and west facing walls in cities like Tucson and Sierra Vista. Plant with other succulents like *Agave deserti*, *Ferocactus acanthodes*, *Fouquieria splendens*, as well as shrubs with showy flower displays like *Calliandra californica*.

Precautions Plants might suffer some twig and stem damage when winter lows drop below 25° F.

Bursera microphylla

Calibanus hookeri
Mexican Boulder Plant
SHRUB-LIKE SUCCULENT

SIZE (H x W)	1–3 feet x 1–2 feet
FLOWER COLOR	Creamy-white
FLOWER SEASON	Spring to summer
EXPOSURE	Full sun, filtered sun
WATER	Low to moderate
GROWTH RATE	Slow
PRUNING	None
HARDINESS	10°–15° F, zones 8a–11

Etymology Author and botanist Charles Lemaire named this interesting plant in honor of William Hooker, an English botanist and first director of the Royal Botanic Gardens, Kew.

Field Notes Plants can be difficult to spot in habitat because the large caudex looks like a boulder with grass leaves on top. In July 2007, three friends and I were hopping around on large boulders in the state of San Luis Potosí when we spotted grass-like leaves and round reddish fruit growing out from a mass of large rocks. Closer inspection revealed the swollen **caudex** of a *Calibanus hookeri* that was wedged between the rocks. These are found growing in the open and among boulders and rocks on hillsides from about 3,300–7,550 feet elevation.

Description These are evergreen plants that develop a large aboveground **caudex** covered with tufts of gray-green grass-like leaves. The **caudex** can eventually get 1–2 feet across and with the many tufts of leaves the overall plant height can reach 1–3 feet. Plants are **dioecious** and flowers appear mostly in spring or summer.

Culture The San Marcos Growers website indicates that plants are cold hardy to the 10°–15° F range and are suitable for growing in the ground in USDA zones 8a–11. They can be grown in filtered sunlight or full sun in most any low- and mid-elevation city in the desert southwest. The growth rate is slow and it will take several years for the **caudex** to achieve the size of a softball. In the ground, they are low-water-using, but when grown in pots they can tolerate some supplemental water from spring through summer. Do not let the soil get soggy wet or the roots will drown, and the caudex will rot.

Identification Plants of *Calibanus hookeri* are very distinctive and larger ones cannot be confused with any others. However, young ones can be mistaken for young ***Beaucarnea gracilis*** until those start to develop their elongated trunk.

Landscape Application Grow these in large containers until big enough to be visible in the ground. Look for a spot in the landscape that is highly visible, maybe on a raised mound complete with large rocks. Grow with smaller cacti and other succulents like ***Agave schidigera***, ***Astrophytum myriostigma***, ***Ferocactus glaucescens***, and ***Yucca linearifolia***. Perennials and small shrubs that go well with these include *Bahia absinthifolia*, *Conoclinium dissectum*, *Glandularia gooddingii*, *Justicia longii*, *Penstemon triflorus*, and *Zinnia acerosa*. A couple suggestions for small trees would include *Acacia willardiana*, *Bursera microphylla*, and *Eysenhardtia orthocarpa*.

Precautions Leaves and possibly the **caudex** may be susceptible to damage by rabbits and packrats, while whole plants might be uprooted by javelina, so screen newly planted specimens for at least the first 2–3 years.

Carnegiea gigantea
Saguaro
COLUMNAR CACTUS

SIZE (H x W)	10–30 (or more) feet x 5–6 (or more) feet
FLOWER COLOR	White
FLOWER SEASON	Late spring to early summer
EXPOSURE	Full sun
WATER	Drought tolerant
GROWTH RATE	Very slow
PRUNING	None
HARDINESS	Mid-teens F, zones 9a–11

Etymology In describing this plant, botanist George Engelmann used the Greek *gigan-* meaning large to note that this was the largest cactus at that time.

Field Notes These iconic plants are easily spotted from any major highway or interstate while traveling in the Sonoran Desert of Arizona and Sonora, Mexico. Drive through either Saguaro National Park East or West to see incredible examples of this stately cactus. Take an early morning hike in May on any trail in the Tucson Mountains and you are likely to see plants with their large white flowers. Plants grow on rocky hillsides and gentle outwash slopes throughout the Sonoran Desert of southwestern Arizona and western Sonora. They tend to favor south-facing slopes and grow at elevations below 4,000 feet.

Description Young plants are typically thin to fat with spear-shaped single bodies 10–18 inches in diameter with the numerous ribs allowing for expansion and contraction. The individual plants can grow to 10–30 feet (rarely more) high and, with arms, can get 5–6 feet (sometimes more) wide. The 15–30 sharp **spines** are in clusters evenly spaced along the ribs. White funnel-shaped flowers are over 2 inches wide and appear in late spring to early summer. Fleshy fruits are red at maturity and have long been harvested to be eaten and made into wine. A wide variety of birds are important for pollination and seed dispersal.

Culture Distribution is limited in the north by cold, although mature plants can withstand winter lows to mid-teens F and are adaptable to USDA zones 9a–11. Young plants will need some frost protection and shading from summer sun, but older plants prefer full sun. Plants have a very slow growth rate and should not be pushed. They are drought tolerant once established.

Identification *Carnegiea gigantea* tends to have a higher rib count and a dark green body compared to the fewer ribs and bluish cast to the body of *Pachycereus pringlei*. These tend to have darker green epidermis and darker **spine** color than *Trichocereus terscheckii*.

Landscape Application Plants are best used as a focal point in the landscape in cities with hot summers like Phoenix, Tucson, and Yuma. They can be planted singly or grouped for a spectacular effect. This classic Sonoran Desert icon can be used in a **xeriscape** with Sonoran Desert native trees, shrubs, and perennials. Ideal companion trees are *Acacia constricta*, *Acacia greggii*, *Olneya tesota*, and *Parkinsonia microphylla*. Some great shrubs and perennials would include *Baileya multiradiata*, *Calliandra eriophylla*, *Celtis pallida*, *Encelia farinosa*, *Glandularia gooddingii*, and *Justicia californica*.

Precautions Mature naturally occurring Saguaro plants are frequently transplanted from habitat only after permits have been obtained from the Arizona Department of Agriculture. Be aware that large plants, generally over 6 feet tall, do not transplant with great success.

Cephalocereus senilis
Old Man Cactus, Viejo
COLUMNAR CACTUS

Etymology English botanist Adrian Haworth used the Latin *senil-* meaning old to refer to the "old-man-look" of plants with long white wooly fibers.

SIZE (H x W)	3–30 (45) feet x 8–12 inches stem diameter
FLOWER COLOR	Yellowish pink
FLOWER SEASON	Spring to summer
EXPOSURE	Full sun
WATER	Drought tolerant to low
GROWTH RATE	Very slow
PRUNING	None
HARDINESS	25° F, zones 9b–11

Field Notes In June 2006, I traveled to the Barranca de Metztitlán in Hidalgo, Mexico and was greeted by an extensive stand of these desert sentinels guarding the arid hillsides. As I scanned the hillsides with binoculars, many adult plants were apparent; however, young seedlings were not plentiful. Plants grow on dry rocky hillsides in Hidalgo and Guanajuato between about 3,000–6,000 feet elevation.

Description Young plants are narrow columns densely covered with 1–5 **central spines** and 20–30, 2-4-inch-long white hair-like **radial spines** giving the plant a shaggy appearance. As the plants age, the single body grows tall and wider with old plants in cultivation reaching 15–18 feet tall with a stem diameter of nearly 1-foot. Funnel-shaped, yellowish pink flowers come from

the **pseudocephalium**, which at first grows only on one side of the plant, but eventually covers the top.

Culture Dan Bach of Bach's Greenhouses in Tucson told me plants have survived winter lows of 25° F with no damage, so they can be considered hardy in USDA zones 9b–11. Young plants will probably need some frost protection until they get larger. Slowly acclimate plants to summer sun so the tips do not sunburn. They are drought tolerant and slow growing but will appreciate receiving some supplemental water every couple weeks in summer.

Identification With their long white **spines** that look like an unruly head of hair, young *Cephalocereus senilis* plants are very distinctive and not easily confused with any other cactus. As the plants grow larger, that distinctive feature becomes less noticeable, but the plants are still easily recognizable.

Landscape Application Group several of these together on a slope to recreate what they look like in habitat. Plant them under the canopy of a sparse tree in cities with hot summers like Phoenix, Palm Springs, and Yuma, but put them in full sun in cities with mild summers such as those along the southern California coast from San Diego to Santa Barbara. A few great tree choices are *Acacia constricta*, *Acacia greggii*, *Acacia willardiana*, *Bauhinia macranthera*, and *Parkinsonia microphylla*. Plant these among perennials, and small and medium-size shrubs to help protect young plants. Try using *Buddleja marrubiifolia*, *Leucophyllum laevigatum*, and *Salvia greggii*; while excellent flowering perennials would include *Baileya multiradiata*, *Glandularia gooddingii*, and *Thymophylla pentachaeta*. Grow with other cacti and succulents such as *Agave xylonacantha*, **Dasylirion acrotrichum**, **Echinocactus platyacanthus**, and **Yucca rostrata**.

Precautions Be sure to keep the tender tips from sunburning by slowly acclimating the plants to full sun.

Cleistocactus hyalacanthus
Silver Torch Cactus
COLUMNAR CACTUS

SIZE (H x W)	2–4 feet x 2–3-inch stem diameter, clusters to 2–4 feet or more
FLOWER COLOR	Orange-red with darker tips
FLOWER SEASON	Spring to summer
EXPOSURE	Filtered sun
WATER	Low to moderate
GROWTH RATE	Moderate
PRUNING	None
HARDINESS	20° F, zones 9a–11

Etymology Karl Moritz Schumann used the Greek *hyalo-* meaning glass and the Greek *acantho-* for spine to indicate the nearly transparent or glass-like nature of the spines.

Field Notes I was on a trip to Argentina led by Guillermo Rivera and got to see these plants growing on a rocky slope with some stems showing off their bright red narrowly tubular flowers. *Cleistocactus hyalacanthus* is found growing on rocky slopes in mountains of northwestern Argentina and southern Bolivia from about 5,300–9,200 feet elevation.

Description These shrubby plants have many stems growing to about 2–4 feet tall with individual stems about 2–3 inches in diameter. Plants will produce

Photo by Scott Calhoun

stems from near the base with clusters sometimes reaching 2–4 feet or more across. Stems have 15–25 ribs (it's hard to count them all beneath all those **spines**) and are densely covered by white, yellow, or yellowish-brown **spines**. The 20–30 hair-like **radial spines** are fine-textured and about 1-inch-long while the 3–4 **central spines** are slightly stiffer and longer. Pink, purplish-pink, orange, or red flowers are ever so slightly curved, about 1½-inch-long, and appear in late spring to summer.

Culture Plants have been in southwestern U.S. horticulture for several years and have survived winter lows of about 20° F with tips covered and are fine for USDA zones 9a–11. Small plants should be protected from frost and shaded from summer sun. Larger plants that have been acclimated can tolerate more sun and cold but still prefer a little bit of mid-day and afternoon shade in the hottest cities of the desert southwest. Plants have a moderate growth rate, and prefer receiving supplemental water in the hottest cities of the desert southwest to prevent tips from dying. Keep extra water to a minimum in winter though.

Identification *Cleistocactus hyalacanthus* is more densely **spined** with shorter flowers than *Cleistocactus baumannii*. *Cleistocactus hyalacanthus* has thinner stems with fewer **spines** and slightly shorter flowers than *Cleistocactus strausii*.

Landscape Application Try using these in groups scattered throughout a landscape complete with small or medium-sized desert shrubs and perennials. Some suggested perennials and shrubs include *Chrysactinia mexicana*, *Conoclinium dissectum*, *Penstemon triflorus*, and *Salvia greggii*. One or two strategically placed small trees such as *Acacia constricta*, *Acacia greggii*, and *Acacia willardiana* can provide dappled light for those plants that need it.

Precautions Drape frost cloth over the plants or place styrofoam cups on the growing tips when winter lows are expected to dip into the mid-20s F.

Cleistocactus strausii
Silver Torch Cactus
COLUMNAR CACTUS

Etymology Emil Heese was a German botanist who named this in honor of L. Straus, a German merchant and cactus enthusiast who was a co-founder of the German Cactus Society.

Field Notes *Cleistocactus strausii* can be found in the mountains of southern Bolivia and northern Argentina. We were not quite far enough north when I visited northern Argentina in November 2022, but am determined to go see these. Plants grow on rocky open to forested hillsides in Tarija Department of Southern Bolivia and adjacent northern Argentina from about 7,500–9,000 feet elevation.

SIZE (H x W)	3–8 feet x 2–3 inch stem diameter, clusters to 2–6 feet
FLOWER COLOR	Burgundy red
FLOWER SEASON	Spring to summer
EXPOSURE	Full sun, filtered sun
WATER	Low to moderate
GROWTH RATE	Moderately fast
PRUNING	None
HARDINESS	25° F, zones 9b–11

Description These form narrow columns to about 3–8 feet tall with stems about 2–3 inches in diameter. Plants will sparingly cluster from near the base with clusters sometimes reaching 2–6 feet across. Stems are light green with 25–30 ribs and are densely covered by white **spines**. There are 30–40, white, hair-like **radial spines** that measure ½–2 inches long. Bright red to deep magenta, slightly curved, tubular, 3-inch-long flowers appear in spring and summer.

Cool Cacti and Succulents for Hot Gardens

Culture These have been in cultivation in the southwestern U.S. for many years and have survived winter lows of 25° F with no damage and are hardy in USDA zones 9b–11. Small plants need some frost protection and shading from summer sun. Older plants will tolerate full sun even in the hottest southwestern U.S. cities. Plants have a moderately fast growth rate, and prefer receiving supplemental water on a regular schedule in spring and summer to prevent tips from drying out and  dying. Keep moderately dry in winter to avoid any chance of rotting the roots.

Identification *Cleistocactus strausii* has upright stems densely covered with white **spines** while *Cleistocactus baumannii* has thinner, upright to arching stems less densely covered with golden yellowish **spines**, and *Cleistocactus hyalacanthus* has thinner stems with fewer **spines** and slightly shorter flowers.

Landscape Application Group several of these together along with other cacti and succulents for a stunning effect. Intersperse spring perennials and small shrubs to provide color throughout much of the year. Some suggested perennials and shrubs include *Dalea capitata*, *Glandularia gooddingii*, *Justicia candicans*, *Leucophyllum candidum*, *Penstemon pseudospectabilis*, *Salvia greggii*, *Thymophylla pentachaeta*, and *Zinnia grandiflora*. Place a couple small trees in a cactus and succulent garden to give dappled light for those plants that need it. Two great tree choices are *Acacia constricta*, and *Acacia willardiana*.

Precautions Shade the tips from summer sun until they get acclimated and cover plants with frostcloth if winter lows are forecast to be in the low 20's F.

Corryocactus erectus
Red Hot Chili Poker Cactus
COLUMNAR CACTUS, SHRUB-LIKE CACTUS

SIZE (H x W)	12–48 inches x 1-inch stem diameter (clumps to 30 inches or more)
FLOWER COLOR	Orange
FLOWER SEASON	Late spring and summer
EXPOSURE	Filtered sun, part shade
WATER	Low
GROWTH RATE	Moderate
PRUNING	None
HARDINESS	25° F, zones 9b–11

Etymology Horticulturist Curt Backeberg named this species using the Latin *erect-* to describe the upright stems.

Field Notes In 2018, Carol and I went on a tour to Peru and Ecuador to see all the touristy stuff (Machu Picchu, Cusco, Galapagos, etc.), and I just took pictures of any plant that I saw hoping to figure out ID's later. By shear coincidence, I took a picture of a cactus that my friend and cactus fanatic, Tristan Davis, identified as *Corryocactus erectus*.

It is one that Tristan grows, so much of the information was provided by him. Plants are native to the mountains around the Cusco area in Peru. They grow on rocky steep slopes from about 7,800–16,100 feet elevation.

Description Stems are slender, semi-prostrate to erect, about 1–4 feet tall and 1-inch in diameter with shrub-like aspect to nearly 3 feet across. There are 8–18 light colored **spines** that radiate out in all directions and not differentiated into **central spines** and **radial spines**. Scarlet to orange funnel-shaped flowers are 1–1½ inches long and appear in summer.

Culture Provide some frost protection for young plants, but as they get larger and older they are hardy to about 25° F and are excellent for landscapes in USDA zones 9b–11. They grow best in either filtered sun or part shade in the hot summer cities of the southwest, but can tolerate full sun in cooler summer coastal California cities. They are low-water-using in summer, and soil should be kept dry in winter. They have a moderate growth rate when given supplemental water on a regular schedule in summer. Pruning should be restricted to stems that get too floppy.

Identification *Corryocactus erectus* tends to be a little shorter with narrower stems than the slightly taller *Corryocactus squarrosus*, a plant that has slightly thicker stems and can make a wider cluster with age.

Landscape Application Use several of these scattered throughout a landscape complete with small shrubs and perennials such as *Baileya multiradiata, Chrysactinia mexicana, Conoclinium dissectum, Glandularia gooddingii, Penstemon triflorus, Thymophylla pentachaeta*, and *Salvia greggii*. One or two strategically placed small trees in a cactus and succulent garden would provide the dappled light for the plants that need it. A couple great tree choices are *Acacia constricta, Acacia greggii*, and *Acacia willardiana*. These fit in nicely with a variety of cacti and other succulent plants such as **Agave schidigera, Aloe striata, Bursera microphylla, Echinocactus grusonii**, and **Thelocactus rinconensis**. These small scale plants can be used in smaller residential yards, in small commercial landscapes, or even street medians in residential neighborhoods.

Precautions These seem to look their best when grown in a bit of shade in summer. Inspect your plants carefully for any signs of **mealybugs** and remove them if found.

Coryphantha erecta
Erect Coryphantha
CLUSTERING CACTUS

SIZE (H x W)	15–20 inches x 2–3 inches (clumps to 12–24 inches)
FLOWER COLOR	Yellow
FLOWER SEASON	Summer
EXPOSURE	Full sun, filtered sun
WATER	Low to moderate
GROWTH RATE	Moderate
PRUNING	None
HARDINESS	25° F, zones 9b–11

Etymology Charles Antoine Lemaire was a 19th Century French botanist who used the Latin *erect-* to signify the upright stems of this species.

Field Notes The first time I saw *Coryphantha erecta* was in July 2007. I was with friends exploring around the ruins of an old mining settlement near Mineral de Pozos in Guanajuato, Mexico. We had just missed flowering by a day or two, but there were several large clusters of stems. In June 2021, Tristan Davis and I were tracking down a locality for an unknown *Agave* species in Guanajuato and saw plants with flower buds very close to opening, but we were probably one or two days too early. *Coryphantha erecta* grows in rocky soil on flat land, roadcuts, or on mountainsides in Guanajuato, Hidalgo, and Querétaro from about 4,300–8,200 feet elevation.

Description Plants start as a single short body becoming cylindrical to short columnar to 15–20 inches tall. They branch from the base eventually having several stems and forming small clusters to about 12–24 inches

Cool Cacti and Succulents for Hot Gardens

across. The bright green to blue-green body color is highly visible beneath the sparse **spines**. Conical **tubercles** are about ½-inch-high and topped by 2–4 nearly 1-inch-long yellowish brown **central spines**, and 8–13, straight spreading light yellowish or brownish ½-inch long, **radial spines**. Yellow funnelform flowers are 2–2½ inches long and appear in summer.

Culture Plants are hardy in USDA zones 9b–11 and grow well in southwestern U.S. cities where winter lows rarely hit 25° F. Protect young plants from frost for the first couple winters, but once established they will be fine in cities such as Palm Springs, Phoenix, Tucson, and Yuma. While older fully established plants will tolerate full sun, young ones need to be shaded until they are fully acclimated. Plants have a moderate growth rate when given supplemental water on a regular schedule in spring and summer but prefer to be kept dry in winter.

Identification *Coryphantha erecta* plants are easily recognized by long, thick, cylindrical, upright to spreading stems.

Landscape Application Plants of *Coryphantha erecta* can be used in a cactus and succulent garden along with other cool cacti. Group them with other low growing cacti such as *Astrophytum ornatum*, other *Coryphantha* species, *Echinocereus* species, and *Thelocactus* species. Use some taller short columnar cacti such as *Cleistocactus strausii* and *Oreocereus celsianus*. For seasonal color, mix in perennials and small shrubs such as: *Baileya multiradiata, Calliandra eriophylla, Dalea frutescens, Glandularia gooddingii, Penstemon triflorus,* and *Scutellaria suffrutescens*. For a little bit of shade, plant *Acacia constricta* or *Acacia willardiana*. These can also be grown in large decorative containers and moved around for the best display.

Precautions Be sure to protect young plants from frost and prevent sunburning by slowly acclimating them to full sun.

Coryphantha macromeris
Nipple Beehive Cactus
CLUSTERING CACTUS

Etymology George Engelmann used the Greek *macro-* for large and the Greek *meri-* for part, most likely a reference to the large flower parts.

SIZE (H x W)	6–12 inches x clumps to 24–36 inches
FLOWER COLOR	Rose-pink, magenta
FLOWER SEASON	Summer
EXPOSURE	Filtered sun
WATER	Low
GROWTH RATE	Slow
PRUNING	None
HARDINESS	10° F, zones 8a–11

Field Notes In early April 2024, Carol and I went with a group of friends to Cuatrociénegas in Coahuila. While there, we were scouring the desert for interesting plants and came upon a few clusters of these tucked beneath various shrubs. None of the clusters had the bright rose pink flowers, so I will have to continue traveling into the Chihuahuan Desert Region hoping to find *Coryphantha macromeris* in bloom. The species occurs from New Mexico and Texas south into northern Mexico. Plants are found in a variety of substrates from nearly pure gypsum, gravelly, sandy, or clay and grow in the open under shrubs from near sea level to close to 5,000 feet elevation.

Description Plants have small globose to cylindrical dark green stems about 6–12 inches tall and 2–3 inches in diameter. They produce numerous stems with clumps reaching 24–36 inches across. Conspicuous **tubercles** are narrowly

conical to cylindrical about ½-inch-tall and topped by 1–6, ½-inch-long, black or brown **central spines** and 9–15 thin **radial spines**. Flowers are magenta or rose-pink, about 2–3 inches across, and last for only one day. Prime flowering is during summer monsoons.

Culture Established plants are hardy to about 10° F and can be grown in USDA zones 8a–11. These are perfect for desert cities with hot summers such as Palm Springs, Phoenix, and Tucson. Plants prefer to be in some shade as they will burn in full sun. Plants are low-water-using but will tolerate extra water in summer. Place them in a soil that is fast draining to avoid any rot problems. Leave your clippers in their holster.

Identification The clustering nature, elongated **tubercles**, and brilliant rose-pink to magenta flowers are very distinctive for this species.

Landscape Application Plants can be used in a xeric garden and should be placed in the shade of a large desert shrub like *Aloysia gratissima*, *Larrea divaricata*, or *Senna wislizeni*, or small desert trees like *Acacia constricta* or *Eysenhardtia orthocarpa*. Grow with a variety of other colorful cacti and succulent plants such as ***Astrophytum coahuilense***, ***Coryphantha poselgeriana***, ***Echinocereus stramineus***, ***Hesperaloe funifera***, ***Thelocactus bicolor***, and ***Yucca rostrata***. These are best grown in a smaller home landscape where the showy flowers will be visible. They can also be grown in a large bowl-shaped pot that has some depth to allow the large roots to fully develop.

Precautions Young plants or newly planted ones in an open exposed landscape are best protected from packrats, rabbits, and javelina. Inspect plants for **mealybugs** between the tubercles and near the flowers, and pick them off with sharp tweezers.

Coryphantha macromeris

Coryphantha poselgeriana
Poselger's Coryphantha
SMALL CACTUS

Etymology   Nineteenth century German botanist, Albert Dietrich described this species, naming it in honor of fellow German botanist Heinrich Poselger.

SIZE (H x W)	4–7 inches x 3–6 inches (clumping to 15 inches)
FLOWER COLOR	Yellow or purplish pink
FLOWER SEASON	Late spring and summer
EXPOSURE	Full sun
WATER	Drought tolerant to low
GROWTH RATE	Moderately-slow
PRUNING	None
HARDINESS	10° F, zones 8a–11

Field Notes   In April 2010, Brian Kemble and I were traveling south of Cuatrociénegas on Mexico Highway 30 and stopped for *Fouquieria shrevei*. While walking around taking photos of those plants we came face to face with these hefty *Coryphantha poselgeriana* plants and their beautiful pinkish flowers. I returned to the area in June 2016, May 2019, and April 2024 and saw more robust plants but none in bloom. Plants grow on alluvial plains in sandy or gravelly soil from central Chihuahua south through Coahuila, eastern Durango, eastern Zacatecas, and northern San Luis Potosí from about 3,300–5,900 feet elevation.

Description   Plants start as small rounded balls and grow slightly taller than wide with age; rarely do they cluster with more than one stem. The blue-green bodies have rounded to broadly conical **tubercles** topped by one 1–2-inch-long

rigid whitish or blackish **central spine**. There are 8–14 brownish red or blackish red **radial spines** that turn gray with age. Flowers are large, 1½–2½ inches across, either yellow or pinkish purple, appearing in late spring and summer.

Culture Mature plants are hardy to at least 10° F and can be grown in USDA zones 8a–11. Young ones should be protected from extreme cold for the first couple winters. These are perfect for desert cities with hot summers such as Palm Springs, Phoenix, and Tucson. Older plants will tolerate full sun, but young ones need to be shaded from summer sun until they are fully acclimated. They have a moderately-slow growth rate but will grow a little faster when given periodic supplemental water in spring and summer. No pruning is necessary.

Identification *Coryphantha poselgeriana* can be distinguished from other species of *Coryphantha* commonly grown by the combination of blue-green body, prominent **tubercles**, and thick **spines**.

Landscape Application These are perfect for use in a xeric garden and look great when grown with other low growing cacti such as ***Astrophytum capricorne***, ***Echinocereus stramineus***, ***Neolloydia conoidea***, and ***Thelocactus rinconensis***. For a little height, mix in short columnar cacti such as ***Cleistocactus strausii*** and ***Oreocereus celsianus***. Add seasonal color by planting perennials and small shrubs such as: *Bahia absinthifolia*, *Calliandra eriophylla*, *Glandularia gooddingii*, *Justicia longii*, *Penstemon parryi*, and *Salvia greggii*. Add a couple small trees for light shade in the garden. Try *Acacia constricta*, *Acacia willardiana*, or ***Bursera microphylla***. These can also be grown in decorative pots and kept with a cactus and succulent collection.

Precautions Acclimate plants slowly to full sun and protect from packrats and rabbits until they are established.

Coryphantha recurvata
Santa Cruz Beehive Cactus
CLUSTERING CACTUS

SIZE (H x W)	4–8 inches x 4–8 inches (clumps to 30 inches)
FLOWER COLOR	Yellow
FLOWER SEASON	Summer
EXPOSURE	Full sun
WATER	Low
GROWTH RATE	Moderately-slow
PRUNING	None
HARDINESS	20° F, zones 9a–11

Etymology German-born, American-trained botanist George Engelmann named this species using the Latin *recurv-* for the downward curving central spine.

Field Notes In July 2021, after a month of exceptional rainfall, my friend Rob Romero and I traveled along the Ruby Road in southern Arizona to look for cacti, *Agave parviflora*, and anything else of interest. Rob knew of a spot where we could see a couple incredible plants of *Coryphantha recurvata*. We went back in January 2022, and the area was very dry compared to the previous July, but the plants looked healthy even though the surrounding hills were brown and barren. The species has a restricted distribution and occurs only in southern Arizona and south into northeastern Sonora. Plants are found in open grasslands and on rocky slopes in oak woodland from about 3,950–5,900 feet elevation.

Description Stems are rounded to elongate, about 4–8 inches tall and 4–8 inches wide near the base. They cluster with age, and old specimens can get up to 30 inches across. Bodies are dark green and have low rounded **tubercles**. The color is nearly obscured by the dense **spine** clusters of 1–2, white, rigid, downward curving **central spines** just shy of 1-inch-long, and 12–20 white **radial spines**. Flowers are ½–1-inch-wide, light yellow or yellow with green at the base of the **tepals** and appear in response to summer monsoons.

Culture Plants are hardy to at least 20° F and can be grown in USDA zones 9a–11. Protect young plants from extreme cold for the first couple winters. While older fully established plants will tolerate full sun even in the hottest cities, young plants need to be shaded from summer sun until they are fully acclimated. The moderately-slow growth rate will speed up some when given supplemental water on a regular schedule in spring and summer. Even so, it will take a few years for small plants to become large enough to flower and be a force in the landscape. Leave the pruners in their holster!

Identification *Coryphantha recurvata* is readily identified by the downward curving **central spine** and pale yellow to yellow-green flowers.

Landscape Application Because these are slow growing, they are best grown in containers until large enough to plant in the ground. Grow them with cacti such as *Echinocereus engelmannii*, *Mammillaria geminispina*, and *Neolloydia conoidea*. Add seasonal color by planting perennials and small shrubs such as *Dalea frutescens*, *Glandularia gooddingii*, and *Telosiphonia brachysiphon*. These can also be grown in decorative pots and kept with a cactus and succulent collection.

Precautions Be sure to keep young plants from sunburning by slowly acclimating the plants to full sun. Physically remove any **mealybugs**.

Dasylirion acrotrichum
Brushy-tip Green Desert Spoon
SUCCULENT ROSETTE

SIZE (H x W)	5–7 feet x 4–5 feet
FLOWER COLOR	Tan (male), greenish (female)
FLOWER SEASON	Late spring to summer
EXPOSURE	Full sun, reflected heat
WATER	Low to moderate
GROWTH RATE	Moderately fast
PRUNING	None
HARDINESS	At least 15° F, zones 8b–11

Etymology The German botanist Joseph Zuccarini used the Greek *acro-* meaning the tip and the Greek *trich-*, meaning hair, to describe the hair-like tips of the leaves

Field Notes In 2014, Jeff Chemnick, Brian Kemble, and I were scouting locations for an upcoming Cactus and Succulent Society field trip and stopped at a hillside in Hidalgo laden with some of the most striking and symmetrical specimens of *Dasylirion acrotrichum*. This attractive species with green leaves and brushy tips is found on stony or rocky hills and slopes in Puebla and Hidalgo from about 5,700–9,000 feet.

Description The beautifully symmetrical **rosette** of leaves is generally about 4–5 feet in diameter and sits atop a short trunk. Occasionally, ancient specimens will develop a taller single trunk that may or may not be hidden by the skirt of dead leaves with the plant reaching an overall height of 5–7 feet. Numerous bright green leaves are about 2–2½ feet long by ½-inch-wide and have countless small yellowish prickly **teeth** that mostly point out or curve

forward toward the tip. Leaf tips are unbroken when new and fray with age to create the distinctive brushy tips from which this draws its common name. I imagine a talented painter could use these tips to create a masterpiece. In late spring or early summer, the flower stalk begins to emerge from the top of the plant. This stalk grows rapidly to 12–15 feet tall with male and female flowers on separate plants, so to get seed, both a mom and a dad are needed.

Culture Plants are hardy to at least 15° F and can be used in USDA zones 8b–11. The growth rate is moderately fast and these can reach a reasonable size in a few years. It is best to start with plants in at least a #5 nursery container. Low-water-using once established, these will appreciate receiving supplemental water once every two weeks during the growing season. They will grow and look best when planted in full sun or even against a south or west facing wall. They are tolerant of most desert soils if the drainage is good, which allows roots to dry between waterings.

Identification *Dasylirion acrotrichum* is one of the green-leaved toothy species that are difficult to distinguish from one another.

Landscape Application This is an ideal plant to use as a single eye-catching specimen surrounded by low shrubs and perennials, or mass-planted among a field of flowering plants. Some great companion plants would include *Baileya multiradiata*, *Calliandra eriophylla*, *Chrysactinia mexicana*, *Dalea frutescens*, *Galphimia glauca*, *Menodora longiflora*, and *Penstemon superbus*. The bright green leaves look great when planted alongside gray-leaved shrubs such as *Buddleja marrubiifolia*, *Eremophila hygrophana*, or *Leucophyllum candidum*. Add some height to the landscape by including a couple trees with thin and open canopies such as *Acacia willardiana* and *Bauhinia macranthera*.

Precautions Sometimes those pesky rabbits and packrats will nibble on the leaves.

Dasylirion gentryi
Gentry's Desert Spoon
SUCCULENT ROSETTE

SIZE (H x W)	3–5 feet x 3–5 feet
FLOWER COLOR	Tan (male), fruits reddish-purple to tan (female)
FLOWER SEASON	Late spring to summer
EXPOSURE	Full sun, reflected heat
WATER	Low to moderate
GROWTH RATE	Moderate
PRUNING	None
HARDINESS	20° F, zones 9a–11

Etymology *Dasylirion* specialist, David Bogler, named this species in honor of Dr. Howard Scott Gentry.

Field Notes In March 1984, I climbed up the Sierra de Alamos in southern Sonora and came upon a green-leaved species of *Dasylirion* that I had never seen before. I collected a voucher for the herbarium, which *Dasylirion* expert David Bogler later identified as his newly described *Dasylirion gentryi*. There are easier places to see this plant, such as along Mexico Highway 16 between Yecora, Sonora, and Basaseachi, Chihuahua. Plants are found on rocky hills and slopes among oaks and grasses in the Sierra Madre Occidental in Sonora and Chihuahua from about 2,000–5,900 feet. There are reports of this species growing in the hills near San Carlos, Sonora, but there has not been reliable confirmation.

Description Plants can have a tidy **rosette** of leaves about 3–5 feet in diameter, frequently without a trunk but sometimes with a short trunk of 2–3 feet tall. Green leaves are about 2–3 feet long by ½–1-inch-wide and have many small forward-pointing **teeth**. These are **dioecious**, with the female plants producing colorful reddish-purple fruits when fresh turning tan when ripe.

Culture Plants have been through winter lows of 20° F without damage and based on distribution, should be hardy in USDA zones 9a–11. The growth rate is moderate, but it will still take several years for them to reach substantial size, so start with plants in at least a #5 nursery container. Although low-water-using once established, these will appreciate receiving supplemental water every two weeks during the growing season. Plants grow best when in full sun or with the reflected heat off a south or west facing wall. They prefer a soil which has excellent drainage allowing roots to dry some between water applications.

Identification Mature **rosettes** of *Dasylirion gentryi* can have an untidy appearance and be on a short trunk that may not be visible under the new and old leaves while ***Dasylirion acrotrichum*** rosettes are generally more symmetrical and will grow a noticeable trunk in time.

Landscape Application *Dasylirion gentryi* can be a stand-alone accent plant in a **xeriscape**. Mass several together and weave in perennials and small shrubs for color and texture contrast. Plants can be massed together with ***Cleistocactus strausii***, ***Echinocactus grusonii***, ***Ferocactus gracilis***, ***Fouquieria splendens***, ***Mammillaria standleyi***, or ***Yucca rostrata***. A selection of compatible companion plants would include *Acacia berlandieri*, *Aloysia wrightii*, *Berlandiera lyrata*, *Chrysactinia mexicana*, *Dalea frutescens*, *Ericameria laricifolia*, *Glandularia gooddingii*, *Leucophyllum laevigatum*, *Menodora longiflora*, *Penstemon pseudospectabilis*, *Thymophylla pentachaeta*, and *Zinnia grandiflora*.

Precautions Screen young plants to prevent damage done by javelina, rabbits, and packrats.

Dasylirion leiophyllum
Smooth-leaf Desert Spoon, Sotol
SUCCULENT ROSETTE

SIZE (H x W)	4–6 feet x 4–6 feet
FLOWER COLOR	Tan (male), greenish (female)
FLOWER SEASON	Summer
EXPOSURE	Full sun, reflected heat
WATER	Low to moderate
GROWTH RATE	Moderately slow
PRUNING	None
HARDINESS	0° F, zones 7a–11

Etymology German-born botanist George Engelmann used the Greek *leio-* for smooth and the Greek *phyll-* for leaf to describe the relatively smooth leaf of these plants.

Field Notes While driving to northeastern Mexico in summer of 2008, Chad Davis and I stopped for a couple shots of these green leaved Desert Spoons west of Van Horn, Texas. This is commonly found growing on limestone hills in southern New Mexico, western Texas, and northern Mexico from about 4,300–6,800 feet elevation.

Description Plants will develop a short trunk of about 2–3 feet obscured by a combination of dead and fresh leaves. The smooth leaves are lightly **glaucous** when young aging to glossy green, about 2–2½ feet long by 1-inch-wide with **teeth** that curve back toward the trunk. The leaf crown is moderately dense and irregular sometimes with an unkempt look. The flower stalk is 12–15 feet tall and appears from late spring to summer with male and female flowers on separate plants. The female plants are the ones to produce seed.

Culture Plants are hardy to 0° F and can be used in USDA zones 7a–11. They have a moderately slow growth rate, taking several years to reach a substantial size, so start with plants in at least a #5 nursery container and be prepared to grow old along with your specimens. Give the plants supplemental water on a consistent basis in spring and summer for the best appearance. Plant them in full sun or reflected heat and a desert soil with very good drainage.

Identification This species is one of several with green leaves, but is distinguished by its smooth darker green leaves with **teeth** that mostly curve back toward the trunk.

Landscape Application These Desert Spoon plants can be used in any southwestern **xeriscape**. Plant one or several with flowering shrubs and perennials that will provide color for most of the year. Try using *Baileya multiradiata*, *Calliandra eriophylla*, *Chrysactinia mexicana*, *Dalea formosa*, *Ericameria laricifolia*, *Glandularia gooddingii*, *Larrea divaricata*, *Leucophyllum candidum*, *Poliomintha incana*, *Telosiphonia brachysiphon*, and *Zinnia acerosa*. Combine with cacti and other succulents such as ***Agave ovatifolia***, ***Ferocactus emoryi***, ***Fouquieria splendens***, ***Hesperaloe campanulata***, ***Nolina nelsonii***, and ***Yucca rostrata***. These are tough plants that can be used along freeways and in street medians if there is ample room. Keep them away from spots where there will be a lot of foot traffic because the prickly **teeth** can be a hazard. Do not prune off the old leaves except to lift them off the ground to prevent snakes from hiding in the shade.

Precautions Screen young plants to prevent damage done by javelina, rabbits, and packrats.

Dasylirion leiophyllum

Dasylirion miquihuanense
Miquihuana Desert Spoon
SUCCULENT ROSETTE

Etymology David Bogler, an American botanist, used the town name of Miquihuana to note this plants' nearby occurrence.

SIZE (H x W)	3–8 feet x 4–7 feet
FLOWER COLOR	Tan (male), greenish (female)
FLOWER SEASON	Late spring to summer
EXPOSURE	Full sun, reflected heat
WATER	Moderate
GROWTH RATE	Moderate
PRUNING	None
HARDINESS	At least 15° F, zones 8b–11

Field Notes My first encounter with these awesome plants was in September 1986 while hunting for new landscape plants around the town of Miquihuana in southern Tamaulipas. The next time was while traveling along the logging road that heads up into the high reaches of Cerro Peña Nevada. *Dasylirion miquihuanense* grows on open gravelly bajadas and hillsides on the western side of the Sierra Madre Oriental in southern Tamaulipas and southern Nuevo León from about 5,500–6,300 feet elevation.

Description These robust plants typically have a single large symmetrical **rosette** of leaves that gets about 4–7 feet in diameter and sits atop a short trunk for an overall height of up to 8 feet. Numerous green leaves are smooth, about 2½–3 feet long by ½-inch wide and have countless small yellowish prickly **teeth** that mostly curve forward toward the tip. Leaf tips are narrow and brushy. The 10–13-foot-tall flower stalk appears in spring and grows rapidly with male and female flowers on separate plants. Both sexes are needed to produce seed.

Culture Plants are hardy to at least 15° F and can be used in USDA zones 8b–11. The growth rate is moderate, and these beauties will take several years to reach substantial size, so start with as large a plant that you can find. They naturally receive about 30 inches of annual rainfall so give plants supplemental water every couple weeks in spring and summer and they will thank you profusely. Place these in full sun, and they will reward you with a dense crown of leaves. They are tolerant of most desert soils if the drainage is good; allow roots to dry some between water applications. No need to prune these plants.

Identification *Dasylirion miquihuanense* leaves have yellow **teeth** (they should see a dentist) along the edge and are quadrangularly thickened at the base while the leaves of ***Dasylirion quadrangulatum*** lack **teeth**.

Landscape Application These stately plants are perfect to use as a single eye-catching specimen surrounded by low shrubs and perennials. Some great companion plants would include *Aloysia macrostachya, Anisacanthus quadrifidus, Galphimia glauca,* and *Leucophyllum pruinosum*. The bright green leaves look great when planted alongside gray-leaved shrubs such as *Buddleja marrubiifolia, Eremophila hygrophana,* or *Leucophyllum candidum*. Combine with cacti and other succulents like ***Agave ovatifolia, Ferocactus pilosus, Fouquieria splendens****,* and ***Yucca rostrata***.

Precautions Screen young plants to prevent damage done by javelina, rabbits, and packrats. Protect young plants from extreme cold.

Dasylirion quadrangulatum
Toothless Desert Spoon
SUCCULENT ROSETTE

SIZE (H x W)	4–10 feet x 5–9 feet
FLOWER COLOR	Tan (male), greenish (female)
FLOWER SEASON	Spring
EXPOSURE	Full sun
WATER	Moderate
GROWTH RATE	Slow
PRUNING	None
HARDINESS	20° F, zones 9a–11

Etymology American botanist Sereno Watson described this species using the Latin *quad-* meaning four and the Latin *angul-* meaning angled to describe the four-angled leaves.

Field Notes In the fall of 1986, Ron Gass and I were driving along a dirt road in southern Tamaulipas scouting for intriguing landscape plants when we saw a hillside of these plants off in the distance. I have since made it a point to stop for these incredibly majestic plants whenever possible. There are many incredible specimens growing with ***Dasylirion miquihuanense*** on the southern slopes of Cerro Peña Nevada in southern Tamaulipas. *Dasylirion quadrangulatum* is found on dry open rocky limestone hills, slopes, and arroyos on the western side of the Sierra Madre Oriental in southern Tamaulipas and southern Nuevo León from about 5,300–6,600 feet elevation.

Description Ancient plants can have a trunk to 5 feet or more tall that is most often covered by a skirt of dead leaves and topped by a single large symmetrical

rosette of leaves to 4–5 feet in diameter. Numerous green leaves are wire-thin, growing up spreading out and arching down. They are four-angled, about 2½–3 feet long by ¼-inch-wide and lack **teeth**, except the occasional hybrid with *Dasylirion miquihuanense* that has small **teeth** at the base of the leaf. The massive inflorescence is 10–20 feet tall, appears in spring and grows rapidly with male and female flowers on separate plants. The plants pictured on page 122 are probably 200 years old, so pass your plants down to your great-grandchildren.

Culture Plants are hardy to at least 20° F and can be used in USDA zones 9a–11. These slow growing beauties will take several years to reach massive proportions, so start with plants in at least a #5 nursery container and be prepared to grow old with them. Although they hail from the dry western side of the Sierra Madre Oriental, they should still be given supplemental water every couple weeks in spring and summer. They grow best when located in full sun and desert soil with very good drainage.

Identification This is one of two species lacking **teeth** along the leaf edges. *Dasylirion longissimum* has a skinnier trunk, more open leaf crown, and blooms later in the year.

Landscape Application Although it will take several years for these statuesque plants to develop their trunk, they can be used either singly or in groups in southwestern **xeriscapes**. Surround these with low shrubs and perennials such as *Chrysactinia mexicana*, *Conoclinium dissectum*, *Dalea frutescens*, *Galphimia glauca*, and *Salvia greggii*. Combine them with cacti and other succulents like **Agave gentryi**, **Ferocactus pilosus**, **Fouquieria splendens**, **Nolina nelsonii**, and **Yucca rostrata**.

Precautions Rabbits and packrats will sometimes treat the leaves as a buffet and munch them to nubs. Protect young plants from extreme cold.

Dasylirion wheeleri
Desert Spoon, Sotol
SUCCULENT ROSETTE

SIZE (H x W)	4–6 feet x 4–6 feet
FLOWER COLOR	Tan (male), greenish (female)
FLOWER SEASON	Summer
EXPOSURE	Full sun, reflected heat
WATER	Low to moderate
GROWTH RATE	Moderate
PRUNING	None
HARDINESS	0° F, zones 7a–11

Etymology Sereno Watson described this species naming it in honor of First Lieutenant George Wheeler.

Field Notes These are very common plants at the right elevation in southern Arizona and are easily seen while out exploring the countryside. I like to see them whenever I get into their range while out looking for cool cacti and other succulents in southern Arizona. *Dasylirion wheeleri* is found on gravelly mesas and rocky hillsides at the upper edge of the Sonoran Desert zone in southern Arizona across to western Texas and south in Chihuahua and Sonora, Mexico from about 4,000–6,000 feet elevation.

Description It may take several years, but these plants will eventually develop a trunk 3–4 feet or more tall that is covered by the skirt of old dead leaves. Numerous thin blue-gray leaves are about 2–2½ feet long by ¾-inch wide with **teeth** that curve back toward the trunk. These leaves radiate out from the central growing point and form a nearly perfect hemisphere that sits atop the trunk. The flower stalk is 10–15 feet tall and plants are **dioecious**, so both male and female plants are needed to produce seed. Flowers are mostly wind or bee pollinated.

Culture Plants are generally hardy to 0° F and can be used in USDA zones 7a–11. They are slow growing and will take several years to reach a substantial size, so start with plants in at least a #5 nursery container and sit back to watch your specimens get incrementally larger each year. Because they come from a little bit higher elevation, these should be given supplemental water on a consistent basis in spring and summer. Plant them in full sun or reflected heat and a soil with very good drainage.

Identification These are easily distinguished by the blue-gray leaves compared to the green leaves of the others in cultivation.

Landscape Application They look great in nearly any **xeriscape** throughout much of the southwestern U.S., even in the very hot cities if they receive enough water in the summer. Plant singly, or if there is enough room, group several together for an eye-catching display. They are great for large open spaces such as along roadsides, on/off freeway ramps, or in front of large commercial buildings. Use flowering shrubs and perennials to provide color throughout the year. Mix these with *Bahia absinthifolia, Calliandra eriophylla, Dalea pulchra, Ericameria laricifolia, Penstemon superbus,* and *Salvia greggii.* Combine with cacti and other succulents like **Agave parryi**, **Ferocactus acanthodes**, and **Fouquieria splendens**.

Precautions Rabbits will treat the leaves as a buffet and munch them to nubs. The teeth on the leaves curve toward the trunk allowing you to reach in to pull a weed, but tearing up your arm as you extract it.

Dasylirion wheeleri

Denmoza rhodacantha
Red-spine Denmoza
BARREL CACTUS, SMALL BARREL-LIKE CACTUS

Etymology The genus name, *Denmoza*, is an anagram of the Argentine city Mendoza, which is near where the plant was first collected. The species name is a combination of the Greek *rhod-* for rose and the Greek *acanth-* spine, alluding to the red (rose colored) spines.

SIZE (H x W)	2–4 feet x 8–12 inches
FLOWER COLOR	Scarlet-red
FLOWER SEASON	Spring and summer
EXPOSURE	Full sun
WATER	Low
GROWTH RATE	Slow
PRUNING	None
HARDINESS	20° F, zones 9a–11

Field Notes In 2022, I latched onto a trip to Argentina and Chile led by Guillermo Rivera, and he promised that we would get to see plants of *Denmoza rhodacantha*. Well, he was true to his word and took us to see them along RN149 as we made our way back from the Chile-Argentina border to Córdoba. We saw them growing on rocky slopes and rock ledges above the road with *Larrea* species, *Deuterochonia* species and *Trichocereus strigosus*. There were young plants with few stout **spines**, and larger plants with their narrowly tubular red flowers poking out above the densely clustered **spines**. Plants have been recorded as growing on the east side of the Andes and a few isolated mountains in the northern half of Argentina from about 2,600–7,500 feet elevation.

Cool Cacti and Succulents for Hot Gardens

Description   Plants have a single body that is globose when young, becoming a short stout column with age, eventually reaching about 2–4 feet tall and 8–12 inches in diameter. Young plants have few spines that are stout. Older plants typically have longer **spines** along with several thin bristle-like **spines**. There are two forms in cultivation - one with red **spines** and one with yellow **spines**. Scarlet-red, tubular, slightly curved flowers are produced near the top of the plant in spring and summer.

Culture   Plants are reported to be hardy to about 20° F and are considered hardy in USDA zones 9a–11. They can be grown in full sun throughout those zones in the southwestern U.S., except for the hottest cities of Palm Springs, Phoenix, and Yuma. The growth rate is slow, so look for as large a plant as you can find and afford. Put them in a soil that has very good drainage and provide supplemental water every 10–14 days to plants that are established in the ground. Be sure to let the soil dry before watering again.

Identification   There are no other species of *Denmoza* and, even though spination is variable, these plants are usually easy to identify. Seedlings and young plants look very different than adult plants, and can be mistaken for some species of *Melocactus*, *Neoporteria*, or *Gymnocalycium*.

Landscape Application   Mass several of these in a cactus and succulent garden along with other barrel-like plants with colorful spines such as **Echinocactus grusonii**, **Ferocactus acanthodes**, and **Ferocactus gracilis** and spiky **rosette** forming plants such as **Agave parryi**, **Agave schidigera**, and **Dasylirion acrotrichum**. Surround these with colorful low growing perennials such as *Baileya multiradiata*, *Glandularia gooddingii*, *Tetraneuris acaulis*, and *Thymophylla pentachaeta*.

Precautions   I am not aware of any insect problems, although **mealybugs** may find their way to potted plants.

Denmoza rhodacantha

Echinocactus grusonii
Synonym: Kroenleinia grusonii
Golden Barrel
BARREL CACTUS

SIZE (H x W)	1–3 (rarely to 6) feet x 1–2½ feet
FLOWER COLOR	Yellow
FLOWER SEASON	Spring and summer
EXPOSURE	Full sun
WATER	Drought tolerant to low
GROWTH RATE	Moderately-slow
PRUNING	None
HARDINESS	15° F, zones 8b–11

Etymology Heinrich Hildmann, a 19th century German plantsman and nursery owner, named this for the German engineer, Hermann Gruson.

Field Notes In May 2013, Brian Kemble and I drove out to see the population of *Echinocactus grusonii* growing in Zacatecas. The drive took a long time, and we did not have any camping gear, so we had limited time to explore the area. In May 2014, Jeff Chemnick, Brian Kemble, and I were looking for cacti and succulents and stopped at a pullout to have a look around. We walked to a canyon and looked across, spotting two large *Echinocactus grusonii* growing on a steep slope. Plants favor steep rocky slopes and semi-arid vegetation from about 4,600–6,500 feet elevation.

Description Individual stems are rounded in youth, becoming short thickened columns with age reaching about 1–3 (rarely to 6) feet tall and 1–2½ feet wide. Initially solitary, plants will sometimes branch from the base or higher up. Bodies are green with bright golden yellow **spines** lining the 30–40 ribs.

The apex is flat to slightly depressed and densely covered with wool. Yellow flowers are about 1–2 inches wide and appear mostly in spring and summer.

Culture Plants in Tucson have survived 15° F without damage and are hardy in USDA zones 8b–11. These are great landscape plants for cities with hot summers such as Palm Springs, Phoenix, Tucson, and Yuma, and those with moderate summer temperatures such as Deming, Las Cruces, and Sierra Vista. They are best grown in full sun but young ones should be acclimated slowly to prevent sun burn.

Although drought tolerant, plants should receive supplemental water every 2–3 weeks or so during summer to minimize heat stress in cities with very hot summer temperatures. No pruning is necessary for these big barrels.

Identification These are very distinctive and not easily confused with any other cactus. There are some South American barrel-like cacti with yellow **spines**, but they are easily distinguished from *Echinocactus grusonii*.

Landscape Application These make spectacular specimens in any southwestern **xeriscape** or cactus and succulent garden. Use alongside plants such as *Agave gentryi*, *Dasylirion acrotrichum*, *Echinocereus viereckii*, *Hesperaloe campanulata*, and *Pedilanthus macrocarpus*. Add seasonal color by planting perennials and small shrubs such as *Baileya multiradiata*, *Calliandra eriophylla*, *Dalea versicolor*, *Ericameria laricifolia*, *Glandularia gooddingii*, *Justicia candicans*, *Penstemon parryi*, *Salvia greggii*, and *Thymophylla pentachaeta*. Plant a couple *Acacia willardiana* trees in the garden for added interest.

Precautions Be sure to keep young plants from sunburning by slowly acclimating them to full sun.

Echinocactus horizonthalonius
Eagle-claw Cactus, Blue Barrel Cactus
SMALL BARREL CACTUS

SIZE (H x W)	4–12 (–18) inches x 5–8 – (–12) inches
FLOWER COLOR	Pink
FLOWER SEASON	Spring and summer
EXPOSURE	Full sun
WATER	Drought tolerant to low
GROWTH RATE	Slow
PRUNING	None
HARDINESS	10° F, zones 8a–11

Etymology   Charles Lemaire named this species using the Latin *horizontalis-* for the horizontally oriented areoles.

Field Notes   *Echinocactus horizonthalonius* occurs in both the Chihuahuan Desert Region and the Sonoran Desert. I got to see plants in flower near Cuatrociénegas in central Coahuila in April 2010. I have also come across these near Saltillo, Coahuila growing on flat stony ground derived from limestone. There are plants in the Waterman Mountains northwest of Tucson, and they are a favorite to see whenever I go look at the *Agave simplex* there. The distribution is widespread, being found in both the Chihuahuan Desert and the Sonoran Desert. Plants prefer flat stony or rocky ground derived from limestone and are found from about 2,000–5,000 feet elevation.

Description   There are two subspecies with slightly different forms as adult plants. Those of subsp. *horizonthalonius* from the Chihuahuan Desert tend to be shorter overall, reaching about 4–12 inches tall by 5–7 inches in diameter. Subspecies *nicholii* in the Sonoran Desert can grow to as much as 16–18 inches tall by 8 inches in diameter and sometimes spiraling. The stems are blue-gray with 7–13 ribs, with stiff and rigid **spines** that are pink, red, gray, yellowish, whitish, brown, black, or a combination of two or more colors. Bright pink to rose-pink flowers are 2–3 inches long and 2–3 inches wide, appearing in spring and summer.

Culture In nature, plants are found growing where winter lows dip to 10° F, so they should be hardy in USDA zones 8a–11. These are not overly large but are perfect for **xeriscapes** in most low and mid-elevtion cities in the southwest. They grow well in full sun once acclimated by slowly exposing them to more sun a little at a time. Plants are slow growing and will take several years for little ones to reach flowering size. They are drought tolerant to low-water-using.

Identification Blue-gray bodies and pink to rose-pink flowers distinguish these from *Echinocactus grusonii*, *Echinocactus parryi*, and *Echinocactus platyacanthus*, and their yellow flowers.

Landscape Application These can be grown in a cactus and succulent garden, but they will not make an overwhelming statement. Place them in an open exposure where they can be showcased for the flower display, but acclimate slowly to full sun. They look great when used near large boulders and mixed with plants such as *Agave schidigera*, *Echinocereus engelmannii*, *Euphorbia antisyphilitica*, *Neolloydia conoidea*, and *Thelocactus rinconensis*. Add seasonal color by planting perennials and small shrubs such as: *Baileya multiradiata*, *Calliandra eriophylla*, *Ericameria laricifolia*, *Glandularia gooddingii*, *Justicia longii*, and *Salvia greggii*. These look great when placed in decorative pots in a cactus collection.

Precautions Be sure to keep young plants from sunburning by slowly acclimating them to full sun.

Echinocactus horizonthalonius

Echinocactus parryi

Synonym: *Homalocephala parryi*
Parry's Barrel Cactus
SMALL BARREL CACTUS

SIZE (H x W)	6–18 inches x 6–12 inches
FLOWER COLOR	Yellow with red center
FLOWER SEASON	Spring
EXPOSURE	Full sun
WATER	Drought tolerant to low
GROWTH RATE	Moderately slow
PRUNING	None
HARDINESS	15° F, zones 8b–11

Etymology German-born, American-trained botanist George Engelmann named this species for American botanist Dr. Charles Parry.

Field Notes I have never had a reason to cross the U.S.-Mexico border at El Paso and consequently have never been where these plants grow. My friend Rob Romero has been to see them, and he indicated they grow in open exposure on flat ground in sandy or rocky soil, sometimes with small grasses or scattered shrubs. The range is very limited, encompassing about 40–50 square miles south of Juarez, Chihuahua. Plants are found from about 3,900–4,600 feet elevation.

Description These are usually solitary with a globose to short cylindrical body about 6–18 inches tall and 6–12 inches in diameter. The body is gray-green with about 13 ribs covered with **spine** clusters along the ribs. The usually 4 central spines are about 2 inches long straw-colored to magenta when young and aging to gray. The 6–11 **radial spines** are yellowish to magenta when young and

aging to gray. Yellow flowers have a red center, are 2–3 inches across, and appear mostly in late spring.

Culture   These hardy plants can tolerate a winter low of about 15° F without sustaining damage and are great landscape plants in USDA zones 8b–11. They are best grown in full sun even in the hottest cities of the southwestern U.S. including Las Vegas, Palm Springs, Phoenix, Tucson, and Yuma. Plants have a moderately slow growth rate and are drought tolerant once established in the ground, but will grow a little faster when given some supplemental water in spring and summer. They grow well in most any soil type if watering is adjusted accordingly.

Identification   With their yellow flowers and gray-green body, *Echinocactus parryi* plants are readily distinguished from those of *Echinocactus horizonthalonius* with their blue-green body and pink flowers.

Landscape Application   Because of their smaller size, these lend themselves to mass plantings in either a cactus and succulent garden or a **xeriscape** complete with a variety of perennials and small shrubs. Some suggested cacti and other succulents would include *Agave deserti*, *Echinocereus stramineus*, *Euphorbia antisyphilitica*, *Fouquieria splendens*, *Hesperaloe funifera*, and *Yucca rostrata*. Add colorful perennials and small shrubs like *Asclepias subulata*, *Calliandra eriophylla*, *Chrysactinia mexicana*, *Dalea capitata*, *Hibiscus denudatus*, *Penstemon eatonii*, and *Zinnia acerosa*. These can also be grown in large decorative pots and incorporated into a collection of *Ferocactus* and other *Echinocactus*.

Precautions   The snout moth, *Cactobrosis fernaldialis*, has been known to feed on species of *Ferocactus* and other barrel-like cacti, tunneling into the plant and providing an open wound for plant-killing pathogens to invade. Treat all your *Echinocactus* and *Ferocactus* with a systemic insecticide in spring and summer as a profilactic measure.

Echinocactus platyacanthus

Synonym: *Echinocactus ingens*
Giant Barrel Cactus
BARREL CACTUS

SIZE (H x W)	1–8 feet x 1⅓–2⅔ feet
FLOWER COLOR	Yellow
FLOWER SEASON	Spring and summer
EXPOSURE	Full sun
WATER	Drought tolerant to low
GROWTH RATE	Slow
PRUNING	None
HARDINESS	20° F, zones 9a–11

Etymology Link and Otto teamed up and used the Greek *platy-* for flat and the Greek *acantho-* for spines to describe the flat spines on these giants.

Field Notes *Echinocactus platyacanthus* has a very widespread distribution, and the southern plants are generally more massive than the northern ones. In 2009, I was looking for interesting plants in southern Nuevo León with my friend, Scott Calhoun, when we came across both juvenile and adult forms. Young plants have blue-gray bodies and prominent purple chevron stripes, while adults have green bodies and lack any other coloration. The largest plants I have seen were growing in the Barranca de Metztitlán in Hidalgo. These grow on flat ground or gentle slopes in much of eastern Mexico from about 3,200–6,500 feet elevation.

Description Juvenile plants are very distinct and look quite different from adult plants. Young plants are rounded blue-gray to green bodies marked with distinctive purplish or reddish-purple stripes. They have four thick flattened

central spines and 8–10 **radial spines**. Older plants are short columns and can reach 7–8 feet tall by nearly 3 feet across. Showy yellow 2–3-inch-wide flowers poke out of the densely wooly apex in spring and summer.

Culture   I have plants from three disparate localities in the ground that have all been subject to a temperature of 20° F with no damage. These are ideal for use in low and mid-elevation cities in the southwest. They grow well in full sun and in soil with good drainage. Plants are drought tolerant once established but are slow growing and will take several years for little ones to reach flowering size, so be prepared to pass them down to grandkids.

Identification   *Echinocactus platyacanthus* are closest in looks to *Echinocactus grusonii* but have heavier gray **spines**.

Landscape Application   These are perfect for a **xeriscape** filled with flowering perennials and small shrubs. Grow in an open exposure near large boulders and mix with plants such as *Agave gentryi* and *Dasylirion acrotrichum*. Add seasonal color by planting perennials and small shrubs such as: *Calliandra* 'Sierra Starr', *Chrysactinia mexicana*, *Dalea frutescens*, and *Glandularia gooddingii*. They are spiny so keep them away from high traffic areas!

Precautions   Treat all your *Echinocactus* and *Ferocactus* with a systemic insecticide to prevent the snout moth, *Cactobrosis fernaldialis*, from invading your plants.

A young *Echinocactus platyacanthus*

Echinocactus platyacanthus

Echinocereus bonkerae
Bonker's Hedgehog
CLUSTERING CACTUS

Etymology Botanist John James Thornber named this species for Frances Bonker in the book The Fantastic Clan: The Cactus Family.

Field Notes While looking for agaves in central Arizona, I came upon a handful of these plants with their gorgeous magenta purple flowers prominently displayed and looking for bees to take pollen from one plant to another. The primary distribution is in the grasslands of central Arizona, growing among rocks and boulders. Plants occur mostly from about 2,800–5,600 feet elevation.

SIZE (H x W)	5–10 inches x clumps to 10–15 inches
FLOWER COLOR	Magenta to reddish purple
FLOWER SEASON	Spring to early summer
EXPOSURE	Filtered sun
WATER	Drought tolerant to low
GROWTH RATE	Moderate
PRUNING	None
HARDINESS	10° F, zones 8a–11

Description These start life with a single stem that can get 5–10 inches tall with a diameter of 1½–3 inches, and with age will produce multiple stems clustering to 10–15 inches across. There is one rigid **central spine** that is white, yellow, or gray with a darker tip and measuring about ⅓-inch-long. The 11–14 **radial spines** are similar in color to the **central spine** and measure ½–1-inch-long. Large showy magenta-purple flowers are about 2–2½ inches wide and appear in late spring and early summer.

Culture Plants are generally cold hardy to about 10° F and can be grown in USDA zones

136 Cool Cacti and Succulents for Hot Gardens

8a–11. They can be used in the landscape throughout much of the southwestern U.S., performing nicely in cities with moderate summers, but need some shade in cities with hot summers. Plants have a moderate growth rate and can reach flowering size in just a handful of years from seed. They are drought tolerant to low-water-using when grown in the ground but will appreciate receiving some supplemental water during summer. They require supplemental water on a regular schedule in spring and summer when grown in pots. The soil should have excellent drainage to prevent roots from rotting.

Identification *Echinocereus bonkerae* is a more compact plant with shorter **spines** than *Echinocereus fasciculatus*. *Echinocereus bonkerae* has more ribs and a slightly longer **central spine** than either *Echinocereus fasciculatus* or *Echinocereus fendleri*.

Landscape Application These are best grown in containers until they get some size before planting in a landscape. Once large enough, they do well in a cactus and succulent garden or a mixed garden with flowering perennials and small shrubs. In cities with hot summers and intense sunlight, plants would benefit from being under the shade of a small tree, while they can tolerate full sun in cities with mild summers. Mix with plants such as *Agave parryi*, *Dasylirion wheeleri*, *Ferocactus acanthodes*, and *Fouquieria splendens*. Add seasonal color by planting perennials and small shrubs such as *Baileya multiradiata*, *Calliandra eriophylla*, *Dalea formosa*, *Ericameria laricifolia*, *Glandularia gooddingii*, *Melampodium leucanthum*, *Menodora scabra*, *Penstemon superbus*, and *Salvia greggii*. Plant *Acacia constricta* or *Acacia willardiana* trees in the garden for some dappled shade and added interest.

Precautions Protect young plants from intense sun and hungry packrats, and be on the lookout for **mealybugs** that like to hide between the ribs.

Echinocereus dasyacanthus
Texas Rainbow Cactus
SMALL CACTUS

SIZE (H x W)	6–14 inches x 2½–4 inches stem diameter
FLOWER COLOR	Yellow, rarely pink, orange, or purplish
FLOWER SEASON	Spring to early summer
EXPOSURE	Filtered sun
WATER	Drought tolerant to low
GROWTH RATE	Moderate
PRUNING	None
HARDINESS	0° F, zones 7a–11

Etymology German-born, American-trained George Engelmann described this cactus using the Greek *dasy-* for dense and the Greek *acantha-* for spine to denote the dense spination.

Field Notes Although I have made many trips into the range of this species, it had always eluded having its picture taken until recently. Cactus expert Rob Romero gave me coordinates for a locality in west Texas, and I made the stop on the way to see the total eclipse in Mexico in April 2024. there were small plants, but none in flower yet. These grow on limestone soil from southeastern New Mexico to Big Bend area of Texas and south into adjacent Mexico. They occur mostly from about 1,700–4,700 feet elevation.

Description Typically, plants have a single cylindrical to elongated stem that grows to 6–14 inches tall with a diameter of 2½–4 inches. Body color is obscured by the densely packed **spines**, but there are 15–18 ribs. All **spines** are stiff and straight, white, yellow, reddish, or brownish, usually with darker tips. The 3–12 **central spines** are about ¼-inch-long while the 12–24 **radial spines** are ¼–1-inch-long. Showy flowers are 4 inches long and nearly 5 inches wide, usually yellow with green at the base of the **tepals**, but sometimes pale to deep pink, orange, or purplish and erupt through the spines in spring and summer.

Culture These are hardy to 0° F and can be grown in USDA zones 7a–11. They are difficult to keep alive for several years when planted in the ground, but can be displayed in decorative pots throughout the southwestern U.S., but like some summer shade in cities with very hot summers. Plants have a moderate growth rate and can reach flowering size when not too large. They are drought tolerant to low-water-using needing very little supplemental water even when grown in pots. Be sure the soil has perfect drainage to prevent rotting of roots.

Identification With their yellow, magenta, or orange flowers, *Echinocereus dasyacanthus* plants are readily separated from the purplish-pink flowered *Echinocereus reichenbachii*.

Landscape Application These make great potted plants that can be moved around to take advantage of the showy flower display in spring. Plant them in a cactus and succulent garden along with spring or summer flowering perennials. In cities with hot summers and intense sunlight, place them under the shade of a small wispy tree like *Acacia willardiana* or at the canopy edge of a small tree like *Acacia constricta*. In cities with mild summers, plant with other cacti and succulents. Grow alongside *Agave parviflora*, *Ariocarpus fissuratus*, *Astrophytum asterias*, *Echinocactus horizontha-lonius*, *Mammillaria grusonii*, and *Thelocactus bicolor*.

Precautions Bodies on old plants have been known to split. **Mealybugs** will hide under **spine** clusters, and **spine mealies** have been seen on the spines.

Echinocereus engelmannii
Engelmann's Hedgehog
CLUSTERING CACTUS

SIZE (H x W)	6–24 inches x clumps to 18–36 inches
FLOWER COLOR	Magenta purple
FLOWER SEASON	Late winter and spring
EXPOSURE	Full sun
WATER	Drought tolerant to low
GROWTH RATE	Moderate
PRUNING	None
HARDINESS	0° F, zones 7a–11

Etymology Charles Parry named this for German born, American botanist, George Engelmann.

Field Notes I see these near my home on the west side of Tucson on a regular basis. Bob Webb and I were in the southern end of the Sierra San Pedro Mártir in northern Baja California in March 2011. We set up camp in the afternoon so I had time to look at the plants nearby and found *Echinocereus engelmannii* in bloom. These have a wide-spread distribution, occurring throughout much of the desert southwest

from central Nevada and Utah to Baja California, and Sonora. They grow on flats, hillsides, and alluvial fans mostly from near sea level to 5,000 feet elevation.

Description This is a clumping species with young plants having 5–10 stems, and large clumps having up to 70 stems and reaching 36 inches across. Individual stems are cylindrical, 6–24 inches tall with a diameter of 1½–3½ inches with 10–13 ribs. **Spines** are needle-like, white, brown, yellow, red or a combination of the colors; 2–6 stout **central spines** are straight to curving and measure about 1–3½ inches long while the 6–12

radial spines are straight to twisted and shorter than the centrals. Flowers are large and showy, magenta purple, dark lavender, or pinkish purple, and about 3 inches wide. They appear high up on the stem but below the apex in late winter and spring.

Culture These are cold hardy to at least 0° F and can be grown in USDA zones 7a–11. Plants from central Nevada are probably hardy to -10° F, so look for nursery plants grown from seed collected in Nevada if you live in USDA zones 6a or 6b. Grow in full sun and a fast-draining soil for best growth and flowering in most major metropolitan areas in the desert southwest. The growth rate is moderate but can reach flowering size in 6-inch pots. They are drought tolerant to low-water-using when grown in the ground but require supplemental water in spring and summer when grown in pots.

Identification *Echinocereus engelmannii* typically has more than one **central spine** while *Echinocereus fasciculatus* and *Echinocereus fendleri* both have one **central spine**.

Landscape Application These fit well in any **xeriscape** garden in the desert southwest. Plants can be eye-catching in late winter or spring when they are alive with bright magenta purple flowers. Plant with non-cactus succulents such as *Agave parryi*, *Hesperaloe campanulata*, and *Yucca rostrata*. Mix in spring or summer flowering perennials and small shrubs for a spectacular color display. Try using *Calliandra eriophylla*, *Chrysactinia mexicana*, *Dalea frutescens*, *Ericameria laricifolia*, *Glandularia gooddingii*, *Gutierrezia microcephala*, and *Thymophylla pentachaeta*.

Precautions Plants are relatively carefree in most situations, but there has been an increase in piercing sucking insect attacks of some cacti that have resulted in the introduction of fungal problems.

Echinocereus enneacanthus
Strawberry Hedgehog
CLUSTERING CACTUS

Etymology German-born botanist George Engelmann used the Greek *ennea-* for nine, and the Greek *acantha-* meaning **spine**, for the number of spines on the original plants.

Field Notes These are fairly easy to find in the Chihuahuan Desert Region. Plants with some of the fattest stems I have seen were on Mexico Highway 30 south of Cuatrociénegas in Coahuila. They were relatively low-growing, topping out at about 15–18 inches tall but spreading to nearly 36 inches across. The species is widespread in the Chihuahuan Desert Region and plants grow on flats, gravelly hillsides, and sandy alluvial fans mostly from 1,800–4,000 feet elevation.

SIZE (H x W)	clusters 10–24 inches x 18–36 inches
FLOWER COLOR	Magenta, purplish pink, or crimson
FLOWER SEASON	Late spring
EXPOSURE	Full sun
WATER	Drought tolerant to low
GROWTH RATE	Moderately fast
PRUNING	None
HARDINESS	15° F, zones 8b–11

Description Plants will form large clumps with 30–100 stems reaching 10–24 inches tall and 36 inches across. Individual stems are cylindrical, either slender or thick 6–8 inches long with a diameter of 2½–6 inches. Stems are light to medium green with 7–10 ribs visible beneath the **spine** clusters. There are 1–4 **central spines** each about 3 inches long and 6–13 stiff **radial spines** that measure about 1½-inch-long. All **spines** are white to yellow and turn gray with age. Flowers are magenta, purplish pink, or crimson, about 3–5 inches wide and appear in spring.

Cool Cacti and Succulents for Hot Gardens

Culture Plants are reasonably cold hardy tolerating winter lows to at least 15° F and can be grown in USDA zones 8b–11. They should be grown in full sun and a fast-draining soil for best growth and optimal flowering in most major metropolitan areas in the southwestern U.S. The growth rate is moderate, but plants are of flowering size when in 6-inch pots. They are low-water-using when grown in the ground, but require supplemental water on a regular schedule in spring and summer when grown in pots.

Identification These plants are readily identified by the fat green stems highly visible beneath the **spine** clusters, magenta or purplish pink flowers, and strawberry red fruits.

Landscape Application As with other clumping species of *Echinocereus*, these can be used in any cactus and succulent garden throughout the desert southwest. With their showy spring flower display, these supplement other cacti such as **Coryphantha poselgeriana**, **Echinocereus bonkerae**, **Echinocereus engelmannii**, and **Thelocactus rinconensis**. Plant with non-cactus succulents such as **Agave parrasana** and **Fouquieria splendens**. Mix in a few spring or summer flowering perennials and small shrubs to create a spectacular color display. Try using *Chrysactinia mexicana, Dalea capitata, Thymophylla pentachaeta*, and *Zinnia grandiflora*.

Precautions Plants are relatively carefree but a piercing sucking insect has been found on some cacti that may result in the introduction of fungal problems.

Echinocereus enneacanthus

Echinocereus fasciculatus
Hedgehog Cactus
CLUSTERING CACTUS

SIZE (H x W)	10–14 inches x clumps to 12–15 inches
FLOWER COLOR	Magenta to purplish
FLOWER SEASON	Spring
EXPOSURE	Full sun
WATER	Drought tolerant to low
GROWTH RATE	Moderate
PRUNING	None
HARDINESS	15° F, zones 8b–11

Etymology In Latin *fasci-* means bundle or cluster and was used by German-born botanist George Engelmann to indicate the cluster of stems.

Field Notes This species grows not far from my home on the west side of Tucson and is an eye-opener when it blooms. I have come across a handful of these clustering plants in the Waterman Mountains northwest of Tucson while out looking at *Agave simplex*. Plants occur in the desert and isolated mountains around Tucson in southeastern Arizona. They typically grow on flat rocky ground, gravelly hillsides, and sandy alluvial fans mostly from 2,000–2,600 feet elevation.

Description Individual stems are about 10–14 inches tall and 1½–2½ inches thick with clusters usually growing to about 12–15 inches across with the exceptional plant reaching 30–36 inches across. Stems are medium to dark green with 9–12 ribs and only partially obscured by the **spines**. There are 1–3

straight **central spines**, each gray with distinctive black or dark brown tips. The 7–15 **radial spines** are ¼–½-inch-long, white, gray, or yellowish. Large flowers are about 2½ inches across, magenta, or purplish, the outermost **tepals** with green or brown mid-stripes. Flowering is mostly in April.

Culture Plants are cold hardy and can tolerate winter lows to at least 15° F meaning they can be grown in USDA zones 8b–11. They should be placed in full sun and a fast-draining soil for best growth and optimal flowering in most major metropolitan areas in the southwestern U.S. The growth rate is moderate, and plants can reach flowering size when in 6-inch pots. This is one of the most xeric species of *Echinocereus* and ashould be grown in native rocky soil. They are drought tolerant once established in the ground and can mostly be left to live on 10–12 inches of annual rain. They are trickier to grow in pots, so find a good spot for them in the landscape and enjoy the blooms in spring.

Identification *Echinocereus fasciculatus* is identified by the dark magenta throat of the flowers.

Landscape Application Plant alongside other Sonoran Desert native cacti and tough desert shrubs that require minimal supplemental water. Use these with spring and summer blooming cacti such as ***Coryphantha poselgeriana*** and ***Opuntia macrocentra***, and non-cactus succulents such as ***Agave parryi*** and ***Fouquieria splendens***. Mix in a few spring blooming perennials and small shrubs native to the Sonoran Desert or try small shrubs and perennials from the Chihuahuan Desert to create a tapestry of color and textures. Some Sonoran Desert companion plants would include *Baileya multiradiata*, *Ericameria laricifolia*, and *Glandularia gooddingii*.

Precautions These plants are very xeric and should not be watered too heavily lest they become subject to rot.

Echinocereus nicholii
Nichol's Hedgehog
CLUSTERING CACTUS

SIZE (H x W)	12–24 inches x clumps to 18–36 inches
FLOWER COLOR	Pink to purplish-pink
FLOWER SEASON	Spring
EXPOSURE	Full sun
WATER	Drought tolerant to low
GROWTH RATE	Moderately slow
PRUNING	None
HARDINESS	15° F, zones 8b–11

Etymology Andrew Nichol found plants in the Silverbell Mountains, and Lyman Benson named it as a variety of *Echinocereus engelmannii*. Later Bruce Parfitt raised it to species status.

Field Notes While hiking in the Waterman Mountains looking at *Agave simplex*, I occasionally see nice clusters of this *Echinocereus*, but am always there at the wrong time of year to see them in flower. I once saw several plants while driving past rocky hills on my way to look for *Agave pelona* in northwestern Sonora. These striking hedgehog plants favor steep rocky slopes and limestone soil where they can avoid competition from other plants. They are found in the Silverbell and Waterman Mountains northwest of Tucson, in southwestern Arizona, and across the border in northwestern Sonora from about 1,000–3,000 feet elevation.

Description Mature clumps of this species can have up to 70 or more stems and grow to 36 inches or more across. Individual stems are cylindrical, 12–24

inches tall and 2½–3½ inches in diameter. Stems have 10–14 ribs with 3–4 **central spines** that are mostly bright yellow and nearly 3 inches long, and 9–11 yellow **radial spines** that are shorter than the **central spines**. Pink to purplish-pink flowers are about 2½ inches wide and appear in spring.

Culture These are cold hardy to at least 15° F and are perfect for USDA zones 8b–11. Plants are best grown in full sun and a fast-draining soil in most major metropolitan areas in the southwestern U.S. The growth rate is moderately slow, but they can reach flowering size in 8-inch diameter pots. They are drought tolerant when grown in the ground but require supplemental water in summer when grown in pots.

Identification The flowers are a little smaller and lighter pink than those of *Echinocereus engelmannii*.

Landscape Application These are a perfect fit for any **xeriscape** in the desert southwest. With their yellow **spines**, these stunning plants are attractive even when they are not in flower, but for a couple weeks in mid spring the flower display is nearly unrivaled. Plant with non-cactus succulents such as *Agave deserti*, *Fouquieria splendens*, and *Yucca rostrata*. Mix with spring or summer flowering plants such as *Calliandra eriophylla* and *Chrysactinia mexicana*.

Precautions Plants are relatively carefree once established, but keep supplemental watering to a minimum to prevent them from rotting.

Echinocereus nicholii

Echinocereus parkeri
Parker's Hedgehog
CLUSTERING CACTUS

SIZE (H x W)	Clusters 6–12 inches x 10–20 inches
FLOWER COLOR	Magenta
FLOWER SEASON	Late spring
EXPOSURE	Filtered sun
WATER	Low
GROWTH RATE	Moderate
PRUNING	Only cut out dead stems
HARDINESS	Low 20's F, zones 9a–11

Etymology Nigel Taylor honored English cactus collector David Parker when naming this species.

Field Notes In July 2008, my friend Chad Davis and I drove the long bumpy dirt road that climbs up into the Sierra Lampazos where *Agave ovatifolia* was first discovered. Along the way, we encountered plants of *Echinocereus parkeri* growing out of cracks in the limestone on the road cuts and on the flat ground at the top. Plants are found mostly on limestone soil in the Sierra Madre Oriental and a few outlying mountain ranges in Nuevo León, Tamaulipas and San Luis Potosí from about 2,400–7,200 feet elevation.

Description These form small clusters to about 6–12 inches tall by 10–20 inches across. In nature, plants frequently grow on road cuts and slopes and will have trailing stems that curve up near the tips. Individual stems are medium to dark green, narrowly cylindrical, about 5–10 inches long and 1-inch in diameter. There are 7–9 ribs, and 1–5 **central spines** up to 1-inch-long and 10–13 **radial spines** that are about ½-inch-long. Large funnel-shaped magenta to purple flowers are about 2 inches long and 2½ inches across. Prime blooming season is late spring.

Culture I have had these since 2008, and they have breezed through winter lows in the 22–23° F range with no damage and should be perfect for USDA zones 9a–11. Plants can tolerate morning sun, but should be given filtered sun in mid-day. They like a fast draining soil and are low-water-using whether in pots or in a landscape. Be sure the soil has good drainage to prevent rot. They have a moderate growth rate and can make a sizable cluster of stems in just a handful of years. No pruning is required unless a stem happens to die, which could then be removed.

Identification *Echinocereus parkeri* has smaller flowers (about 2½ inches across) and more **radial spines** (10–13) that are darker than *Echinocereus viereckii* with its slightly larger flowers (2½–3 inches across) and fewer **radial spines** (7–9) that are typically more golden yellow.

Landscape Application Plant these under a small tree with a sparse canopy for the filtered sunlight. Some likely options would include *Acacia constricta*, *Eysenhardtia orthocarpa*, or *Parkinsonia microphylla*. Mix with other shade tolerant cacti and succulents such as **Agave bovicornuta**, **Agave ovatifolia**, *Dioon edule*, and **Mammillaria sonorensis**. Put these on a terraced slope held in check by a rock wall and let the stems drape down. Plant shade tolerant perennials and groundcovers such as *Calylophus drummondianus*, *Conoclinium dissectum*, or *Hibiscus denudatus*.

Precautions Protect plants from packrats and rabbits.

Echinocereus parkeri

Echinocereus pentalophus
Ladyfinger Cactus
CLUSTERING CACTUS, SPRAWLING CACTUS

SIZE (H x W)	4–15 inches x ½–1-inch stem diameter, clumps to 12–36 inches across
FLOWER COLOR	Purplish pink with white throat, rarely all white
FLOWER SEASON	Spring to early summer
EXPOSURE	Filtered sun
WATER	Low
GROWTH RATE	Moderate
PRUNING	None
HARDINESS	20° F, zones 9a–11

Etymology Swiss botanist Augustin de Candolle combined the Greek *penta-* meaning five and the Greek *lophos-* meaning crest, in reference to the five ribs.

Field Notes One of my favorite Mexican states in which to botanize is Nuevo León, where I have seen these sprawling plants growing on gentle slopes, in open exposures, underneath shrubs, and along roadsides in several spots in the Sierra Madre Oriental. With three subspecies, this has a wide-ranging distribution from southern Texas south to Querétaro and Guanajuato. They typically grow on flat sandy limestone, among limestone boulders, or metamorphic rock, in mesquite scrub to oak-juniper vegetation, from about 70–6,700 feet elevation.

Description Each stem can reach 4–15 inches long and about ½–1-inch in diameter. These stems are **decumbent** and sprawling, and the whole plant will grow 12–36 inches across. Medium green stems have 5 ribs with 5–6, ½–2-inch-long, straight, needle-like, yellow, or brown **spines** in each cluster. Flowers are about 4–5 inches across, purplish pink with a white throat or rarely all white. Flowering is mostly in spring or early summer.

Culture Plants are cold hardy to the low 20's F and can be used in USDA zones 9a–11. They need some shade in hot summer cities of Palm Springs, Phoenix, and Tucson, but can be planted in full sun in cities with mild summers such as San Diego and Santa Barbara. The growth rate is moderate, and they are low-water-using when in the ground. However, they will flower profusely with supplemental water applied every 2–3 weeks beginning in spring. Keep the plants dry in winter and though stems will shrivel, they will respond to supplemental water applied during warm weather.

Identification *Echinocereus pentalophus* is easily identified by the **decumbent** stems, five ribs, and purplish pink flowers with the white throat.

Landscape Application These plants are best used beneath the canopy edge of a desert tree such as *Acacia constricta* or *Parkinsonia microphylla*. Use them as a sprawling groundcover on a terraced slope with small boulders forming low walls and let the stems flow over the rocks and through any cracks or slots between rocks. Plant with other cacti and succulents that tolerate light summer shade such as ***Agave schidigera*** and ***Echinocereus viereckii***. Plant with shade loving perennials such as *Conoclinium dissectum* and *Justicia longii*.

Precautions If planted in the right spot, there do not seem to be any problems with growing *Echinocereus pentalophus*.

Echinocereus pentalophus

Echinocereus reichenbachii
Black Lace Cactus, Reichenbach's Hedgehog
SMALL CACTUS

Etymology Botanist Wilhelm Walpers named this species for German cactus collector Friedrich Reichenbach.

Field Notes In June 2016, I was in the Chihuahuan Desert looking for cactus and other succulents with Jeff Chemnick and Brian Kemble. We stopped at a low hill between the town of General Cepeda and Saltillo in Coahuila and spotted a couple plants of *Echinocereus reichenbachii*. There are three subspecies of *Echinocereus reichenbachii*, so the distribution is widespread. These occur from southern Colorado to Oklahoma south through parts of eastern New Mexico and central Texas and into northeastern Mexico. Plants are fond of rocky or sandy soil and are frequently found on limestone in grasslands and oak-juniper woodland below 6,000 feet elevation.

SIZE (H x W)	3–12 inches x 2–4 inches
FLOWER COLOR	Magenta, purplish-pink, crimson, whitish-pink
FLOWER SEASON	Spring
EXPOSURE	Full sun, filtered sun
WATER	Low
GROWTH RATE	Slow
PRUNING	None
HARDINESS	10–15° F, zones 8a–11

Description Plants frequently have a single body 3–12 inches tall and 2–4 inches in diameter but can have as many as 12 stems and reach 10–12 inches across. There are 10–19 ribs with low **tubercles** holding the **spine** clusters.

Central spines are usually lacking, but there can be as many as 7. The 12–36 slightly curved and appressed **radial spines** are pure white or white with reddish or brownish tips. The large showy flowers are pink to magenta, 2–3 inches across, and can nearly hide the plant when they appear. Peak blooming season is primarily in spring, although the rogue flower can appear in summer.

Culture These are reliably hardy to about 10–15° F and are perfectly suited for USDA zones 8a–11. They can tolerate full sun in cities where summer temperatures rarely climb above 90° F, but need shade in hot summer cities like Palm Springs, Phoenix, and Tucson. Although they are low-water-using, plants will tolerate being given supplemental water on a weekly basis in summer if the soil is fast draining. The growth rate is slow, but they can flower when only 2–3 inches tall, and the large flowers are quite the show stopper even from a distance.

Identification *Echinocereus reichenbachii* has finer **spines** and a softer body than both *Echinocereus pectinatus* and *Echinocereus dasyacanthus*.

Landscape Application Use several of these small plants in a cactus and succulent garden, and place them for their spring surprise when the spectacularly showy flowers burst forth. If you are in a hot summer city and use them in a landscape, mix in small grasses, perennials, and small shrubs to provide some cover for these sun-sensitive plants. Suggestions would include *Bouteloua gracilis*, *Bouteloua curtipendula*, *Hibiscus coulteri*, and *Tetraneuris acaulis*. For a truly riotous spring flower show, plant *Echinocereus engelmannii*, *Echinocereus fasciculatus*, and *Thelocactus bicolor*. Put several in a large decorative pot with a jumble of rocks atop the soil, and incorporate that into your cactus and succulent collection.

Precautions Packrats and rabbits find these plants to be quite tasty, so take precautions to protect them from the little critters.

Echinocereus stramineus
Strawberry Hedgehog
CLUSTERING CACTUS

Etymology The prolific author George Engelmann used the Latin *stram-* to refer to the straw-colored spines of these plants.

Field Notes In June 2007, I traveled to northeastern Mexico where I saw large clusters of these densely spined plants growing on Cerro Bola in Coahuila. Nine years later, I was back in the area with Jeff Chemnick and Brian Kemble and saw more large clumps of this species, some with brown spines and others with pure white ones. Plants are native from southern New Mexico to western Texas, south to Chihuahua, Coahuila, and Nuevo León. These are Chihuahuan Desert natives that grow in soil derived from limestone and occur from about 3,000–7,600 feet elevation.

SIZE (H x W)	6–12 inches x clumps to 12–36 inches
FLOWER COLOR	Magenta purple with crimson throat
FLOWER SEASON	Spring to early summer
EXPOSURE	Full sun
WATER	Drought tolerant to low
GROWTH RATE	Moderate
PRUNING	None
HARDINESS	5° F, zones 7b–11

Description These clustering plants have individual stems growing out and up to about 6–12 inches high with a diameter of 2–4 inches. Clusters are typically about 12–24 inches in diameter with some large ones reaching 36 inches across. Stems are light green and mostly obscured by the dense **spine** clusters. There are 2–4 **central spines** measuring 1½–4 inches long and 7–10 **radial**

Cool Cacti and Succulents for Hot Gardens

spines that are ½–1½ inches long. **Spines** are needle-like, stiff, straight, adpressed to spreading, pure white, yellow, or brown. Large flowers are about 4–6 inches across, magenta with a darker crimson throat. Flowering is mostly in spring or early summer.

Culture These are very cold hardy shrugging off winter lows of 5° F and are ideal plants for USDA zones 7b–11. They will tolerate full sun even in hot summer cities of Las Vegas, Palm Springs, Phoenix, Tucson, and Yuma. The growth rate is moderate to moderately slow, depending on amount of water received during the growing season. They are drought tolerant once established in the ground; I have had a couple survive on 10–12 inches of annual rainfall in Tucson, but can handles supplemental water in summer and should be kept dry in winter.

Identification *Echinocereus stramineus* is distinguished by its dense **spine** clusters, large magenta flowers, and strawberry red fruit.

Landscape Application These are ideal for use in an open exposed cactus and succulent garden along with other drought tolerant plants. Locate them among small boulders or strategically arranged rock clusters, and plant with other full sun lovers such as *Agave parryi*, *Carnegiea gigantea*, *Euphorbia antisyphilitica*, *Ferocactus acanthodes*, *Fouquieria splendens*, and *Hesperaloe campanulata*. Mix in a few wildflowers and small shrubs that bloom in spring to give more color to the garden. Use *Baileya multiradiata*, *Calliandra* 'Sierra Starr', *Glandularia gooddingii*, *Isocoma tenuisecta*, and *Penstemon superbus*.

Precautions If planted in the right spot, *Echinocereus stramineus* is an easy-to-care-for plant. However watch for a Leaf-footed bug that might pierce the skin and cause open wounds that are an invitation to other pathogens.

Echinocereus viereckii
Viereck's Hedgehog
CLUSTERING CACTUS, SPRAWLING CACTUS

SIZE (H x W)	6–10 inches x 12–48 inch spread
FLOWER COLOR	Magenta purple
FLOWER SEASON	Spring
EXPOSURE	Filtered sun
WATER	Drought tolerant to low
GROWTH RATE	Moderate
PRUNING	None
HARDINESS	25° F, zones 9b–11

Etymology   Botanist Erich Werdermann named this species for German cactus collector Hans-Wilhelm Viereck.

Field Notes   The three subspecies of this beautiful plant (subsp. *huastecensis*, subsp. *morricalii*, and subsp. *viereckii*) all occur in small areas in northeastern Mexico. In 1989, Carol and I stopped to look at Cola de Caballo where I spotted plants of subsp. *morricallii* growing among the dense vegetation. Years later, I saw subsp. *viereckii* on a rock slab in Tamaulipas. Plants grow in rocky wooded areas on limestone soil in Tamaulipas and Nuevo León from about 2,300–5,000 feet.

Description   Plants form clusters of upright to sprawling stems 6–10 inches long by about 12–48 inches across. Individual stems are medium green to dark green, and mostly trailing along the ground but turning up slightly at the tips. There are 5–7 ribs, and when present, 8 radial **spines**. Magenta flowers are about 2½–3 inches across, appearing mostly in late spring.

Culture I have subspecies *morricalii* in the ground under the open canopy of a hybrid *Parkinsonia* tree. The plant receives summer shade and winter sun and has withstood winter lows of 22° F with no damage. Plants will benefit from being in filtered sunlight in hot summer cities of Las Vegas, Phoenix, and Tucson. Although drought tolerant once established in the ground, the moderate growth rate will speed up slightly with supplemental water in summer. Potted plants need water in summer, but can go nearly all winter without water.

Identification *Echinocereus viereckii* is easily distinguished from other ***Echinocereus*** species by the combination of growth form, **spine** color, and flower color. Subspecies *morricalii* lacks **spines** or has very short **spines**.

Landscape Application Use these plants under the canopy of a sparsely branched desert tree such as *Acacia constricta*, *Acacia willardiana*, *Eysenhardtia orthocarpa*, or *Parkinsonia microphylla*. Plant with other shade tolerant cacti and succulents such as ***Agave schidigera*** and ***Peniocereus greggii***. Plant on a terraced slope held in check by a rock wall and let the stems drape over the rock. Tuck in with small to large boulders or among strategically arranged rock clusters. Plant shade tolerant perennials and groundcovers for extra color.

Precautions Put them in some shade and protect from packrats and rabbits for the first two or three years.

Echinocereus viridiflorus var. *canus*
Graybeard Cactus
SMALL CACTUS

SIZE (H x W)	6–12 inches x 1½–2½ inch stem diameter
FLOWER COLOR	Light green to yellowish green
FLOWER SEASON	Spring
EXPOSURE	Full sun to filtered light
WATER	Low
GROWTH RATE	Moderately slow
PRUNING	None
HARDINESS	15° F, zones 8b–11

Etymology   The species name is from the Latin *viridis* for green and *florus* for flower, while the variety name is the Latin *canus* for grayish-white and refers to the white spines.

Field Notes   I have not yet made the journey to see these in habitat and still hope to make the trip someday. Plants were discovered in 1984 by graduate student James Jeff Clark while conducting a vegetative survey as part of his Master of Science project. Plants grow on the exposed Caballos Novaculite ridge crests and south-facing slopes, and on rhyolite and sandstone at elevations between 4,400–4,800 feet in Presidio County in the Trans-Pecos of western Texas.

Description   In habitat, plants are usually solitary while in cultivation they can develop multiple stems, each growing to 6–12 inches tall and about 1½–2½ inches thick. Seedlings and very young plants are covered with long soft shaggy white hair-like **spines**, but as they grow older, the **spines** become stiffer. Older plants are densely covered with white or red and white ½–1-inch-long **spines**. Light green to yellowish-green or even golden-green flowers are about 1-inch-long, appear in spring, and have a delicate lemony fragrance.

Cool Cacti and Succulents for Hot Gardens

Culture Plants are hardy to at least 15° F and can be grown in USDA zones 8b–11. They can be grown in full sun in cities like Sierra Vista and Tucson, but should be given some mid-day shade in the hottest cities of Palm Springs, Phoenix, and Yuma. They are low-water-using but plants in full sun should be watered more frequently during summer than plants in some shade. Growth rate is moderately slow, but they do flower at a small size.

Identification These are readily identified by the long soft hair-like **spines** as seedlings, and older plants are notable for the dense covering of white **spines**.

Landscape Application Place these in a highly visible spot in a small cactus and succulent garden: someplace where they will not be hidden by other plants. These would go well with other small cactus and succulents such as *Agave victoriae-reginae*, *Ariocarpus trigonus*, *Astrophytum coahuilense*, *Coryphantha poselgeriana*, *Echinocereus reichenbachii*, and *Mammillaria candida*. Use small perennials to add seasonal color and shade the surrounding soil. Some suggestions include *Amoreuxia palmatifida*, *Dalea nana*, *Menodora scabra*, *Tetraneuris acaulis*, and *Zinnia grandiflora*. These are perfect for growing in decorative pots and incorporating into a cactus and succulent collection.

Precautions Keep these away from any potential packrat or rabbit encounters. No telling what those critters will eat when summer rolls around and food is scarce.

Echinocereus viridiflorus var. canus

Erythrina flabelliformis
Coral Bean
SHRUB-LIKE SUCCULENT

SIZE (H x W)	3–6 (20) feet x 3–6 feet
FLOWER COLOR	Bright red
FLOWER SEASON	Late spring to summer
EXPOSURE	Full sun, reflected heat
WATER	Drought tolerant to low
GROWTH RATE	Moderately fast
PRUNING	Remove frozen stems
HARDINESS	25–30° F, zones 9b–11

Etymology American botanist Thomas Kearney used the Latin *flabell-* for fan and the Latin *form-* for shape to describe the fan-shaped **leaflets**.

Field Notes I see these plants growing as shrubs in southern Arizona. Here they routinely freeze back because they are at the northern edge of their range. They become small or medium-size trees in frost-free areas of Mexico. Plants are found on slopes and cliffs in canyons and arroyos from southeastern Arizona south throughout much of Mexico from about 30–6,000 feet elevation.

Description As the weather heats up in late spring and summer, so do these xerophytic shrubs. Plants will first sprout their signature clusters

of 2–3-inch-long narrowly tubular bright red flowers in late spring and early summer followed by the new leaves with their three fan-shaped **leaflets**. Flowers appear on growth from the previous year, so if the stems are frozen, flowering will be delayed until summer or even the next year. Flowers are regularly visited by hummingbirds, and then later woody pods develop that open to reveal bright red seeds. These seeds are toxic if ground up and ingested, but are very hard and difficult to break open without breaking several teeth first. The leaves are composed of three fan-shaped **leaflets** each about 2–3 inches long and

wide. These are typically seen as medium to large shrubs 3–6 feet tall and wide in southwestern landscapes, but can be grown as a 20-foot-tall tree in cities that do not experience frost.

Culture Plants will freeze back when subjected to temperatures in the mid-20's F, but will not be killed outright, so they are suitable for USDA zones 9b–11 and possibly 9a if grown in a warm microclimate. When frozen repeatedly, these will develop a large underground **caudex** from which plants generate new stems if frozen to the ground. Plant in full sun or reflected heat to minimize frost damage. They are low-water-using to drought tolerant once established and prefer to grow in a rocky soil with good drainage.

Identification The three fan-shaped **leaflets**, bright red flowers, and stems with **prickles** readily distinguish this from other *Erythrina* species.

Landscape Application These could be considered specialty plants and used to fill a specific spot in a patio or **xeriscape** garden. Find a spot in full sun or the reflected heat of a south or west-facing wall to maximize flowering and minimize frost damage. Place them in a warm micro-climate and plant low growing cactus, succulents, perennials, and even small shrubs with these intriguing plants. They can be used to fill a south and west-facing corner niche on a patio where you can enjoy the bright red flowers prior to new leaves appearing.

Precautions Plants are susceptible to frost and should be placed in a warm micro-climate to minimize damage.

Erythrina flabelliformis

Escobaria vivipara
Beehive Cactus
CLUSTERING CACTUS

SIZE (H x W)	2–8 inches x 12–20 inches for cluster
FLOWER COLOR	Pink to lavender
FLOWER SEASON	Early summer
EXPOSURE	Filtered sun
WATER	Drought tolerant to low
GROWTH RATE	Moderate
PRUNING	None
HARDINESS	0° F, zones 7a–11

Etymology Englishman Thomas Nuttall based the species name on the Latin for viviperous, possibly for the clustering stems.

Field Notes I have seen these in flower in mid-May while seeking out Agaves in the New River Mountains of central Arizona. Cactus aficionado Rob Romero and I found plants while looking for *Echinomastus erectocentrus* in southeastern Arizona. The species has a very wide-ranging distribution from California east to Texas and north into Canada with plants growing in desert scrub, grasslands, and oak-juniper to pine woodland from about 2,200–7,200 feet elevation.

Description Individual stems are small, growing to 2–8 inches tall and 2–4 inches in diameter, but plants can cluster with age and reach 12–20 inches across. Dark green stems are mostly visible beneath the clusters of colorful **spines**. There are 5–6 **central spines** and 15–18 **radial spines** all about ½-inch-long and colored a mixture of white, gray, brown, and pink. Colorful flowers are various shades of pink or lavender, are 1½–2 inches wide, and appear in summer.

Culture The species has a wide-ranging distribution, from the desert southwest to Canada, so hardiness can be difficult to pinpoint depending on where the seed originated. However, it is safe to say these can tolerate 0° F with no problem and are able to be grown in USDA zones 7a–11 if kept dry in winter. They may be able to tolerate full sun in high elevation cities with summer temperatures rarely over 80° F, but elsewhere they should be given some shade in summer to take the edge off the heat. Established plants are drought tolerant, surviving on 10–15 inches of annual rainfall, but those growing in pots will like a drink of water every week or two in hot weather: less frequently in cooler climates. Make sure the soil has good drainage to prevent roots from rotting.

Identification *Escobaria vivipara* can be identified by its colorful **spines**, large colorful flowers, and beehive-shaped body.

Landscape Application Grow these plants in pots until large enough to put in the ground. Once they are big enough, find a spot with a little bit of summer shade in a cactus and succulent garden or a more extensive **xeriscape** garden, and plant several in a grouping. If you live in a hot summer city such as Phoenix or Tucson, put the plants beneath a tree canopy. A couple interesting shrubs/trees to use would be *Acacia berlandieri*, *Acacia constricta*, or *Bauhinia macranthera*. Other intriguing options for some shade would be to plant several on the east side of a large *Fouquieria splendens* or near native grasses such as *Aristida purpurea* or *Eragrostis intermedia*.

Precautions Sometimes **mealybugs** will target these plants, but those can be picked off with a good pair of sharp tweezers. If you see signs of a **spider mite** infestation look into using a miticide.

Escobaria vivipara

Espostoa blossfeldiorum
Synonym: *Thrixanthocereus blossfeldiorum*
Blossfeld's Espostoa
COLUMNAR CACTUS

SIZE (H x W)	6–12 feet x 2–4 inch stem diameter, clusters up to 4 feet across
FLOWER COLOR	Yellowish cream
FLOWER SEASON	Late spring to summer
EXPOSURE	Full sun
WATER	Low
GROWTH RATE	Moderate
PRUNING	None
HARDINESS	mid-20's F, zones 9b–11

Etymology German-born botanist Erich Werdermann named this species for German horticulturists Robert Blossfeld and his son Harry.

Field Notes I have been to Peru once, but not to the mountains in the north where these grow. Looks like another trip to the southern hemisphere is in my future. These are found growing on open dry slopes and rocky outcrops in the mountains of northern Peru from about 2,300–7,500 feet elevation.

Description Plants have narrow columnar stems 2–4 inches in diameter with each growing to 6–12 feet tall. They may be solitary as young plants, but can produce more stems from the base and form clusters up to 4 feet across. The 18–25 ribs are covered with 1–4 dark brown central spines and 20–25 glassy white radial spines. Slender funnelform 3-inch-long creamy yellow flowers poke out of the **cephalium** that is near the top of the stem. Prime flowering season is mostly from late spring into summer.

Photo by Tristan Davis

Cool Cacti and Succulents for Hot Gardens

Culture These are cold hardy to mid-20's F and can be used in USDA zones 9b–11, but might need protection on the really cold nights. They can tolerate full sun and are low-water-using even in the hottest southwestern U.S. cities that experience triple digit temperatures for much of the summer such as Palm Springs, Phoenix, and Tucson. Keep the soil dry in winter though as the plants tend to shut down and do not need extra water. They have a moderate growth rate and take a few years to start to develop clusters.

Photo by Tristan Davis

Identification *Espostoa blossfeldiorum* forms a **cephalium** a lot sooner than other species, and has fewer radial spines (20–25) than the similar sized *Espostoa melanostele* with 40–50.

Landscape Application These versatile plants can be grown in large decorative pots and placed on an open patio in the sun or planted in a low-water-use landscape. If you can only find single-stemmed plants, put three together in the same hole to get an immediate clustering effect. Use them in a xeriscape with plants such as *Agave ocahui*, *Coryphantha recurvata*, *Dasylirion acrotrichum*, *Echinocactus grusonii*, *Ferocactus gracilis*, and *Fouquieria splendens*. Add a few flowering perennials to provide seasonal color and moderate the micro-climate around the plants. Use plants such as *Calliandra eriophylla*, *Dalea frutescens*, *Justicia longii*, *Scutellaria suffrutescens*, *Tetraneuris acaulis*, *Thymophylla pentachaeta*, and *Zinnia acerosa*.

Precautions Protect stem tips if temperatures are expected to dip below about 25° F. Be sure to provide supplemental water in spring and summer.

Photo by Tristan Davis

Espostoa lanata
Peruvian Old Man
COLUMNAR CACTUS

SIZE (H x W)	2–15 feet x 2–6-inch stem diameter
FLOWER COLOR	White to purple
FLOWER SEASON	Late spring to summer
EXPOSURE	Full sun, filtered sun
WATER	Low
GROWTH RATE	Slow
PRUNING	None
HARDINESS	25° F, zones 9b–11

Etymology German-born botanist Carl Kunth used the Latin *lana-* for wool when describing this hairy species.

Field Notes My only trip to Peru to date found me south of the range of these beautiful plants, and I hope to one day get to where they grow. Plants are found on the western slopes of the Andes Mountains in southern Ecuador and northern Peru from about 2,600–7,200 feet elevation.

Description Initially, these shrubby plants have a single stem that can grow to 2–15 feet tall and 2–6 inches in diameter, but over time they will develop several stems with clusters attaining a 3–6-foot diameter. Light green stems are mostly obscured by the long white hairs that are responsible for the common name of Peruvian Old Man. There are 30–40 short reddish or yellowish-brown **radial spines** less than ½-inch-long. White or purple bell-shaped flowers are about 2 inches long and appear in the **cephalium** in late spring to summer.

Culture These are very popular plants in the cactus and succulent industry because of their hairy look when young. They reportedly are able to tolerate winter lows of 25° F with no problem and can be grown in USDA zones 9b–11 if kept dry in winter. They should be able to tolerate full sun in cities where summer temperatures rarely climb over 100° F, but elsewhere they should be given some afternoon shade in summer to take the edge off the heat. Established plants are low-water-using, preferring a periodic drink of water in hot weather, but keep the soil dry in winter. Make sure the soil has good drainage so excess moisture does not drown the roots.

Identification The **central spine**, if present, is about 1-inch-long on *Espostoa lanata*, while the **central spines** on *Espostoa melanostele* can be up to 4 inches long.

Landscape Application These can be grown in large pots until they get large enough to be planted in a southwestern **xeriscape**. Try planting several together for an immediate clustering effect. Use these in a cactus and succulent garden along with plants such as **Agave ovatifolia**, **Coryphantha poselgeriana**, **Dasylirion quadrangulatum**, **Echinocactus grusonii**, **Echinocereus stramineus**, **Fouquieria splendens**, **Mammillaria standleyi**, and **Parodia leninghausii**. Add a few flowering perennials to provide seasonal color and moderate the micro-climate around the plants. Use plants such as *Calliandra eriophylla*, *Dalea frutescens*, *Glandularia gooddingii*, *Justicia xylosteoides*, *Salvia greggii*, and *Tetraeuris acaulis*.

Precautions Protect the stem tips if temperatures are expected to dip below about 25° F. Be sure to provide supplemental water in spring and summer, but keep soil dry in winter.

Espostoa melanostele
Peruvian Old Lady
COLUMNAR CACTUS

SIZE (H x W)	2–6 feet x 2–4-inch stem diameter
FLOWER COLOR	White
FLOWER SEASON	Summer
EXPOSURE	Full sun, filtered sun
WATER	Low
GROWTH RATE	Slow
PRUNING	None
HARDINESS	25° F, zones 9b–11

Etymology The German botanist Friedrich Vaupel used the Greek *melan-* meaning black and the Greek *stele-* meaning column for the species name. The spines can turn black with age.

Field Notes I have been to Peru only one time and that was to the south of where these plants grow. Looks like I should be visiting South America more. Plants occur in the mountains of central and northern Peru on exposed rocky slopes from about 2,000–8,200 feet elevation.

Description These are shrubby plants with many narrow columnar stems, each stem growing 2–6 feet tall and about 2–4 inches in diameter. In time, clusters of stems can eventually grow 2–3 feet across. Stems are light green with 18–25 ribs and densely covered with ½-inch-long white or brownish hairs. **Central spines** are about 1½–4 inches long, yellow when young and turn black with age, and poke out beyond the fine hairs. White bell-shape flowers appear in summer and only in the lateral **cephalia** found near the top of the stems. Subspecies *nana* (pictured here) is a shorter plant with fewer **spines**.

Culture Plants are reported to be hardy to 25° F and can be used in USDA zones 9b–11 with no problems of frost damage. They are best grown in full sun in most major southwestern U.S. cities, but will adapt to very light shade in hot summer cities like Las Vegas, Palm Springs, and Phoenix. These can be grown either in the ground or in large pots if the soil drains very quickly. Plants in the ground are drought tolerant but will grow faster and fill in quicker if given extra water in spring and summer. Plants in pots prefer to have a consistent schedule of supplemental water in spring and summer. No pruning is needed for these unless a stem gets badly damaged by frost and needs to be removed.

Identification *Espostoa melanostele* are shorter plants that branch from the base while *Espostoa lanata* grows taller and can branch in the upper parts. *Espostoa melanostele* has more **radial spines** (40–50) than the similar sized *Espostoa blossfeldiorum* with 20–25 **radial spines**.

Landscape Application These can be grown in large pots and placed on a patio or planted in a southwestern **xeriscape**. Unless you can find plants that already have multiple stems, try planting several together for an immediate clustering effect. Use these in a cactus and succulent garden along with plants such as *Agave parryi*, *Astrophytum myriostigma*, *Coryphantha poselgeriana*, *Echinocactus grusonii*, *Fouquieria splendens*, and *Thelocactus bicolor*. Add a few flowering perennials to provide seasonal color and moderate the micro-climate around the plants. Use plants such as *Baileya multiradiata*, *Dalea capitata*, *Glandularia gooddingii*, *Justicia longii*, *Scutellaria suffrutescens*, and *Tetraeuris acaulis*.

Precautions Protect the tips of stems if temperatures are expected to dip below about 25° F. Be sure to provide supplemental water in spring and summer.

Euphorbia antisyphilitica
Candelilla
SHRUB-LIKE SUCCULENT

SIZE (H x W)	2–3 feet x 2–4 (–6) feet
FLOWER COLOR	Pink-and-white
FLOWER SEASON	Late spring to fall
EXPOSURE	Full sun
WATER	Drought tolerant to low
GROWTH RATE	Fast
PRUNING	None
HARDINESS	10°F, zones 8a–11

Etymology German-born botanist Joseph Gerhard Zuccarini described this species and noted that the "milk juice is used by the Indians as a cure for gonorrhea."

Field Notes I was with plant buddies Ron Gass and Dave Palzkill when we saw large stands of the distinctive pencil-thin, gray stemmed plants in western Texas along State Highway 285 between Fort Stockton and Big Bend National Park. Plants are found primarily on flat desert soil or perched among large rocks and boulders in the Chihuahuan Desert in southern New Mexico, western Texas, and northern and east-central Mexico. They occur mostly between 3,000–4,500 feet, rarely to 7,000 feet elevation.

Description *Euphorbia antisyphilitica* starts life as a single thin stem eventually transforming into an intriguing mass of gray-green or gray-white, slender, upright, succulent stems reaching 2–3 feet tall. The plants spread by **rhizomes**, which results in the formation of large clusters to 2–4 feet or even up to 6 feet across. Leafless stems are coated with high-grade wax that was the object

of commercial harvesting during World Wars I and II. Pink-and-white flowers grace the length of the stem from late spring and summer and even fall.

Culture Plants in the ground are hardy to 10° F and probably lower, while those in pots might suffer root damage if the soil freezes. As a landscape plant, they can be used in USDA zones 8a–11. To keep the plants dense and give the best stem color, place them in full sun, in a soil type that has very good drainage, and keep supplemental water to a minimum. The growth rate of individual stems is fast, but clump development is rather slow. No pruning is required for these plants.

Identification *Euphorbia antisyphilitica* is shorter with thinner stems and small pink-and-white flowers compared to the taller **Pedilanthus macrocarpus** with its thicker stems and bright red slipper-shaped flowers.

Landscape Application Candelilla was made to be scattered about in a xeric landscape with other low-water-use plants or tucked in among large boulders in a cactus and succulent garden. Mix it with perennials and shrubs such as *Chrysactinia mexicana*, *Dalea frutescens*, *Ericameria laricifolia*, *Glandularia gooddingii*, and *Parthenium incanum*. These get along well with cacti and other succulents such as **Aloe ferox**, **Agave ovatifolia**, **Echinocactus grusonii**, **Fouquieria splendens**, **Opuntia santa-rita**, **Oreocereus celsianus**, and **Yucca rostrata**.

Precautions If you get the white milky sap on your hands, wash immediately and thoroughly using soap and water.

Euphorbia antisyphilitica

Euphorbia resinifera
Moroccan Mound
SHRUB-LIKE SUCCULENT

SIZE (H x W)	1–2 feet x 2–6 feet
FLOWER COLOR	Yellow
FLOWER SEASON	Spring to early summer
EXPOSURE	Full sun
WATER	Drought tolerant to low
GROWTH RATE	Moderately slow
PRUNING	None
HARDINESS	20°F, zones 9a–11

Etymology 20th Century German botanist Otto Berg named this species for its aromatic resin that was sometimes used medicinally as a drug.

Field Notes I have never traveled to Morocco but have read that this species is native to the slopes of the Atlas Mountains in the central part of the country. These mountains separate the Sahara Desert from both the Mediterranean Sea and Atlantic ocean. There are observation records on iNaturalist.org indicating that plants have been seen on the northwest side of the mountains growing in dry soil from about 2,300–4,300 feet elevation.

Description *Euphorbia resinifera* is a mounding plant that typically grows to about 1–2 feet tall with numerous four-sided succulent stems about 1-inch thick. Plants slowly grow more stems and with enough time will reach 2–6 feet across. Leafless pale green stems, sometimes with a slight bluish cast, grow upright like short columns. Stems have small, white or brown **spines** on the ribs, and bear small yet colorful yellow flowers in spring to early summer.

Culture These are hardy to at least 20° F and make superb landscape plants in USDA zones 9a–11. Grow them in full sun to achieve the dense form and buckets of flowers in spring and summer. Established plants are very low-water-using to drought tolerant, and prefer soil that has very good drainage. These are moderately slow growing, so avoid pruning any stems, unless one dies back for some reason. If you do have to prune a stem, wear gloves to prevent contact with the milky latex.

Identification *Euphorbia resinifera* is readily identified by its thick four-ribbed stems.

Landscape Application Use these as succulent shrubs in a xeriscape in nearly all low- and mid-elevation southwestern U.S. cities. Allow ample room for plants to fully develop without encroaching into neighboring plants. These mix nicely with cacti and other succulent plants like **Aloe ferox**, **Aloe striata**, **Ferocactus acanthodes**, and **Hesperaloe funifera**. Plant with small perennials such as *Tetraneuris acaulis* and *Thymophylla pentachaeta*, but they should keep their distance from shrubs and trees. *Euphorbia resinifera* plants can be used in wide-open commercial landscapes like street medians, roadsides, and freeway on/off ramps.

Precautions Stems have a milky white latex with a high concentration of resiniferatoxin. The resin does have medicinal uses when dried, but the fresh latex should be thoroughly washed off skin with soap and water.

Euphorbia resinifera

Ferocactus acanthodes

Synonym: *Ferocactus cylindraceus*
Fire Barrel, California Barrel
BARREL CACTUS

SIZE (H x W)	3–6 feet x 1–2 feet in diameter
FLOWER COLOR	Yellow or greenish yellow
FLOWER SEASON	Late spring to summer
EXPOSURE	Full sun
WATER	Drought tolerant to low
GROWTH RATE	Slow
PRUNING	None
HARDINESS	10°–15° F, zones 8a–11

Etymology Frenchman Charles Lemaire used the Greek *acanth-* meaning spine and the Greek *odes-* meaning like, referring to the spiny nature of the plants.

Field Notes The three loosely defined subspecies are spread across the southwest. My favorite is subspecies *acanthodes* (bottom left, this page), which I have seen along Mexico Highway 3, which cuts between the Sierra Juarez and Sierra San Pedro Mártir in northern Baja California. These plants can get nearly 6 feet tall and have beautiful spines. Rob Romero and I saw subspecies *lecontei* (bottom right, this page) in the Tortilita Mountains near Tucson. With three subspecies, the distribution is wide-spread in a variety of habitats from Sonoran Desert to juniper-grassland from about 600–4,600 feet elevation.

Description In habitat these are typically solitary plants growing to 3–6 feet tall with a stem diameter of about 1–2 feet. Individual stems are pale

green to medium green with 20–31 ribs and 12–32 **spines** per cluster with 4 **central spines**. In subsp. *acanthodes*, the colorful **spines** can be red, yellow, or white. In subsp. *eastwoodiae* the **spines** are uniformly whitish or light to bright yellow. Flowers are 1½–2½ inches across, yellow, greenish yellow, sometimes with a red mid-stripe and appear in spring into summer.

Culture I have plants that have been through a low temperature of 20° F without sustaining damage. I suspect they should be able to handle a range of 10°–15° F and can be grown in USDA zones 8a–11. They are best grown in full sun even in the hottest cities of the southwestern U.S., including Las Vegas, Palm Springs, Phoenix, Tucson, and Yuma. They are drought tolerant once established in the ground and will grow well in most any soil type.

Identification *Ferocactus acanthodes* subsp. *acanthodes* has bristle-like outer **radial spines** that are lacking in subsp. *eastwoodiae*. The subsp. *lecontei* has shorter **central spines** than subsp. *acanthodes* and fewer **radial spines** than subsp. *eastwoodiae*.

Landscape Application Use these plants in full sun in a cactus and succulent garden and mix in spring wildflowers for a splash of color. These durable plants grow well alongside Sonoran Desert cactus, shrubs, and perennials. For a hardcore desert look, plant with *Agave deserti*, *Baileya multiradiata*, *Calliandra eriophylla*, *Echinocereus engelmannii*, *Encelia farinosa*, *Fouquieria splendens*, *Glandularia gooddingii*, and *Penstemon parryi*.

Precautions The female of the snout moth, *Cactobrosis fernaldialis*, has been known to lay eggs in species of *Ferocactus*, with the larva tunneling into the plant, and providing an opening for other pathogens.

Ferocactus chrysacanthus
Yellow-spined Barrel
BARREL CACTUS

SIZE (H x W)	8–30 inches x 10–12 inches in diameter
FLOWER COLOR	Yellow, orange-red
FLOWER SEASON	Late spring to summer
EXPOSURE	Filtered sun
WATER	Low
GROWTH RATE	Slow
PRUNING	None
HARDINESS	low 20's F, zones 9a–11

Etymology Charles Orcutt described this species using the Greek *chryso-* meaning gold and the Greek *acanth-* meaning spine to signify the golden yellow spines.

Field Notes These are native to Cedros Island and San Benito Island off the western coast of Baja California. I have been to Cedros twice and both times was able to hire a fishing boat to take me to Punta Norte on the northeast side of the island where there are spectacular specimens of *Agave sebastiana* and *Ferocactus chrysacanthus*. Plants grow in sandy washes or on rocky slopes and outcrops from about 20–1,500 feet elevation.

Description In habitat these are usually solitary plants about 8–30 inches tall with a stem diameter of about 10–12 inches. There are 10–13 ribs on young softball-sized plants with the number increasing to 18–25 on larger plants. On old plants grown slowly, the dense spination mostly obscures the dark green body, but on young plants the **spine** clusters are farther apart revealing the

Cool Cacti and Succulents for Hot Gardens

attractive body color. On young plants there are only 3–4 **central spines** and 7–9 **radial spines**, while on older plants there are more **spines** including several bristle-like **radial spines**. **Spine** color is bright or dull yellow, sometimes red or yellow-red. Flowers are yellow or rarely orange-red, 1½ inches across, and appear in spring and summer.

Culture I have a large potted plant that has remained uncovered through winter low temperatures of 22°–23° F without sustaining any damage. Cactus grower extraordinaire, Steve Plath, had plants make it through upper teens F without damage, so these should be reliably hardy in USDA zones 9a–11. I have tried planting a couple in the ground without success and have decided to keep my smaller ones in pots until they are at least the size of a cantaloupe. Plants prefer to be grown in filtered sun in the hot summer cities of the southwestern U.S. including Las Vegas, Palm Springs, Phoenix, Tucson, and Yuma. These are low-water-using but should be given supplemental water from late spring through summer and kept dry in winter.

Identification *Ferocactus chrysacanthus* generally has **central** and **radial spines** that look alike while *Ferocactus acanthodes* and *Ferocactus gracilis* have distinctly different **central spines** and **radial spines**.

Landscape Application These are best grown in decorative containers and kept in a collection with other potted cacti and succulents, especially in cities that experience low-20's F or lower. My friend Jeff Chemnick has grown these in his Santa Barbara, California landscape. Place them in a prominent location along with other Baja California plants such as *Agave cerulata* and *Echinocereus engelmannii*.

Precautions The snout moth, *Cactobrosis fernaldialis*, has been known to tunnel into species of *Ferocactus*.

Ferocactus emoryi
Emory's Barrel
BARREL CACTUS

SIZE (H x W)	1½–6 feet x 1–2 feet in diameter
FLOWER COLOR	Red
FLOWER SEASON	Summer
EXPOSURE	Full sun
WATER	Drought tolerant to low
GROWTH RATE	Slow
PRUNING	None
HARDINESS	20° F, zones 9a–11

Etymology German-born, American-trained botanist George Engelmann named this species for Major William Emory who oversaw the Mexican boundary survey from 1850–1854.

Field Notes Take a drive through Organ Pipe Cactus National Monument to see these plants growing on gravelly flats and rocky slopes. The tallest plant I have seen there was about 6 feet, but most were 1½–2 feet. Make the trip in late July or early August to see plants with their deep red flowers and look for the occasional plant with yellow flowers. This Sonoran Desert native occurs from south-central Arizona south to about Guaymas, Sonora. Plants grow on gravelly flats and rocky slopes from near sea-level–4,100 feet elevation. Some people include *Ferocactus rectispinus* as a subspecies, but I have that as a separate entry.

Description Plants usually have a single body growing to 2–3 feet and about 1-foot in diameter. Occasionally, a very old plant will grow to 6 feet tall with

a diameter of close to 2 feet. Mature specimens have 15–32 ribs with stout **spines** at each areole. The **central spine** is straight or curved, 2–5 inches long, and usually gray or white, sometimes with a pinkish tinge. **Radial spines** number 6–8 and look much like the **central spine** in color and thickness but are a little shorter. Flowers are red, rarely yellow, about 2 inches across and appear in mid- to late summer.

Culture I have plants that have survived winter low temperatures of about 22°–23° F without sustaining any damage, so these should be able to be grown in USDA zones 9a–11. These are no speed demons when it comes to growth rate, so have patience and they will eventually make extraordinary landscape plants. They grow best in full sun throughout the southwestern U.S., even in cities with hot summers such as Las Vegas, Palm Springs, Phoenix, Tucson, and Yuma. Established plants are drought tolerant but will accept periodic supplemental water from late spring through summer, but should be kept dry through winter.

Identification *Ferocactus emoryi* is easily identified by the single stout curved **central spine**, few **radial spines**, and red flowers.

Landscape Application Grow these plants in full sun along with non-cactus succulents and other cacti, and interspersed with spring flowering perennials and small shrubs to get color nearly all year. A few suggestions for companion succulents and cacti include *Agave simplex*, ***Astrophytum ornatum***, ***Coryphantha recurvata***, ***Echinocactus grusonii***, ***Echinocereus engelmannii***, and ***Fouquieria splendens***. For perennial color use plants like *Baileya multiradiata*, *Calliandra eriophylla*, *Encelia farinosa*, *Glandularia gooddingii*, *Justicia candicans*, and *Zinnia acerosa*.

Precautions The snout moth, *Cactobrosis fernaldialis*, has been known to tunnel into species of ***Ferocactus*** and other barrel-like cacti.

Ferocactus fordii
Ford's Barrel
SMALL BARREL-LIKE CACTUS

SIZE (H x W)	15–20 inches x 8–10 inches in diameter
FLOWER COLOR	Pinkish-rose to purplish
FLOWER SEASON	Spring
EXPOSURE	Filtered sun
WATER	Low to moderate
GROWTH RATE	Moderately slow
PRUNING	None
HARDINESS	High 20's F, zones 9b–11

Etymology Early 20th century explorer/naturalist Charles Orcutt named this species for a Mr. Ford, but more information is scarce.

Field Notes *Ferocactus fordii* is not the easiest plant to spot unless it is laden with flowers. Bob Webb and I found the northern subsp. *borealis* while researching in the sandy parts of Baja California south of Mexico Highway 1 on the way to Punta San Carlos on the Pacific coast. In May 2011, Brian Kemble and I found plants of the southern subsp. *fordii* growing in sandy soil east of Villa Jesus Maria on the way to El Mezquital. *Ferocactus fordii* subsp. *borealis* can be found on the Pacific side of the Sierra San Pedro Mártir from near sea level to about 2,000 feet. *Ferocactus fordii* subsp. *fordii* grows farther south and can be found on the Pacific side in sandy or rocky soil from near sea level to about 1,300 feet elevation in the far southwestern corner of Baja California state and the Vizcaíno Biosphere in northwestern Baja California Sur.

Ferocactus fordii **subsp.** ***borealis***

Cool Cacti and Succulents for Hot Gardens

Description These are usually single stemmed plants growing about 15–20 inches tall and 8–10 inches in diameter. There are about 20–21 ribs on mature plants. Plants have 4 pink, red, gray, or brown **central spines** and about 12–15 **radial spines**. Flowers are pinkish-rose in subsp. *fordii* or purplish in subsp. *borealis*. They measure about 1½ inches long, appear mostly in spring, and might attract the occasional hummingbird.

Culture I have not grown these outside of an unheated greenhouse in winter, and suspect they need frost protection when low temperatures reach about 27°–28° F. Plants should be reliably hardy in USDA zones 9b–11. They grow best in filtered sun in the hot cities of the southwestern U.S. including Las Vegas, Palm Springs, Phoenix, Tucson, and Yuma. These are low- to moderate-water-using, but should be given supplemental water from late spring through summer and kept dry in winter.

Ferocactus fordii* subsp. *fordii

Identification The pinkish to purplish flowers distinguish *Ferocactus fordii* from the yellowish to yellowish-green flowered *Ferocactus viridescens*.

Landscape Application These are best grown in decorative containers and kept in a collection with other potted cacti and succulents, especially in cities that experience winter low temperatures below the mid-20's F. Grow in a cactus and succulent collection with smaller cacti and succulents that also need winter protection. A couple small cacti and succulents that are also great in containers include *Agave albopilosa* and ***Ariocarpus fissuratus***.

Precautions *Cactobrosis fernaldialis*, has been known to tunnel into ***Ferocactus***.

Ferocactus fordii* subsp. *borealis

Ferocactus fordii

Ferocactus glaucescens
Blue Barrel
SMALL BARREL-LIKE CACTUS

SIZE (H x W)	8–15 inches x 8–15 inches in diameter, clusters to 24–36 inches
FLOWER COLOR	Yellow
FLOWER SEASON	Spring
EXPOSURE	Full sun, filtered sun
WATER	Drought tolerant to low
GROWTH RATE	Moderately slow
PRUNING	None
HARDINESS	Low 20's F, zones 9a–11

Etymology Augustin de Candolle was a Swiss botanist who used the Latin *-glaucus* for blue-green and the Latin *-escens* for becoming to note the blue glaucous color of the plant.

Field Notes I first saw these in August 1983 on a vertical limestone outcrop in central San Luis Potosí. In April 2010, Brian Kemble and I saw plants on steep slopes and canyon walls in the Barranca de Tolimán, which is a deep canyon chock full of incredibly interesting plants growing on the steep sides. The species ranges from northern San Luis Potosí south to eastern Guanajuato, Querétaro, and Hidalgo from about 3,900–6,600 feet elevation.

Description Appropriately called Blue Barrel, the plants have a waxy blue body color that contrasts beautifully with the yellow **spines**. Individual bodies grow to 8–15 inches tall by 8–15 inches in diameter. Plants will produce a few offsets and a very large cluster can get 24–36 inches across. Bodies have yellow or cream-colored **spines** that are all similar and about 1-inch long. Yellow 1-inch-diameter flowers appear at the top of the plant in spring.

Culture Plants have made it through low-20's F without flinching, so they are considered hardy in zones 9a–11. They can probably be used in zone 8b with some winter protection. They have a moderately slow growth rate, so start with one that already has some size to it. These are best grown in filtered sun in cities with hot summers such as Phoenix, Tucson, and Yuma, but will be fine in full sun where summer temperatures are mild. These are low-water-using, but should be given supplemental water from late spring through summer and then kept dry through winter.

Identification The blue glaucous body and yellow **spines** are very distinctive and set *Ferocactus glaucescens* apart from all other *Ferocactus*.

Landscape Application These are great candidates for a shady spot in a cactus and succulent garden. Place them under the canopy of a sparse desert tree for the filtered sunlight. A few nice companion plants include *Agave bovicornuta*, *Aloe striata*, *Echinocereus viereckii*, and *Peniocereus greggii*. Add some color by using shade tolerant perennials such as *Conoclinium dissectum*, *Hibiscus martianus*, *Salvia greggii*, and *Zinnia grandiflora*.

Precautions The snout moth, *Cactobrosis fernaldialis*, has been known to feed on species of *Ferocactus* opening a wound for plant-killing pathogens to invade.

Ferocactus glaucescens

Ferocactus gracilis
Baja Fire Barrel
BARREL CACTUS

Etymology Howard Gates named this species using the Latin *gracil-*, meaning slender, to aptly describe the slender plant body.

Field Notes In March 2010, my good friend Scott Calhoun and I had four days for a fast trip to Baja California. We made it to just south of Santa Ynez, which is deep into *Ferocactus gracilis* country. Since then, the peninsula and all its incredible otherworldly plants have drawn me back numerous times frequently searching for *Ferocactus gracilis* with the reddest spines I can find. Plants favor sandy washes of granitic debris and gravelly or rocky granitic slopes in the southern half of the northern state of Baja California from about 100–2,000 feet elevation.

SIZE (H x W)	2–4 (–8) feet x 1-foot in diameter
FLOWER COLOR	Red
FLOWER SEASON	Late spring to early summer
EXPOSURE	Full sun, filtered sun
WATER	Drought tolerant to low
GROWTH RATE	Moderately slow
PRUNING	None
HARDINESS	20° F, zones 9a–11

Description Although an extremely old specimen can reach nearly 8 feet tall, these single bodied plants are most commonly seen at about 2–4 feet tall with a 1-foot stem diameter. Plants have 16–25 ribs mostly hidden beneath the dense **spine** clusters. The 6–13 **central spines** are about 2–3 inches long, slightly twisted, and curved, and fiery red especially when wet. The many **radial spines** are thin, white, and bristle-like. Red funnel-shaped flowers are about 2 inches across and appear in late spring and early summer.

Cool Cacti and Succulents for Hot Gardens

Culture Plants have made it through low temperatures in the low 20's F with no damage and can be considered hardy in USDA zones 9a–11. Cover with grandma's old quilt when temperatures dip below 20°F. The growth rate is moderately slow, so start with a big one when using in the landscape. Plants are best grown in full sun throughout much of the southwestern U.S. even in cities with hot summers such as Las Vegas, Palm Springs, Phoenix, Tucson, and Yuma. These are dought tolerant to low-water-using and grow well when given supplemental water from late spring through summer and then kept dry through winter. They do best in a soil that has very good drainage.

Identification The combination of slender body, brilliant red **spines**, and red flowers distinguish this one from all other species of *Ferocactus*.

Landscape Application These are wonderful plants for any low-water-use southwestern U.S. landscape and do very well when mixed with colorful perennials and small shrubs. They grow well even in hot summer cities such as Palm Springs, Phoenix, and Tucson. A few great companion plants would include *Agave cerulata*, *Echinocereus engelmannii*, and *Fouquieria columnaris*.

Precautions Check for the snout moth, *Cactobrosis fernaldialis,* which feeds on *Ferocactus*.

Ferocactus gracilis

Ferocactus hamatacanthus

Synonym: *Hamatocactus hamatacanthus*
Giant Fishhook Barrel
BARREL CACTUS

SIZE (H x W)	12–24 inches x 6–12 inches
FLOWER COLOR	Yellow
FLOWER SEASON	Summer
EXPOSURE	Full sun, filtered sun
WATER	Drought tolerant to low
GROWTH RATE	Moderately slow
PRUNING	None
HARDINESS	15° F, zones 8b–11

Etymology The German botanist Philipp Friedrich Mühlenpfordt named this species and used the Latin *hamat-* for hooked and the Greek *acanth-* for spine to note the hooked spines.

Field Notes These are astounding plants and usually found growing with hardcore Chihuahuan Desert species such as *Agave lechuguilla*, *Larrea divaricata*, and *Leucophyllum frutescens*. In June 2016, I was with Jeff Chemnick and Brian Kemble scouting localities for cool cacti when we stopped at a hill in central Coahuila loaded with interesting plants. Among those cool cacti were several impressive specimens of *Ferocactus hamatacanthus* with

their long **spines** and showy yellow flowers on full display. Plants are fond of flat sandy or gravelly soil or the rocky slopes of mountains from southern New Mexico and western Texas, south throughout the Chihuahuan Desert Region to San Luis Potosí from about 30–7,000 feet.

Description Plants are usually solitary with globose to cylindrical stems growing 12–24 inches tall and 6–12 inches across. There are 13–27 ribs on mature plants, each lined with clusters of red to gray-white **spines**. There are 4–8 **central spines**, 3–5 inches long, recurved to hooked, and sometimes

Cool Cacti and Succulents for Hot Gardens

twisted. **Radial spines** number 8–20 and are 1–1½ inches long. Large yellow flowers are funnelform, 3–4 inches long and 2½–3 inches wide and appear primarily in summer.

Culture Plants are hardy to about 15° F and can be used in USDA zones 8b–11 without protection. They can be grown in full sun or very light shade in the desert southwest. They are drought tolerant when established in a landscape and low-water-using even when grown in pots. They prefer a sandy soil with good drainage.

Identification Long flexible curved to twisting **central spines** are what set this species apart from other *Ferocactus* species.

Landscape Application Use these singly or in groups mixed with other cacti, succulents, desert shrubs, and perennials in a well-rounded **xeriscape**. Use tough desert shrubs and perennials such as *Anisacanthus quadrifidus*, *Buddleja marrubiifolia*, *Calliandra eriophylla*, *Hibiscus martianus*, *Glandularia gooddingii*, *Larrea divaricata*, *Penstemon superbus*, *Thymophylla pentachaeta*, and *Zinnia acerosa*. Some good companion cactus and succulents could include *Echinocereus enneacanthus*, *Euphorbia antisyphilitica*, *Hesperaloe parviflora*, *Jatropha dioica*, and *Yucca rostrata*. These can be a maintenance nightmare because their long curly **spines** are apt to catch stray papers and other assorted trash, so keep long-handled grabbers handy.

Precautions The snout moth has been known to feed on species of *Ferocactus*, tunneling into the plant and providing an open wound for plant-killing pathogens to invade.

Ferocactus hamatacanthus

Ferocactus histrix
Porcupine Barrel
BARREL CACTUS

Etymology Swiss botanist Augustin Pyramus de Candolle used the Latin for porcupine to describe the spiny nature of these plants.

Field Notes On a June trip with Brian Kemble and Jeff Chemnick, we took the road from Zimapán, Hidalgo west toward Mexico Federal Highway 120 in Querétaro. About 12 miles east of the border between Hidalgo and Querétaro we made a stop to look at some interesting plants and came across a couple dazzling specimens of this stately plant. These grow in a wide area in central Mexico from Durango south to Querétaro from about 4,000–8,500 feet elevation.

SIZE (H x W)	1–2(–3) feet x 1–1½(–2) feet
FLOWER COLOR	Yellow
FLOWER SEASON	Spring to summer
EXPOSURE	Filtered sun
WATER	Low
GROWTH RATE	Slow
PRUNING	None
HARDINESS	25° F, zones 9b–11

Description Plants generally grow to about 1–2 feet tall with a diameter of 1–1½ feet, although some of the larger plants can reach 3 feet tall by 2 feet in diameter. Young plants have about 15–20 ribs while mature plants have 30–40 ribs. There are 7–13 **spines**, with 1–4 of those being **central spines** and the others **radial spines**. All **spines** are a light straw yellow, slender, and straight to slightly curved. Light yellow flowers are about 1–1½ inches long and wide and generally appear in the spring. Flowers are followed by red, juicy, 1-inch-long fruits.

Cool Cacti and Succulents for Hot Gardens

Culture Plants are cold hardy to 25° F and can be used in landscapes in USDA zones 9b–11. Place these under the shade of a desert tree with a sparse canopy that will provide some protection from the scorching desert sun and from cold winter temperatures. They grow best in soil with very good drainage and with some supplemental water when temperatures are on the rise. Although slow growing, these will grow quite well in large decorative pots, which would allow them to be moved to a warm area in winter.

Identification *Ferocactus histrix* are larger plants, have nearly double the number of ribs, and are more densely **spined** than *Ferocactus echidne*. *Ferocactus histrix* has 30–40 ribs, while *Ferocactus alamosanus* has 20 ribs.

Landscape Application These slow growing beasts will take several years to become a focal point in the landscape, so start with larger plants. They look great when several are massed together and mixed with flowering perennials or small desert adapted shrubs. Plant with succulents and other cacti such as ***Agave gentryi***, ***Cleistocactus strausii***, and ***Fouquieria splendens***. Use flowering plants such as *Calliandra eriophylla*, *Chrysactinia mexicana*, *Glandularia gooddingii*, *Salvia greggii*, and *Tetraneuris acaulis*.

Precautions The snout moth, *Cactobrosis fernaldialis*, has been known to feed on species of ***Ferocactus*** and creates open wounds for other pathogens.

Ferocactus histrix

Ferocactus latispinus
Wide-spine Barrel
BARREL CACTUS, SMALL BARREL-LIKE CACTUS

SIZE (H x W)	4–12 inches x 8–14 inches
FLOWER COLOR	Deep purplish pink
FLOWER SEASON	Late fall to early winter
EXPOSURE	Full sun, filtered sun
WATER	Low
GROWTH RATE	Moderate
PRUNING	None
HARDINESS	low 20's F, zones 9a–11

Etymology Adrian Hardy Haworth used the Latin *lati-*, meaning wide and the Latin *spin-*, meaning **spine** a reference to the very wide **central spine**.

Field Notes I have come across these plants in the states of San Luis Potosí and Guanajuato in east central Mexico. They are typically growing on gentle slopes and hunkered down among grasses making them hard to find. One of my favorite places to see these is on the slopes around the once bustling mining town of Mineral de Pozos in Guanajuato. Plants favor gravelly or rocky granitic slopes from Durango in north-central Mexico south to near Mexico City from about 5,900–9,500 feet elevation.

Description These have a depressed globose or flattened body that is wider than tall with plants growing 4–12 inches tall and 8–14 inches across. They have a light green to dark green body with 13–23 sharply angled ribs. There are 4 reddish or yellowish brown **central spines** with the lowest being about 2 inches long and conspicuously wide, flat, and curved or hooked. The 9–15 **radial spines** are thin and white, yellowish, or reddish-brown. Deep purplish pink or rarely white funnel-shaped flowers are 1–2 inches across and appear in late fall to early winter.

Culture Plants will survive the low 20's F and are considered hardy in USDA zones 9a–11. They can be grown in zone 8b if you are willing to sacrifice an old t-shirt or two that can be used to cover the plants if overnight lows are forecast to drop into the high teens. These have a moderate growth rate but will flower at a relatively small size, so enjoy them in decorative containers for a few years before planting in the landscape. Plants can tolerate full sun in cities with mild summers, but should have some afternoon shade in cities with hot summers

like Phoenix, Tucson, and Yuma. They are low-water-using and relish some supplemental water from late spring through summer, but should be kept dry through winter. Plants are not too picky about soil, even growing well with some organic matter added if the drainage is good.

Identification The distinctive wide flat **central spine** and deep purplish pink flowers set this one apart from *Ferocactus macrodiscus*.

Landscape Application These small barrels are perfect for growing in containers and showing off in a cactus and succulent collection. They can also be used in a **xeriscape**, but because they are so low growing, plants should be located in the foreground where they will be highly visible. Plant low growing grasses or perennials around the barrels to help keep them partially shaded and to cool the soil temperature. Use plants such as *Bouteloua curtipendula*, *Bouteloua gracilis*, *Conoclinium dissectum*, *Dalea capitata*, *Glandularia gooddingii*, *Hibiscus coulteri*, *Justicia longii*, *Penstemon triflorus*, *Salvia greggii*, *Thymophylla pentachaeta*, and *Zinnia grandiflora*.

Precautions Inspect your plants for the snout moth, *Cactobrosis fernaldialis*, which has been known to feed on species of ***Ferocactus*** and other barrel-like cacti.

Ferocactus latispinus

Ferocactus pilosus
Synonyms: *Ferocactus pringlei, Ferocactus stainesii*
Fire Barrel
BARREL CACTUS

Etymology Henri Galeotti used the Latin *pilos-*, which means hairy, to describe the numerous, thin white bristly radials.

Field Notes A favorite place for me to see these plants is in the desert between the towns of Miquihuana and Dr. Arroyo in southern Nuevo León. Another special road is San Luis Potosí State Highway 9 to the town of Guadalcázar. Here one can also see ***Agave striata*** and ***Echinocactus platyacanthus***. Plants grow in sandy or rocky soils in the Chihuahuan Desert Region from about 3,700–7,500 feet elevation.

SIZE (H x W)	1–6 (–9) feet x 1–1½-foot stem diameter
FLOWER COLOR	Orange-red
FLOWER SEASON	Spring to summer
EXPOSURE	Full sun
WATER	Low
GROWTH RATE	Slow
PRUNING	None
HARDINESS	15° F, zones 8b–11

Description Young plants have single stems growing to about 1-foot-tall with a diameter of about 7–8 inches. With age, plants eventually offset and form large clusters of stems to 5–7 feet across with stems ranging from 1–9 feet tall and 1–1½ feet across. Grapefruit-size plants usually have 12–13 ribs while larger plants have 24–28 ribs. The brilliant red **central spines** are 1–2 inches long. Numerous white bristly **radial spines** are 1–2 inches long. Orange-red flowers are about 1½ inches long and about 1-inch-wide, appearing in late spring to early summer.

Culture Plants are cold hardy to about 15° F and can be used in landscapes in USDA zones 8b–11. They will tolerate full sun even in the blazing hot desert cities of Phoenix, Tucson, and Yuma if they are given sufficient supplemental water in summer. These should be fine in mid-elevation cities such as Green Valley and Sierra Vista, but might need to be covered in places like El Paso, Las Cruces, and Albuquerque. Plants grow naturally in a sandy or gravelly soil type, so be sure yours has good drainage.  They will benefit from receiving supplemental water from late spring through summer, but should be weaned off extra water for winter. Although slow growing, these will eventually make a statement in a xeric landscape.

Identification With thin red **spines** and orange-red flowers, *Ferocactus pilosus* plants are not easily confused with any other species.

Landscape Application Plant these in a cactus and succulent garden or any southwestern xeriscape at a house you plan to pass along to your grandchildren. These slow growing plants will take several years to become a force in the landscape, so do not expect instant impact. Surround them with colorful perennials to fill the space while these inch skyward.

Precautions The moth, *Cactobrosis fernaldialis*, has been known to create openings that allow for plant-killing pathogens to invade.

Ferocactus pilosus

Ferocactus rectispinus
Synonym: *Ferocactus emoryi* subsp. *rectispinus*
Long-Spine Barrel
BARREL CACTUS

SIZE (H x W)	1–2 (–6) feet x 1–1½ feet
FLOWER COLOR	Yellow
FLOWER SEASON	Summer
EXPOSURE	Filtered sun, full sun
WATER	Drought tolerant to low
GROWTH RATE	Slow
PRUNING	None
HARDINESS	18° F, zones 9a–11

Etymology   German-born, American-trained botanist George Engelmann used the Latin *rectus-* meaning straight and the Latin *spinus-* meaning spine for the name of these long-spined plants.

Field Notes   In April 2010, Brian Kemble and I drove into the Sierra San Francisco in the southern part of Baja California and saw some amazing examples of this species. Bob Webb and I saw super long-spined specimens on Cerro Colorado along Mexico Federal Highway 1 on the way to the Gulf of California. *Ferocactus rectispinus* has a wide-ranging distribution in the southern half of the Baja California peninsula. Plants are frequently found growing among large rocks and boulders in the mountains from about 600–3400 feet elevation.

Description   Plants grow slowly and old ones can get 5–6 feet tall with a diameter of 1–1½ feet, while a more reasonable size would be about 1–2 feet tall with a diameter closer to 1-foot. Large plants have 15–21 ribs, while young

ones have fewer. There is one reddish or yellowish **central spine** that is usually straight but sometimes with a hook and 4–6 inches long. The 7–9 **radial spines** are reddish or yellow. Flowers are about 2 inches long and yellow to orangish-red appearing in late spring or summer.

Culture These have been grown in Tucson where they have been subjected to winter low temperatures of 18° F with no frost damage. They are valuable landscape subjects in USDA zones 9a–11. Plants can tolerate full scorching sun in the desert southwest, even in cities like Palm Springs, Phoenix, and Tucson. They do not seem to be particular about the soil type if the watering schedule is adjusted accordingly. Although drought tolerant, plants will appreciate a drink of water on a regular basis from spring until fall. These are slow growing, so look for a sizable plant for the landscape.

Identification Even young plants of *Ferocactus rectispinus* have a relatively long **central spine** and are not easily confused with any other species.

Landscape Application These are slow growing and will take several years to make an eye-popping specimen in the landscape, so start with larger plants, and group several together for a more immediate impact. Combine with plants such as *Calliandra eriophylla*, *Glandularia gooddingii*, or *Penstemon superbus*. If you have enough space to make a nice cactus and succulent garden, use plants such as **Agave cerulata**, **Echinocereus engelmannii**, or **Fouquieria splendens**.

Precautions The snout moth, *Cactobrosis fernaldialis*, tunnels into the plant and provides an open wound for plant-killing pathogens.

Ferocactus rectispinus

Ferocactus robustus
Mounding Barrel
CLUSTERING CACTUS

SIZE (H x W)	Individual heads 4–5 inches x 4–5 inches, clusters 2 feet x 2–4 feet
FLOWER COLOR	Yellow
FLOWER SEASON	Summer
EXPOSURE	Filtered sun, part shade
WATER	Drought tolerant to low
GROWTH RATE	Moderately slow
PRUNING	None
HARDINESS	25° F, zones 9b–11

Etymology The German duo of Johann Link and Christoph Otto named this using the Latin *robust-* for the robust nature of the plants.

Field Notes In June 1985, Carol and I were with two fern botanists heading to Chiapas and drove past the San Lorenzo Mesa in southern Puebla. We saw large clusters of these plants growing on the open exposed limestone mesa along with giant plants of **Beaucarnea gracilis**. Another spot in southern Puebla where I have seen large clusters of these plants is a hill near the town of Azumbilla. Here, these grow with *Ferocactus haematacanthus* and *Agave potatorum* among other very cool cacti. The distribution is restricted to southern Puebla and northern Oaxaca with plants being found mostly on flat open ground in limestone soil from about 4,900–6,900 feet elevation.

Description Plants start out with a single rounded body that will reach about the size of a softball and, with age they grow multiple stems, eventually forming large mounds about 2 feet tall and 2–4 feet across. While some of the largest clumps in habitat are reported to be 15 feet across, that is rare in cultivation. Each stem is green and has 8 sharply angled ribs. There are 4–7 **central**

Cool Cacti and Succulents for Hot Gardens

spines and 10–14 **radial spines** in each cluster. Yellow flowers are about 2 inches long and 2 inches wide and appear in summer.

Culture According to Brian Kemble, plants at the Ruth Bancroft Garden have done fine when the winter low hit the mid-20's F. I have a couple plants that have been through mid-20's F with no damage, and these can be grown unprotected or with minimal protection in USDA zones 9b–11. Plants grow well in part shade or filtered sun in the hottest cities of the desert southwest like Palm Springs, Phoenix, Tucson, and Yuma.

These have a slow growth rate and will require many years to form sizable clusters. When young, they will tolerate extra water in summer, but older plants become quite drought tolerant.

Identification *Ferocactus robustus* has yellow flowers and fruits and 8 ribs while *Ferocactus flavovirens* has orange-red or red flowers and 11–15 ribs.

Landscape Application These can be planted in a cactus and succulent garden or a **xeriscape** in frost-free areas or those that experience winter lows into the high 20's F infrequently. Some cacti and succulents to plant with these could be *Agave ovatifolia*, *Beaucarnea gracilis*, *Dasylirion acrotrichum*, *Echinocactus platyacanthus*, and *Yucca rostrata*, while perennials and shrubs could include *Acacia constricta* or *Eysenhardtia orthocarpa* to provide filtered light and *Dalea frutescens* for colorful flowers. These can also be grown in large shallow planters that allow the plants to develop large clusters.

Precautions In the desert southwest, packrats and javelina might be tempted to taste test these, while the female snout moth could drill into the bodies and lay her eggs allowing the larva to destroy the plants from inside.

Ferocactus robustus

Ferocactus wislizeni
Fishhook Barrel, Compass Barrel
BARREL CACTUS

SIZE (H x W)	2–5 (–8) feet x 1–2 feet
FLOWER COLOR	Orange, yellow, or red
FLOWER SEASON	Summer
EXPOSURE	Full sun
WATER	Drought tolerant to low
GROWTH RATE	Slow
PRUNING	None
HARDINESS	15° F, zones 8b–11

Etymology German-born, American-trained botanist George Engelmann named this species in honor of Dr. Friedrich A. Wislizenus, a physician in the Mexican-American War of 1846-1847.

Field Notes These plants are common in my neck of the Sonoran Desert on the west side of Tucson. I frequently see them while out biking or hiking when the weather is conducive to such activity. I always look forward to the blooming season because the ring of flowers topping the plants is a special treat during summer monsoon season. After flowering, the plants develop a ring of bright yellow fruits that look like miniature pineapples. *Ferocactus wislizeni* is native to much of the desert southwest and adjacent northern Mexico. Plants grow in rocky, gravelly, or sandy soil on hills, flats, canyons, and wash margins from about 1,000–5,000 feet elevation.

Description Mature plants normally have a single body growing 2–5 feet tall by 1–2 feet across. The exceptional specimen approaches 8 feet tall, but those get too heavy and usually fall over. Plants of flowering size will have 20–30 ribs with closely spaced **spine** clusters. There are 4 (rarely 8) **central spines** with the lowest being 4–5 inches long and typically hooked but rarely straight. The 10–25 **radial spines** are bristle-like and shorter than the centrals. Flowers appear in summer, are about 2 inches across, and are most commonly orange, but sometimes yellow or even red.

Cool Cacti and Succulents for Hot Gardens

Culture These are easily grown in the hotter cities of the desert southwest and will tolerate winter low temperatures down to the mid-teens F making them hardy in USDA zones 8b–11. Place them in full scorching sun even in cities that routinely see high temperatures over 100° F in the summer. They grow well in rocky desert soil and, once established, do not require supplemental water. These transplant well and have been a big hit with the Tucson Cactus and Succulent Society's rescue program.

Identification The **central spine** that is curved like a fishhook gives away the identity of these plants.

Landscape Application These slow growing plants will take several years to get noticed in the landscape, so start with larger plants, ideally those from a sanctioned rescue. Use these in groups in a cactus and succulent garden and mix in several flowering perennials or small sized desert-adapted shrubs for a complete landscape. If you have enough space to make a nice cactus and succulent garden, use plants such as *Agave colorata*, *Echinocactus grusonii*, *Fouquieria splendens*, or *Yucca elata*. Use Sonoran Desert natives such as *Baileya multiradiata*, *Calliandra eriophylla*, *Encelia farinosa*, *Glandularia gooddingii*, *Parthenium incanum*, *Senna covesii*, or *Zinnia acerosa*.

Precautions *Cactobrosis fernaldialis*, commonly called the snout moth, will tunnel into the plant providing an open wound for plant-killing pathogens to invade.

Ferocactus wislizeni

Fouquieria columnaris
Synonym: *Idria columnaris*
Cirio, Boojum
COLUMNAR SUCCULENT

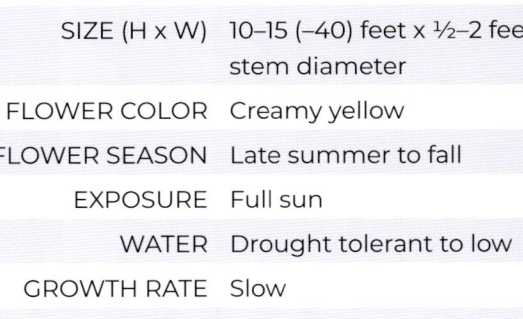

SIZE (H x W)	10–15 (–40) feet x ½–2 feet stem diameter
FLOWER COLOR	Creamy yellow
FLOWER SEASON	Late summer to fall
EXPOSURE	Full sun
WATER	Drought tolerant to low
GROWTH RATE	Slow
PRUNING	None
HARDINESS	Low 20's F, zones 9a–11

Etymology Albert Kellogg described this plant using the Latin *column-* for the column-like growth form.

Field Notes A trip to the Baja California peninsula is not complete without several stops to hug and photograph these bizarre and fascinating plants. Try stomping around the hill off Mexico Federal Highway 5 just north of the usually dry lake called Laguna Chapala that holds an incredible stand of *Fouquieria columnaris*, **Ferocactus gracilis**, and **Agave cerulata**. Plants occur in the central part of the Baja California peninsula and near Puerto Libertad along the coast of Sonora. They favor rocky hillsides, mesas, and alluvial plains from near sea level to about to 4,750 feet elevation.

Description These have one of the most intriguing forms for a succulent plant in the landscape. Once the plant reaches about 5–6 inches tall, the stem resembles an upside-down carrot. After several years, they develop a single upright trunk fattest at the base tapering to the tip. Rarely will a plant have more than one trunk. A reasonable size to achieve in a landscape would be 10–15 feet tall. Leaves are just under 1-inch-long and winter active. Small white flowers appear in summer.

Culture Plants in the ground are hardy to low 20's F, while those in pots might suffer damage at those same temperatures simply because the soil will get colder. As a landscape plant they can be used in USDA zones 9a–11 but protect those in containers. These are winter growing plants that need a rest period in summer. If your plants shed their leaves as the summer heat comes on, they are going dormant, so cut way back on the water to prevent them from rotting. Young plants prefer some summer shade in hot cities, but larger plants can be acclimated to full sun.

Identification These are easily identified by their whitish trunk and upside-down carrot appearance. *Fouquieria fasciculata* and *Fouquieria purpusii* are closest in looks, but both have green trunks and are summer growers.

Landscape Application Use one or more as a focal point in a **xeriscape**, but plants are slow growing so start with a large specimen, if you can afford one, or be very patient. In frost-free cities, go for the whole Baja California look and plant with *Agave avellanidens*, *Agave cerulata*, *Calliandra californica*, *Echinocereus engelmannii*, *Encelia californica*, *Ferocactus gracilis*, *Pachycormus discolor*, and *Ruellia peninsularis*.

Precautions If your plants look like they are going dormant as the weather heats up stop any supplemental watering until the weather cools in the fall.

Fouquieria columnaris

Fouquieria diguetii
Palo Adán
SHRUB-LIKE SUCCULENT, TREE-LIKE SUCCULENT

Etymology Frenchman Philippe van Tieghem honored French explorer Léon Diguet when he named this species.

SIZE (H x W)	8–15 feet x 5–8 feet
FLOWER COLOR	Red
FLOWER SEASON	Nearly any month, better with rains
EXPOSURE	Full sun
WATER	Drought tolerant to low
GROWTH RATE	Moderately slow
PRUNING	None, minimal
HARDINESS	High 20's F, zones 9b–11

Field Notes In May 2011, Brian Kemble and I found these plants growing in flat sandy soil along the road to the Sierra San Francisco in Baja California Sur. The short single trunk was about 1-foot-tall and about 6–8 inches in diameter, with several thick lichen covered branches topped with young inflorescences and even a few open flowers. Plants are common in the southern 2/3 of the Baja California peninsula and grow in deep sandy flats or volcanic rock from near sea level to nearly 4,000 feet elevation.

Description Plants grow to 8–15 feet tall by 5–8 feet wide, and can be large and shrub-like or small trees with a short thick trunk. The bark peels off to reveal the orange-bronze to greenish inner bark. Leaves are green to gray-green and about 1-inch-long. They have a long petiole that sits atop a sharp **spine** that is revealed when the leaf falls off. Red flowers are narrowly tubular, about 1-inch-long, and appear in clusters at the branch tips from late winter until early summer, attracting hummingbirds from around the neighborhood.

Culture Plants in Chandler, Arizona have been through winter low temperatures in the high 20's F with little or no damage. They can be used as landscape plants in USDA zones 9b-11 and grown in containers nearly anywhere with frost protection. These are summer growing and need extra water in summer until they are established, at which point they are very drought tolerant. Plants in containers will need supplemental water while in leaf, but keep them dry in winter. They have a moderately slow growth rate so start with a large plant. Plants need minimal judicious pruning to grow as a small tree or to remove any frost damaged twigs.

Identification *Fouquieria diguetii* has shorter leaves that are ever so slightly wider than those of **Fouquieria macdougalii**.

Landscape Application These can be grown as small trees in frost-free or nearly frost-free cities such as Phoenix, Los Angeles, Palm Springs, or San Diego. Some judicious pruning will be needed to lift the canopy, although it will probably never become a walk-under tree. However, they can provide shade for plants and animals seeking relief from summer sun. In frost-free cities, go for the whole Baja California look and plant with **Agave cerulata**, *Calliandra californica*, *Encelia californica*, **Ferocactus gracilis**, **Fouquieria splendens**, **Pachycormus discolor**, and *Ruellia peninsularis*.

Precautions When growing plants as small trees, be sure to prune branches one or two at a time to prevent sunburning the trunk.

Fouquieria diguetii

Fouquieria fasciculata
Arbol de Barril
SHRUB-LIKE SUCCULENT, TREE-LIKE SUCCULENT

SIZE (H x W)	3–15 feet x 2–8 feet
FLOWER COLOR	White
FLOWER SEASON	Spring to early summer
EXPOSURE	Full sun, filtered light
WATER	Drought tolerant to low
GROWTH RATE	Moderate
PRUNING	Remove dead stems
HARDINESS	25° F, zones 9b–11

Etymology Carl Ludwig Willdenow was a German botanist who described this species using the Latin *fasci-* meaning bundle, possibly referring to the clusters of branches.

Field Notes In summer 2006, I was traveling in the Barrancas de Tolantongo and Metztitlán in Hidalgo with several other plant nerds. This stretch is incredibly rich in cacti and other succulents, and we were obligated to stop numerous times for a variety of plants. I had not seen *Fouquieria fasciculata* before, but we spotted several large plants perched on rock outcrops and rocky hills. Some plants were exposed while others were buried in dense vegetation

with a few in flower. Nine years later, I was in that same stretch of Mexico and got to see more incredible specimens. Plants are found in Querétaro and Hidalgo from about 3,200–4,600 feet elevation.

Description In their native habitat, plants are shrub-like to tree-like, growing to 3–15 feet tall with a spread of 2–8 feet. They can have several swollen trunks that can reach 1–2 feet in diameter at maturity. Trunks on young plants in cultivation are still relatively thickened, but are typically 3–8 inches in diameter and abruptly narrowing. Numerous side shoots occur on the swollen trunks, feeding the girth. Glossy green leaves are **spatulate**, **oblanceolate**, to

elliptic, rounded at the apex, and 1–2 inches long. Slender **spines** are about 1-inch-long. White flowers in clusters 3–4 inches wide appear in spring and early summer.

Culture   These fascinating plants are cold hardy to 25° F and can be grown without protection in zones 9b–11. They will tolerate full sun in cities like Las Cruces, San Diego, Santa Barbara, Sierra Vista, and Tucson, but might prefer filtered light in the hottest cities such as Las Vegas, Phoenix, and Yuma. They are drought tolerant to low-water-using, requiring some supplemental water in summer when grown in pots, but keep the soil dry in winter. Avoid pruning live stems when plants are young as those feed the girth of the trunks.

Identification   *Fouquieria fasciculata* has broadly **oblanceolate** to **spatulate** leaves compared to the more narrowly **elliptic-linear** ones of *Fouquieria purpusii*. *Fouquieria fasciculata* is active in summer while *Fouquieria columnaris* grows in winter and is usually dormant in summer.

Landscape Application   These can be used in a cactus and succulent garden if the soil is kept dry in winter and the overnight low temperature does not drop below 25° F. For those living in zones that get colder, keep them in large pots that can be moved under the protection of a covered patio or even brought indoors for the coldest nights. Try planting with *Agave xylonacantha*, *Dasylirion quadrangulatum*, *Echinocactus platyacanthus*, and with flowering small shrubs.

Precautions   Protect small plants from hungry rabbits and rodents, and cover them when overnight low temperatures will be colder than 25° F.

Fouquieria fasciculata

Fouquieria macdougalii
Torote Verde
SHRUB-LIKE SUCCULENT, TREE-LIKE SUCCULENT

Etymology George Nash was an American botanist who named this species for fellow American botanist Dr. Daniel MacDougal.

Field Notes I routinely see these while driving to Hermosillo, Sonora in the hot Sonoran Desert. They are also common in the foothills of the Sierra Madre

SIZE (H x W)	6–20 feet x 5–18 feet
FLOWER COLOR	Red
FLOWER SEASON	Nearly any month, better with rains
EXPOSURE	Full sun
WATER	Drought tolerant to low
GROWTH RATE	Moderately slow
PRUNING	None, minimal
HARDINESS	High 20's F, zones 9b–11

Occidental along Mexico Federal Highway 16 east of Hermosillo. They can be seen growing in sandy soil closer to the coast not far from Guaymas. Plants grow in a variety of soil types from deep sandy flats to volcanic rock and can be found from near sea level to nearly 4,000 feet elevation.

Description Plants are large and shrub-like, or small trees with a short thick trunk and many wide-spreading branches. The bark peels off to reveal the greenish inner bark. Leaves are narrowly **elliptic**, about 1-inch-long, dark green, and have a long petiole. The long sharp **spines** are quite noticeable after the leaves fall off. Bright red or scarlet flowers are narrowly tubular about 1-inch-long and occur in an openly branched **inflorescence** at the branch tips in spring and fall following rains. Flowers do attract hummingbirds and bees.

Culture I had two plants growing in very large clay pots that had been subjected to a winter low temperature of 20° F and both suffered significant twig damage. I would consider these to be reliably hardy in USDA  zones 9b-11 and half-hardy in zone 9a where they are best planted against a south or west-facing wall for additional heat in winter. They have a moderate to moderately slow growth rate and will take several years to become small tree-like plants. Plants are active in summer and need supplemental water while getting established in the landscape, after which they are low-water-using to drought tolerant. However, plants in containers will need supplemental water while in leaf during the growing season. They will not be using any water when they are leafless in winter, so keep them dry. Plants need minimal judicious pruning to grow as a small tree.

Identification *Fouquieria macdougalii* is distinctive with its open drooping inflorescence.

Landscape Application These can be grown as small trees in cities that are frost-free or nearly frost-free such as Phoenix, Yuma, Los Angeles, Palm Springs, San Diego, or Santa Barbara. Some judicious pruning will be needed to lift the canopy, although they will probably never become walk-under trees. They are perfect for **xeriscapes** in cities where frost is a rare occurrence. They are compatible with other low-water-use plants and look good with ***Agave palmeri***, *Calliandra* 'Sierra Starr', ***Dasylirion wheeleri***, *Encelia farinosa*, ***Ferocactus wislizeni***, and *Ruellia peninsularis*.

Precautions If you intend to grow these as small trees, only prune any extraneous branches one or two at a time to prevent sunburning the trunk.

Fouquieria macdougalii

Fouquieria purpusii
Purpus' Bottle Plant
SHRUB-LIKE SUCCULENT

SIZE (H x W)	1–10 feet x ½–1 foot stem diameter
FLOWER COLOR	White
FLOWER SEASON	Spring to summer
EXPOSURE	Part shade, filtered light
WATER	Drought tolerant to low
GROWTH RATE	Moderately slow
PRUNING	None
HARDINESS	25° F, zones 9b–11

Etymology Botanist Townsend Stith Brandegee named this amazing species for German horticulturist J.A. Purpus.

Field Notes In 2004, I was in Oaxaca looking at agaves and went to see these plants at a limestone hill in southern Puebla, and then on another limestone hill in very northern Oaxaca along Mexico Highway 135D. I have sinced stopped along Highway 135D to look at the *Fouquieria purpusii* growing there and on a separate hill farther off the highway. I finally was able to return to the first hill on which I saw the plants and get updated photos. The species has a restricted distribution, being known from just a few localities in southern Puebla and northern Oaxaca. Plants occur on limestone outcrops and open basaltic slopes from about 3,200–7,500 feet elevation.

Description These shrub-like succulent plants have a very distinctive growth form, usually having one swollen succulent main trunk resembling a green upside down carrot with numerous spiny side shoots. Leaves are dark green, **elliptic-linear** to narrowly **oblanceolate**, and 1–2 inches long by ¼-inch-wide. Tubular white flowers are about ½-inch-long. In their native habitat, flowers appear during the dry season of February to April, while in cultivation the main blooming time is late spring.

Culture My friend Tim Harvey in Thousand Oaks has a large plant that has survived a winter low of 20° F but I still protect mine when temperatures drop below 25° F. They can be grown without protection in zones 9b–11 and with minimal protection in zone 9a, but make great potted plants in any zone. They will tolerate full sun in cities like Los Angeles, San Diego, Santa Barbara, Sierra Vista, and Tucson, but grow best in filtered light in the hottest cities such as Las Vegas, Phoenix, and Yuma. They are drought tolerant to low-water-using, requiring some supplemental water in summer when grown in pots but kept dry in winter.

Identification *Fouquieria purpusii* has narrowly **elliptic-linear** leaves compared to the broadly **oblanceolate** to **spatulate** leaves of *Fouquieria fasciculata*. *Fouquieria purpusii* grows in summer while *Fouquieria columnaris* actively grows in winter and is usually dormant in summer.

Landscape Application These are special plants highly sought after by cactus and succulent enthusiasts around the world. They can be planted in the ground in frost-free or nearly frost-free areas, and a whole world of possibilities becomes available to the lucky collector who lives in one. They grow well in tall decorative containers elsewhere if given some protection during winter. The majority of collectors who have one or more of these plants will need to keep them in containers and move them into a spot that does not freeze in winter.

Precautions There do not seem to be any pest problems although packrats and rabbits might nip off side shoots. The primary concern is to keep plants protected from frost.

Fouquieria shrevei
Shreve's Ocotillo
SHRUB-LIKE SUCCULENT

SIZE (H x W)	3–8 feet x 3–5 feet
FLOWER COLOR	White
FLOWER SEASON	Spring
EXPOSURE	Full sun, partial shade
WATER	Low
GROWTH RATE	Moderate
PRUNING	None, minimal
HARDINESS	Mid-20's F, zones 9b–11

Etymology American botanist Ivan M. Johnston named this species for fellow American botanist and ecologist Dr. Forrest Shreve.

Field Notes In April 2010, Brian Kemble and I were driving north along Mexico Federal Highway 30 looking to spend the night in Cuatrociénegas, Coahuila when we noticed the Ocotillos growing on the tops of the rolling hills looked different than those growing below the hills. We stopped to investigate and discovered the ones on the gypsum hills had white flowers in the leaf axils which we determined were *Fouquieria shrevei*. I have visited the area three more times, and have made it a point to stop for these plants each time. Plants grow in gypsum soil on hills and flats at scattered localities in the Bolsón de Mapimí of western Coahuila from about 3,200–4,000 feet elevation.

Description Plants are large and shrub-like with a very short trunk from which the many upright branches arise. Frequently, the trunk and larger stems will have a coating of a bronze-orange colored resin that looks like candle-wax drippings. Leaves are **elliptic** to **ovate**, green, about 1-inch-long, and have a 1-inch-long petiole that sits atop a sharp spine. White flowers with broadly spreading lobes are mostly solitary in the leaf axils, sometimes in pairs, or rarely in short terminal or axillary racemes. Flowering is primarily in spring.

Culture Although I had three of these die a year or so after planting them in my landscape in Tucson, others have been successful growing them in the ground. They grow quite well in deep pots with extra gypsum added to the soil mix. I do protect them when winter temperatures drop to the mid-20's F. These are summer active plants and  relish supplemental water while they are in leaf and growing. Keep soil dry while plants are leafless in winter, only resuming extra water when leaves appear. Plants will tolerate full sun or a mix of sun and shade. They have a moderate growth rate so will take several years to grow into a sizable specimen. Leave the pruners in their case and avoid the temptation to prune live stems.

Identification *Fouquieria shrevei* plants have nearly rounded leaves which distinguish them from the similar looking ***Fouquieria splendens***.

Landscape Application These plants are hard to come by, and I would recommend growing them in tall ceramic pots placed on a patio or near a front entry where the interesting growth and shape can be enjoyed regularly. They will grow fine without winter protection in cities that are frost-free or nearly frost-free such as Phoenix, San Diego, or Santa Barbara, but might need a bit of winter protection in cities where the winter temperature can dip into the mid-20's F.

Precautions It appears that these are not bothered by any insect pests, but might be nibbled on by packrats or rabbits.

Fouquieria shrevei

Fouquieria splendens
Ocotillo
SHRUB-LIKE SUCCULENT

SIZE (H x W)	8–15 feet x 5–12 feet
FLOWER COLOR	Red
FLOWER SEASON	Spring to summer
EXPOSURE	Full sun
WATER	Drought tolerant to low
GROWTH RATE	Moderately slow
PRUNING	None
HARDINESS	10° F, zones 8a–11

Etymology German-born, American-trained botanist George Engelmann used the Latin *splendens*- a reference to the showy red flowers.

Field Notes *Fouquieria splendens* is one of the most recognizable icons in much of the Sonoran Desert. It is ubiquitous throughout the Chihuahuan Desert Region, and always a favorite whenever I get to travel there. *Fouquieria splendens* is also quite common throughout much of the northern half of the Baja California peninsula. Bob Webb and I frequently saw these while driving on Mexico Federal Highway 5 in northeastern Baja California. We stopped many times to survey the desert vegetation and found these growing on flats and near sandy washes. Plants grow on rocky slopes, hills, flats, and even on sandy substrates in desert scrub from about 100–6,900 feet elevation.

Description These are large and shrub-like with numerous slender spiny branches arising from near ground level and growing upright to spreading to form the distinctive V-shape. They get 8–15 feet tall and spread 5–12 feet across. Narrow wand-like stems have light gray bark and 1-inch-long stiff spines. **Elliptic** to **oblanceolate** leaves are about 1-inch-long, **deciduous** in cold and drought, but can appear within 48 hours of a summer rainstorm. Bright red 1-inch-long flowers adorn the stem tips in spring and summer following rains. Some forms have pink or white flowers.

Culture Plants are hardy to at least 10° F and can be used in USDA zones 8a–11. These are now being grown from seed and have a much higher survival rate than salvaged plants. They will benefit from receiving supplemental water while they are in leaf and growing, but keep soil dry while plants are leafless in winter. Find a spot in full sun in the landscape and fast draining soil. They are slow growing, so look for plants in #5 or #15 containers. No pruning is needed, so holster your clippers.

Identification *Fouquieria splendens* is so distinctive it cannot be confused with any other species once they achieve some size.

Landscape Application Use these singly as a bold focal point in full sun in any southwestern U.S. xeriscape, or group several together for an "Ocotillo Forest." Go for the total Sonoran Desert look and plant with the likes of **Agave deserti**, *Baileya multiradiata*, *Calliandra eriophylla*, **Ferocactus wislizenii**, *Justicia californica*, *Larrea divaricata*, **Opuntia santa-rita**, and *Penstemon parryi*. Create a nice grouping and weave in several of each of the above-mentioned plants. These are equally suitable for home or commercial landscapes, and are beloved by hummingbirds and bees when in flower.

Precautions Salvaged plants usually have over 90% of their root system missing and can be touchy to get established in a landscape, but plants grown from seed are easier to establish in the ground.

Fouquieria splendens

Grusonia bradtiana
Viejo, Organillo
CLUSTERING CACTUS, SPRAWLING CACTUS

Etymology John Merle Coulter was an American botanist who named this in honor of George Bradt, editor of "The Southern Florist and Gardener", at the request of nurserywoman Anna B. Nickels.

SIZE (H x W)	2–3 feet x clumps to 3–10 feet
FLOWER COLOR	Yellow
FLOWER SEASON	Summer
EXPOSURE	Full sun
WATER	Drought tolerant to low
GROWTH RATE	Moderately slow
PRUNING	None
HARDINESS	15° F, zones 8b–11

Field Notes My first trip to the Chihuahuan Desert was in 1986 with Ron Gass, and one night we camped out in the Bolsón de Mapimí amid fantastic stands of tall *Yucca rigida* and mats of *Grusonia bradtiana* covering the ground. Many years later, I was at a hillside north of the old train station at Marte in Coahuila with Jeff Chemnick, Brian Kemble, and Walker Young. The area was filled with cacti including exquisite stands of these plants, some showing off their yellow flowers. Plants grow in sandy or rocky soil on flats and foothills from about 2,300–3,600 feet elevation.

Description Plants are low growing and highly branched with cylindrical stems to about 2–3 feet tall and 2–3 inches in diameter. They form nearly

impenetrable mats to 3–10 feet or more across. Stems have 8–10 ribs with **spine** clusters consisting of 15–25 needle-like yellowish or white 1-inch-long **spines**. Yellow flowers are 1½–2 inches long and appear primarily in summer.

Culture Plants are cold hardy to at least 15° F and can be used in USDA zones 8b–11 without frost damage. They look best when grown in full sun even in the hottest cities of the desert southwest such as Las Vegas, Phoenix, and Yuma. They are drought tolerant once established, but will tolerate occasional applications of supplemental water in summer. They grow at a moderately slow rate which might speed up slightly with the occasional thorough soaking in spring and summer. Plants do not need any pruning, but will require ample space to reach full size.

Identification *Grusonia bradtiana* resembles some ***Echinocereus*** species, but is easily distinguished by its growth habit, **spines**, and yellow flowers.

Landscape Application These are excellent plants for use in any southwestern U.S. **xeriscape**. With their white to silvery-white spines and low-growing habit, they are stunning specimens throughout the year. Plant with cacti and non-cactus succulents such as ***Astrophytum capricorne***, ***Agave striata***, ***Ferocactus hamatacanthus***, ***Fouquieria splendens***, ***Hesperaloe campanulata***, and ***Yucca rostrata***. Mix in flowering perennials and small shrubs for a spectacular color display. Try using *Calliandra eriophylla*, *Chrysactinia mexicana*, and *Glandularia gooddingii*.

Precautions Plants are sometimes susceptible to the fungal disease anthracnose. However, that is generally not a problem in the arid southwest unless plants are given too much water.

Gymnocalycium monvillei
Monville's Gymnocalycium
SMALL CACTUS

SIZE (H x W)	4–8 inches x 6–10 inches
FLOWER COLOR	White or pink
FLOWER SEASON	Summer
EXPOSURE	Filtered sun
WATER	Low to moderate
GROWTH RATE	Moderately slow
PRUNING	None
HARDINESS	15° F, zones 8b–11

Etymology Frenchman Charles Lemaire named this for Baron Hippolyte Boissel de Monville.

Field Notes I was on a trip to Argentina and Chile in November 2022 led by Guillermo Rivera, and these were among the many cacti we saw. The first day out, we left Cordoba heading south and west, and our first stop was for *Gymnocalycium monvillei* and *Gymnocalycium mostii*. Plants of both species were growing in the full sun among large rocks, grasses, ferns, perennials, and small shrubs with many of the plants in flower! Although plants were fully exposed to the sun, the elevation of 6,000 feet plus surrounding vegetation kept the air temperature moderate. Plants grow on slopes and hills among rocks and low growing perennial vegetation in northern Argentina from about 1,600–8,900 feet elevation.

Description These plants are solitary or occasionally clustering after many years when grown in cultivation. The globular body is about the same height as width growing 4–8 inches tall and 6–10 inches in diameter. Rich green bodies have 10–17 strongly **tubercled** ribs underneath the yellowish **spines** that curve back toward the body. White

Cool Cacti and Succulents for Hot Gardens

or pink flowers are about 3 inches across and appear mostly in summer.

Culture Plants should be able to withstand winter low temperatures of 15° F and are considered hardy for USDA zones 8b–11. They are moderately slow growing and will take a while to reach a noticeable size, but they will flower when relatively small. Plants prefer mid-day to afternoon shade in hot summer cities like Palm Springs, Phoenix, Tucson, and Yuma but can tolerate more sun in cities with cooler summer temperatures. Give the plants supplemental water on a consistent basis in spring and summer for the best appearance. These can be grown either in the landscape or featured in a decorative pot.

Identification *Gymnocalycium monvillei* has slightly curved **spines** held away from the body while *Gymnocalycium spegazzinii* has **spines** that hug the plant body.

Landscape Application These make great specimens when incorporated into a cactus and succulent landscape. The plants are not overly large and are well-suited for massing several together. They mix well with flowering perennials and small shrubs in a well-rounded landscape. Some cool companion plants would be *Bahia absinthifolia*, *Conoclinium dissectum*, *Dalea capitata*, *Glandularia gooddingii*, *Justicia longii*, *Telosiphonia macrosiphon*, and *Zinnia grandiflora*. Include other small cacti and succulents such as *Agave parviflora*, *Agave victoriae-reginae*, *Echinocereus engelmannii*, *Ferocactus glaucescens*, and *Mammillaria petterssonii*. Add the occasional small columnar cactus like *Cleistocactus hyalacanthus*, *Oreocereus celsianus*, or even *Fouquieria splendens* for a little variety.

Precautions Protect these from getting eaten by rabbits and packrats whether in the ground or in pots. Provide some mid-day shade in summer in cities with summer temperatures routinely climbing over 100° F.

Gymnocalycium spegazzinii
Spegazzini's Gymnocalycium
SMALL CACTUS

SIZE (H x W)	2–6 inches x 6–10 inches
FLOWER COLOR	White or pale-pink with purplish-red throat
FLOWER SEASON	Late spring, summer, early fall
EXPOSURE	Full sun, filtered sun
WATER	Low to moderate
GROWTH RATE	Moderately slow
PRUNING	None
HARDINESS	15° F, zones 8b–11

Etymology Nathaniel Britton and Joseph Rose honored Carlos Spegazzini, an Italian who moved to Argentina and became a botanist, when they named this species.

Field Notes In the fall of 2022, I went to Argentina and Chile on a trip led by Guillermo Rivera and got to see these plants in habitat. Many were low and wide somewhat like a squashed half melon with most growing out in full open exposure, while a few were in the dappled light under shrubs. We first saw plants near Cafayete where they were growing in rocky soil out in full sun. The next day, we were west of Salta where we encountered more plants in full sun and pebbly soil. Here they tended to have longer spines densely covering the bodies. Plants grow on flats and low foothills in northern Argentina from about 4,600–9,800 feet elevation.

Description These are beautifully spined plants with a solitary, flattened-globose, gray-green to brownish-green body growing to 2–6 inches tall and 6–10 inches diameter. They have 10–15 low ribs and 5–7 white, brown, or gray-brown **spines** that curve back toward the body. Flowers are pure white or pale-pink with purplish-red in the throat and about 2 inches across. Cultivated plants in southern Arizona will bloom periodically from late spring through summer.

Culture Plants are able to withstand winter low temperatures of 15° F and are fine for USDA zones 8b–11. They are moderately slow growing, but will flower when relatively small. Plants prefer mid-day to afternoon shade in hot summer cities like Palm Springs, Phoenix, Tucson, and Yuma but can tolerate more sun in cities with cooler summer temperatures. Give the plants supplemental water on a consistent basis in spring and summer for the best appearance. These can be grown either in the landscape or featured in a decorative pot.

Identification *Gymnocalycium spegazzinii* has **spines** that hug the plant body while *Gymnocalycium monvillei* has **spines** that protrude away from the body.

Landscape Application Plants are ideal for growing in decorative containers as well as incorporating into a cactus and succulent collection. They are not overly large, but when several are grouped in a cactus and succulent garden, they will show off when flowering. Put small flowering shrubs and perennials in the garden for extra color throughout the year. Some other cool plants would be *Calliandra eriophylla*, *Chrysactinia mexicana*, *Dalea capitata*, *Glandularia gooddingii*, *Menodora longiflora*, and *Zinnia grandiflora*. Mix with other small cacti and succulents such as *Agave victoriae-reginae*, *Cleistocactus hyalacanthus*, and *Echinocereus stramineus*.

Precautions Protect these from rabbits and packrats whether in the ground or in pots. Give them some mid-day shade in summer in cities where daytime highs of triple digits F are common.

Hesperaloe campanulata
Bell-flower Hesperaloe
SUCCULENT

SIZE (H x W)	3 feet x 3–4 feet
FLOWER COLOR	Pink-and-white
FLOWER SEASON	Late spring to summer
EXPOSURE	Full sun
WATER	Drought tolerant to low
GROWTH RATE	Moderate
PRUNING	None
HARDINESS	0° F, zones 7a–11

Etymology I used the Latin *campanulatus* for bell-shaped to describe the flowers when fully open in the late afternoon.

Field Notes In September 1986, Ron Gass and I were botanizing on a rocky hillside near Mamulique, Nuevo León when he showed me what he thought was a plant of ***Hesperaloe parviflora*** with a different leaf form. We saw open flowers later that evening and determined it to be an undescribed species. I took up the challenge, and after much research and study, gave it the species name of *campanulata* to describe the bell-shape of fully open flowers. In the years since, I have spotted these plants elsewhere in northeastern Mexico. They can be seen along Mexico Federal Highway 57 between Allende and Sabinas in Coahuila and along Mexico Federal Highway 85 near the Mamulique microwave hill about 1,400–1,800 feet elevation.

Description These are stemless plants with leaves arising from near ground level and forming clusters to about 3 feet tall and 3–4 feet across. Bright green leaves are 2–3 feet long and about ½-inch-wide. They are channeled on the upper surface, stiff and upright to slightly spreading, and adorned with fine threads along the margins. The flower stalk is 6–10 feet tall with 2–7 branches adorned with many pink-and-white bell-shaped flowers in spring and summer that attract bats and hawkmoths at night and hummingbirds and sometimes bees during the day.

Culture Established plants can withstand winter low temperatures to about 0° F and are suitable for use in USDA zones 7a–11. These grow best when located in full sun. Plants are drought tolerant once established, but will benefit from receiving supplemental water every 10–14 days in summer in the very hot cities of the desert southwest. Stop the supplemental water in fall and winter. The growth rate is moderate, so start with plants in #5 containers. Sheath the pruners and resist any temptation to cut off leaves or old flower stalks, which are used as a perch by hummingbirds.

Identification *Hesperaloe campanulata* is a smaller plant with pink and white bell-shaped flowers compared to the larger **Hesperaloe funifera** with its white flowers. *Hesperaloe campanulata* is slightly larger with stiffer brighter green leaves than **Hesperaloe parviflora**, which makes denser clusters with darker green narrower leaves.

Landscape Application Use these singly or group several together in full sun in most any southwestern U.S. city where winter low temperatures do not drop below 0° F. These fit in nicely when mixed with other low-water-use arid adapted plants such as *Agave simplex, Baileya multiradiata, Calliandra eriophylla, Chrysactinia mexicana, Ericameria laricifolia, Isocoma tenuisecta, Justicia californica, Penstemon parryi,* and *Senna covesii.*

Precautions Screen newly planted specimens to deter javelina from uprooting them and stop rabbits from nibbling on leaves. Established plants are less tempting unless there is little else for them to munch.

Hesperaloe funifera
Giant Hesperaloe
SUCCULENT

SIZE (H x W)	4–6 feet x 4–6 feet
FLOWER COLOR	Green and white
FLOWER SEASON	Summer to fall
EXPOSURE	Full sun, reflected heat
WATER	Drought tolerant to low
GROWTH RATE	Slow
PRUNING	None
HARDINESS	0° F, zones 7a–11

Etymology Botanist Karl Koch used the Latin *funi-* for rope and the Latin *fer-* meaning carrying. When combined, they refer to the fibers on the leaf margins.

Field Notes I have been lucky enough to see these plants during several forays into the Chihuahuan Desert Region in Mexico. In 1986, Ron Gass and I saw plants along Nuevo León State Highway 1 near Lampazos. A few years later, we stopped for plants near Entronque de Matehuala (El Huizache, San Luis Potosí) at the junction of Highway 57 and Highway 80. *Hesperaloe funifera* plants grow with *Acacia*, *Larrea*, *Leucophyllum*, and *Prosopis* on rocky slopes and flats in Coahuila, Nuevo León, and San Luis Potosí from about 1,400–2,200 feet elevation.

Description These stemless rosettes have many 4–5-foot-long green to dark green leaves that stand upright to slightly spreading, giving the plant an overall V-shape appearance about 4–6 feet tall and 4–6 feet across. Stiff leaves are about 2–2½ inches wide and have coarse white fibers along the margins. The 10–15-foot-tall flower stalk shoots from the center of the plant and has 3–8 side branches, with 1-inch-long green and white flowers sometimes tinged with purplish on the outside. Flowers open in the evening and are pollinated by bats and/or hawkmoths or bees during the day.

Culture These are hardy to at least 0° F and can be used in USDA zones 7a–11 without threat of frost damage. Plants are best grown in full sun or reflected heat situations in the desert southwest. They are very drought tolerant once established, but will tolerate supplemental water in summer, especially in the very hot cities of Palm Springs, Phoenix, Tucson, and Yuma. Keep soil dry in winter. Plants are slow growing and will take several years to get big so plan for the maximum size and have patience, even if you start with plants in #5 or #15 containers. With proper planning, you will only need to break out the pruners to cut off old flower stalks unless you leave them as a perch for hummingbirds.

Identification *Hesperaloe funifera* is easily identified by its overall giant size and long, stiff, upright leaves.

Landscape Application The bold form stands out when planted among small and medium-size shrubs and flowering perennials in a southwestern U.S. xeriscape. Some great complementary plants include *Calliandra* 'Sierra Starr', *Ericameria laricifolia*, *Justicia californica*, and *Telosiphonia brachysiphon*. If there is ample room, plant several throughout the landscape. These are great for wide-open spaces along interstates and large natural desert-like landscapes around big buildings.

Precautions Javelina are fond of tearing young plants out of the ground and eating the roots, while packrats might nibble on the leaves of even older plants.

Hesperaloe parviflora
Red False-Yucca, Red Hesperaloe
SUCCULENT

SIZE (H x W)	2–3 feet x 3–6 feet
FLOWER COLOR	Pink, red, coral, yellow
FLOWER SEASON	Late spring and summer
EXPOSURE	Full sun, reflected heat
WATER	Drought tolerant, low, moderate
GROWTH RATE	Moderate
PRUNING	None
HARDINESS	-10° F, zones 6a–11

Etymology   John Torrey was an American botanist who combined the Latin *parvus-* meaning small and the Latin *florus-* meaning flower to indicate the small flowers.

Field Notes   These are very common in cultivation, but less so in the wild. Plants were highly sought after in the early 1900's and were taken from habitat and sold to collectors in U.S. and Europe. Ron Gass, Dave Palzkill, and I stumbled upon a handful of plants in west Texas while returning from an excursion to northeastern Mexico. These are now known only from a few scattered populations in western Texas and Coahuila, Mexico from about 1,400–6,000 feet elevation.

Description   These are stemless plants that slowly produce offsets and eventually form clusters to about 2–3 feet tall and 3–6 feet across. Dark green arching leaves are about 2 feet long by ½-inch-wide, and deeply channeled with thin white fibers along the edges. In late spring and early summer, one or more 3–7-foot-tall flower stalks hold the many 1–2-inch-long, pink, red, coral,

or yellow flowers that open during the day and draw in hummingbirds and bees. 'Brakelights' has dark red flowers and a compact habit, and 'Desert Flamenco' has pinkish orange flowers.

Culture   Plants are hardy to at least -10° F and can be used in USDA zones 6a–11 without suffering any frost damage. They will grow best in full sun and even in reflected heat situations in the desert southwest. These are very drought tolerant once established but will also do well with supplemental water in summer, especially in the very hot southwestern U.S. cities. Keep soil dry in winter and resume watering as temperatures heat up in April or May. Plants have a moderate growth rate, so start with larger plants. Hummingbirds will perch on old flower stalks.

H. parviflora 'Brakelights'

Identification   *Hesperaloe parviflora* is readily distinguished from the other *Hesperaloe* species by its dark green leaves and narrowly tubular flowers.

Landscape Application   Plants work well as a stand-alone accent plant in a cactus and succulent garden or when mixed with a variety of small shrubs and perennials. Some companionable cacti and succulents include **Echinocactus grusonii**, **Euphorbia antisyphilitica**, **Fouquieria splendens**, and **Yucca rostrata**. Some compatible shrubs include *Ericameria laricifolia*, *Dalea frutescens*, and *Telosiphonia hypoleuca*. These are a natural for wide-open spaces such as along interstates and street medians.

Precautions   Rabbits and packrats have a habit of eating the leaves of young plants, while javelina are fond of ripping plants out of the ground and eating the succulent roots.

Hesperaloe parviflora   **225**

Jatropha dioica
Sangre de Drago, Leatherstem
SHRUB-LIKE SUCCULENT

SIZE (H x W)	2–3 feet x 3–6 feet
FLOWER COLOR	Whitish
FLOWER SEASON	Spring to summer
EXPOSURE	Full sun, reflected heat
WATER	Drought tolerant to low
GROWTH RATE	Moderately fast
PRUNING	None
HARDINESS	15° F, zones 8b–11

Etymology Vicente Cervantes was a Spanish botanist who used the Latin *dioicus-* meaning **dioecious** when he named this species.

Field Notes These can be common in the Chihuahuan Desert Region and are easily overlooked because plants are not flashy and lack large showy flowers. I was in the valley between Viesca and Cerro Bola in Coahuila looking at various cacti and managed to find a couple isolated plants showing off their succulent wand-like stems. I have seen these plants elsewhere in my forays into the Chihuahuan Desert, notably while looking for **Agave nickelsiae** in the hills east of Saltillo. Plants are widespread from western and southern Texas south to Puebla and Oaxaca. They are common on limestone soil and occur from about 1,800–4,000 feet elevation.

Description These small succulent-stemmed shrubs grow to about 2–3 feet tall and spread by underground rootstocks to about 3–6 feet across. The wand-like stems are rounded and succulent, about pencil thickness, and very

flexible. When wounded, the stems ooze a yellowish sap that turns blood red when exposed to air, hence the name Sangre de Drago, or Blood of the Dragon. Leaves are **linear** to **spatulate**, **fasciculate** at the nodes and **deciduous** in cold or drought. Plants are **dioecious** with whitish male flowers occuring in small clusters and small pinkish white female flowers appearing singly and followed by the three-lobed fruits.

Culture Plants are hardy to at least 15° F and can be used in USDA zones 8b–11. Place these in full sun or even reflected heat in low and mid-elevation cities of the desert southwest such as Las Cruces, Los Angeles, Palm Springs, Phoenix, Sierra Vista, Tucson, and Yuma. Although stems are slow to fill in, they have a moderately fast growth rate once they do emerge from underground. Young plants or those newly planted in the ground will need supplemental water while actively growing for the first two or three seasons, but they are drought tolerant once established in the landscape. There is no need to prune any stems.

Identification The **fasciculate linear** to **spatulate** leaves and red stems separate *Jatropha dioica* from the white stemmed *Jatropha cuneata* with its wedge-shaped leaves.

Landscape Application These carefree plants can be used in any low-water-use landscape throughout much of the desert southwest. Use them in concert with cacti and other succulents that have a steady consistent appearance throughout the year. Offset the upright wand-like stems of these by mixing with rosette forming plants like *Agave gentryi*, *Agave parryi*, *Aloe ferox*, *Dasylirion acrotrichum*, and *Yucca rostrata* or globular shaped plants like *Echinocactus grusonii*, *Ferocactus acanthodes*, or *Mammillaria petterssonii*.

Precautions These do not seem to have any problems with pests or diseases, and no wildlife appear to eat the plants, although javelina may go after roots.

Leuchtenbergia principis
Agave Cactus
SMALL CACTUS

Etymology Englishman William Hooker used the Latin *princip-* meaning principal or first because this was the first and only species in the genus *Leuchtenbergia*.

SIZE (H x W)	8–14 inches by 6–10 inches
FLOWER COLOR	Yellow
FLOWER SEASON	Spring and summer
EXPOSURE	Filtered light
WATER	Drought tolerant to low
GROWTH RATE	Slow
PRUNING	None
HARDINESS	15° F, zones 8b–11

Field Notes These like to hide beneath shrubs and among rocks, grasses, and *Agave lechuguilla*. I have seen nice specimens on the flats in central San Luis Potosí in 2014 and on a limestone hill in central Coahuila in 2016. The largest plant I have seen was close to 12 inches tall and about 8 inches in diameter. This is the only species in the genus and has a widespread distribution in the Chihuahuan Desert of northern and central Mexico. Plants grow on limestone or sandy soil from about 4,500–7,200 feet.

Description Plants are usually solitary, rarely with one or two offsets, and grow to 8–14 inches tall and 6–10 inches across. This is a most unusual looking cactus with **tubercles** 3–5 inches long, radiating out from a central stem, so the plants somewhat mimic the look of an agave. Yellow or gray papery **spines** are in clusters at the ends of the **tubercles**. Large yellow flowers are 2–2½ inches wide and appear mostly in late spring and summer.

Culture These have been through low temperatures in the high teens, so they can be considered hardy in USDA zones 8b–11. Plants prefer a bit of shade in summer, especially in the hottest southwestern U.S. cities. They are drought tolerant once established in a landscape, but will tolerate occasional supplemental water in summer. Stop supplying extra water if summer rains are plentiful and definitely stop in winter.

Identification The plants are unique and not easily confused with any other cacti.

Landscape Application These are great as potted plants and can be staged nicely to show off the unusual growth form. They work well in any xeric garden and combine nicely with other small cacti and succulents as well as flowering perennials and small shrubs. Try using them in a landscape with plants such as *Agave striata*, *Astrophytum capricorne*, *Coryphantha macromeris*, *Echinocereus stramineus*, *Euphorbia antisyphilitica*, *Ferocactus hamatacanthus*, and *Thelocactus rinconensis*. Some great perennials and small shrubs would include *Baileya multiradiata*, *Dalea frutescens*, *Hibiscus denudatus*, *Menodora longiflora*, *Senna covesii*, and *Zinnia acerosa*.

Precautions Keep packrats and rabbits away from these tasty plants, and be sure to keep the soil dry through winter.

Leuchtenbergia principis

Lophocereus schottii
Senita
COLUMNAR CACTUS

SIZE (H x W)	10–12 (25) feet x 3–8 (10–15) feet
FLOWER COLOR	Pink, lavender, white
FLOWER SEASON	Late spring to summer
EXPOSURE	Full sun, reflected heat
WATER	Drought tolerant to low
GROWTH RATE	Slow
PRUNING	None
HARDINESS	Mid-20's F, zones 9b–11

Etymology German-born, American-trained botanist George Engelmann named this in honor of German naturalist Arthur Schott.

Field Notes To see these in habitat, head to Baja California and look for plants growing in sandy flats and on rocky hillsides. They occur along Mexico Federal Highway 5 from San Felipe to where it connects with Mexico Federal Highway 1 near Laguna Chapala. They can be found growing in or near dry washes and in the rocky hills along the way. Brian Kemble and I spotted one in flower during early May of 2011 in those hills. Bob Webb and I found a monstrose form while driving around in the central part of the peninsula. Plants occur throughout much of the Sonoran Desert in Sonora, both states on the Baja California peninsula, and a few plants in extreme southwestern Arizona from about sea level to nearly 3,000 feet elevation.

Description Plants will slowly produce several stems that are 4–5 inches in diameter growing from the base and creeping ever skyward over the years. Ancient plants will eventually reach about 25 feet tall and fill out a

Cool Cacti and Succulents for Hot Gardens

space 10–15 feet in diameter. A more realistic size for the home landscape would be 10–12 feet tall and 3–8 feet across. Light green to gray-green stems have 5–10 ribs, each sparsely armed with clusters of short gray **spines**. When the stems reach flowering age, they grow dense clusters of long yellow to gray **spines** where the pink, lavender, or white, 1–1½-inch-long flowers are produced from late spring until late summer.

Culture Established plants are hardy to about the mid-20's F and can be used in USDA zones 9b–11. Plants are best grown in full sun and will need reflected heat in zone 9a to be grown in the landscape. Established plants are very drought tolerant, but will look healthier when given periodic supplemental water in summer, especially in the very hot southwestern U.S. cities of Phoenix, Tucson, and Yuma. Stop giving supplemental water in winter. These are slow growing, so start with large plants. Plants do not require any pruning.

Lophocereus schottii 'Monstrose'

Identification *Lophocereus schottii* is readily identified by the section of dense long spines that harbor the flowers.

Landscape Application These are best used as a stand-alone accent plant in a cactus and succulent garden and surrounded with a variety of perennials and small to medium shrubs. Go hardcore Sonoran Desert theme, and plant ***Agave cerulata***, ***Echinocereus engelmannii***, ***Ferocactus gracilis***, and ***Fouquieria splendens*** along with shrubs and perennials such as *Calliandra californica*, *Justicia californica*, and *Penstemon parryi*. These are perfect for wide-open spaces such as along interstates and large commercial lots.

Precautions Javelina and deer might taste test young or newly planted plants, so keep them screened until they become established.

Mammillaria candida
Snowball Mammillaria
SMALL CACTUS

SIZE (H x W)	5–12 inches x 4–6 inches
FLOWER COLOR	Rose-pink or white
FLOWER SEASON	Late winter to late spring
EXPOSURE	Filtered sun
WATER	Low to moderate
GROWTH RATE	Moderate
PRUNING	None
HARDINESS	20° F, zones 9a–11

Etymology German-born botanist Michael Joseph Scheidweiler used the Latin *candid-*, a reference to the white **spines** when he named this species.

Field Notes When seen in habitat, *Mammillaria candida* plants look like snowballs tucked in among rocks, boulders, or other plants. My first encounter with these was in September of 1986 when, after camping out near Palmillas in southern Tamaulipas, I went out exploring and came across a cluster of snowballs. As I recall, the night had been chilly but remember not seeing any other evidence of snow falling and decided the "snowballs" were *Mammillaria candida* plants. Plants occur in rock crevices on flats and hillsides in soil derived from limestone in the northeastern Mexican states of Coahuila, Nuevo León, San Luis Potosí, and Tamaulipas from about 1,500–8,000 feet elevation.

Description The relatively small globular bodies are about 5–9 (–12) inches tall and 4–6 inches across. The bodies are densely covered with white **spines**, over 120 per **areole**, each about ½-inch-long. When grown hard, the **spines** will obscure the green epidermis. Small rose-pink, rarely white, flowers can appear from late winter to late spring.

Culture Plants are hardy to about 20° F and can be grown as a landscape plant in USDA zones 9a–11. They make excellent potted specimens in nearly any major city in the desert southwest, and with some protection they can be used in a landscape in USDA zone 8b. These seem to prefer a bit of summer shade in the very hot cities of the southwest such as Las Vegas, Phoenix, Tucson, and Yuma, but will tolerate more sun in mild summer cities like San Diego and Santa Barbara. Even established plants respond well to receiving supplemental water in summer, but prefer to have the soil kept dry through the  cold months. They have a moderate growth rate and are rewarding to grow when starting with a small plant. As with most other cacti, these plants do not require any pruning, so keep the snippers holstered.

Identification *Mammillaria candida* has shorter and more numerous **spines** than *Mammillaria geminispina*.

Landscape Application Because these are on the small side, they can be used as filler plants in a cactus and succulent garden composed of larger plants that command attention. Not that these will get overlooked though, as the white bodies are eye-catching. Plant alongside companions such as ***Agave colorata***, ***Agave schidigera***, ***Astrophytum myriostigma***, ***Coryphantha poselgeriana***, other ***Mammillaria*** species, and short columnar cacti like ***Cleistocactus strausii*** and ***Oreocereus celsianus***. Add seasonal color by using perennials like *Glandularia gooddingii*, *Hibiscus martianus*, and *Zinnia acerosa*.

Precautions Screen these from rabbits, packrats, and javelina until they are established. Acclimate shade grown nursery plants slowly to full sun so they do not burn.

Mammillaria chionocephala
Snowy-head Mammillaria
SMALL CACTUS

SIZE (H x W)	5–9 inches x 4–5 inches
FLOWER COLOR	Pale rose-pink to white
FLOWER SEASON	Spring to summer
EXPOSURE	Filtered sun
WATER	Low to moderate
GROWTH RATE	Moderately slow
PRUNING	None
HARDINESS	20° F, zones 9a–11

Etymology Joseph Anton Purpus, a botanical collector, named this species using the Greek *chion-* for snow and the Greek *cephal-* for head to emphasize the white wool between the **tubercles**.

Field Notes In July 2008, my friend Chad Davis and I saw these plants while looking for *Agave parrasana* in the Sierra Patagalana near Parras de la Fuente in Coahuila. I have also seen nice specimens growing with *Agave nickelsiae* east of Saltillo. Plants occur in limestone soil on rocky hillsides in the Mexican states of Coahuila, Nuevo León, and Durango from about 5,900–7,900 feet elevation.

Description These plants have small globular single stemmed bodies to about 5–9 inches tall and 4–5 inches across. Dark green bodies are mostly visible through the dense **spines** and rings of white wool. Plants have 2–4 (rarely 6) **central spines** and 22–24 **radial spines**, all very short measuring less than ½-inch-long. Pale rose-pink or white flowers are just under ½-inch-long and ½-inch-wide and usually appear in spring and summer. Flowers are followed by carmine red fruits.

Culture These are hardy to about 20° F and can be used in USDA zones 9a–11. Plants prefer mid-day shade in summer in the very hot cities of the southwest such as Las Vegas, Palm Springs, Phoenix, Tucson, and Yuma, but tolerate more sun in mild summer cities like San Diego and Santa Barbara. Although low-water-using, they appreciate receiving supplemental water when actively growing. However, keep the soil dry through the cold months. These have a moderately slow growth rate and are gratifying to grow when purchased in a 3-inch pot and fawned over for several years. No pruning is needed on these plants, but you might want to have a pair of 12-inch-long tweezers to pull weeds from potted specimens.

Identification The dense wool between the **tubercles** on *Mammillaria chionocephala* distinguish them from *Mammillaria candida*. The solitary short columnar bodies of *Mammillaria chionocephala* separate those plants from the low clustering bodies of *Mammillaria formosa* plants.

Landscape Application Strategically placed plants in a cactus and succulent garden can command attention. Use them to fill in between larger plants or tuck them near boulders and large rocks. Use with plants like ***Agave parrasana***, ***Astrophytum capricorne***, ***Euphorbia antisyphilitica***, ***Echinocereus enneacanthus***, ***Pedilanthus macrocarpus***, short columnar cacti such as ***Cleistocactus strausii***, ***Corryocactus erectus***, and ***Oreocereus celsianus***. Add seasonal color by using perennials like *Bahia absinthifolia*, *Glandularia gooddingii*, *Hibiscus martianus*, *Penstemon triflorus*, *Telosiphonia brachysiphon*, and *Zinnia acerosa*. They make excellent potted specimens in nearly any major city in the desert southwest.

Precautions Take precautions to keep rabbits, packrats, and javelina away from these tasty little plants and place them in filtered sunlight to prevent sunburning. Manually remove any **mealybugs** or **spine mealies**.

Mammillaria geminispina
Twin-spine Mammillaria
CLUSTERING CACTUS

SIZE (H x W)	Clusters 12–24 inches x 24–30 inches
FLOWER COLOR	Deep pink to magenta
FLOWER SEASON	Late summer to fall
EXPOSURE	Filtered sun, full sun
WATER	Low to moderate
GROWTH RATE	Moderately slow
PRUNING	None
HARDINESS	Low 20's F, zones 9b–11

Etymology Early 19th Century English botanist, Adrian Haworth used the Latin *gemini-* for twin and the Latin *spinus-* for spines to signify the 2 **central spines** normally seen on these plants.

Field Notes When driving through the famous cactus mecca of the Barranca de Metztitlán in Hidalgo, make it a point to look for *Mammillaria geminispina*. I have seen them several times and it seems as if the clusters are always trying to outdo each other with their number of stems and extremely long **central spines**. One exceptionally large cluster I saw in June 2006 was close to 3 feet across. Plants are frequently seen on limestone rock in very arid parts of the canyon. The distribution is in Hidalgo, San Luis Potosí, and Querétaro from about 3,000–5,000 feet elevation.

Description Plants start out as a single stem, each about 4–6 inches tall and 3–4 inches across, branching over time and eventually producing clusters up to 24–30 inches across, rarely more. Green bodies are mostly obscured by the profusion of white **spines** and the dense white wooly hairs between the **tubercles**. There are 2–4 **central spines** each ½–2 inches long and 16–20 short **radial spines**. Deep pink to magenta flowers are about 1-inch-long and appear mostly in late summer through fall.

Cool Cacti and Succulents for Hot Gardens

Culture Plants are hardy to the low 20's F and are excellent landscape plants for USDA zones 9b–11. They can be grown as potted specimens in nearly any major city in the desert southwest. They grow best with very light mid-day shade in summer in the very hot cities of the southwest such as Las Vegas, Phoenix, Tucson, and Yuma, but prefer full sun in southern California cities like Los Angeles, San Diego, and Santa Barbara. Plants are low to moderate water using and will benefit from receiving supplemental water in summer, but keep the soil dry through winter. These have a moderately slow growth rate and will take several years to make large mounds.

Identification *Mammillaria geminispina* is readily identified by the combination of long **central spines**, clustering habit, and white wooly hairs.

Landscape Application These clustering plants are stand-outs when used singly or in groups in a **xeriscape** or cactus and succulent garden. Place them near large boulders and give ample room for large clusters, or use with other cacti and succulents. Great companion plants would include ***Agave parrasana***, ***Astrophytum ornatum***, and ***Dasylirion quadrangulatum***. Mix in flowering perennials and small shrubs such as *Calylophus hartwegii*, *Conoclinium dissectum*, *Dalea capitata*, *Glandularia gooddingii*, *Hibiscus martianus*, and *Zinnia acerosa*.

Precautions Protect newly planted plants from rabbits and packrats, as both are likely to test them for their tastiness.

Mammillaria geminispina

Mammillaria grahamii
Graham's Pincushion, Graham's Fishhook
SMALL CACTUS, CLUSTERING CACTUS

SIZE (H x W)	6–10 inches x 2–3 inches
FLOWER COLOR	Pink or rarely lavender
FLOWER SEASON	Summer with monsoons
EXPOSURE	Full sun to filtered sun
WATER	Drought tolerant to low
GROWTH RATE	Moderately slow
PRUNING	None
HARDINESS	10° F, zones 8a–11

Etymology The species was named by George Engelmann in honor of early explorer D. Graham.

Field Notes For nearly eleven months of the year, these little beauties are inconspicuous residents of the Sonoran Desert. Yet, when monsoon rains hit the desert southwest, they explode with masses of pink flowers and virtually scream "look at me" to anybody who will pay attention. Plants are seen growing on rocky flats and slopes throughout much of the desert southwest from southern California east to Texas and south into northern Mexico from about 700–5,000 feet elevation.

Description Small cylindrical stems are 6–10 inches tall by 2–3 inches in diameter and are either solitary or more commonly forming small clusters to 6–8 inches across. Dense **spine** clusters consist of 1–2 hooked centrals and 20–30 radials. **Central spines** are reddish-brown while **radial spines** are white. One-inch-wide pink or lavender flowers appear within a few days after a summer monsoon.

Cool Cacti and Succulents for Hot Gardens

Culture These are easy to grow whether in containers or in a landscape. They are hardy to 10° F and are ideal for use in USDA zones 8a–11. They grow well in either full sun or filtered sun and are quite drought tolerant once established in a landscape. Those growing in pots will need some extra water once every week or two in summer and none in winter. There is usually nothing to prune on these, so shelve the pruners.

Identification Plants are readily identified by their hooked **central spines** and showy pink flowers.

Landscape Application Use several of these against fist-size to basketball-size rocks or under the edge of small shrubs in a **xeriscape** complete with other drought tolerant plants. Mix with other cacti and succulents like ***Agave gentryi***, ***Fouquieria splendens***, ***Hesperaloe funifera***, ***Opuntia engelmannii***, and ***Yucca rostrata***. Some suggested perennials and small shrubs would include *Baileya multiradiata*, *Calliandra eriophylla*, *Dalea frutescens*, *Haplophyton crooksii*, *Justicia longii*, *Menodora scabra*, *Senna covesii*, *Tetraneuris acaulis*, and *Zinnia acerosa*. Find a spot in the landscape where the surprise factor will come into play when these are in bloom.

Precautions Protect young plants from rabbit or packrat damage until they have been in the ground a couple years and are firmly established. As with other *Mammillaria* species, be on the lookout for **mealybugs** and **spine mealies**.

Mammillaria grahamii

Mammillaria grusonii
Gruson's Mammillaria
SMALL CACTUS

SIZE (H x W)	6–8 inches x 6–10 inches
FLOWER COLOR	Light pinkish
FLOWER SEASON	Mid- to late spring
EXPOSURE	Filtered sun
WATER	Drought tolerant to low
GROWTH RATE	Moderately fast
PRUNING	None
HARDINESS	15° F, zones 8b–11

Etymology Friedlieb Runge, a German chemist, named this in honor of Hermann Gruson, a German merchant and grower of succulents.

Field Notes In July 2007, I was with three other cactus and succulent enthusiasts camped out on Cerro Bola. We hiked around the hills in the morning and spotted *Mammillaria grusonii* among many other cool cacti. Eight years later, I was back in Coahuila and saw these in the vicinity of Cuatrociénegas, another area rich in cacti and other xeric plants. These are usually seen growing next to rocks on hills and flats in Coahuila and Durango from 2,600–5,900 feet elevation.

Description Plants typically have a single body to about 6–8 inches tall and 6–10 inches across. Dark green bodies are mostly visible through the **spine** clusters that are composed of 2 **central spines** and 12–14 **radial spines**, all less than ½-inch-long. Light pinkish white flowers have a darker pink central stripe and measure about 1-inch-long and 1-inch-wide. Flowering is in mid- to late spring. Although four or five other species names are sometimes included under this one, the classic form is from Cerro Bola in southwestern Coahuila.

Culture Plants are hardy to at least 15° F and can be used in USDA zones 8b–11. They can be planted in the ground or grown in decorative containers, but need a little bit of shade during the summer heat. They are drought tolerant when planted in the ground, but potted ones do require some supplemental water in summer. Use a gritty soil that drains quickly and keep them dry in winter.

Identification These have fewer, yet stouter, **radial spines** and lack the axillary wool seen on *Mammillaria chionocephala*.

Landscape Application These can be grown in a cactus and succulent garden complete with flowering perennials and small shrubs that will add seasonal color. Some suggested perennials and small shrubs would be *Bahia absinthifolia*, *Calliandra eriophylla*, *Chrysactinia mexicana*, and *Zinnia acerosa*. Some nice companion cacti and succulents could include *Agave parrasana*, *Astrophytum coahuilense*, *Coryphantha poselgeriana*, and *Thelocactus bicolor*. These are perfect for growing in decorative containers.

Precautions Be on the lookout for **mealybugs** or **spine mealies** and remove them if present.

Mammillaria grusonii

Mammillaria heyderi
Heyder's Pincushion
SMALL CACTUS

SIZE (H x W)	2–5 inches x 2–6 inches
FLOWER COLOR	White or yellowish
FLOWER SEASON	Spring to summer
EXPOSURE	Filtered sun
WATER	Low
GROWTH RATE	Moderately slow
PRUNING	None
HARDINESS	15° F, zones 8b–11

Etymology This species was named by German botanist Philipp August Mühlenpfordt in honor of the German cactus hobbyist, Eduard Heyder.

Field Notes After good summer monsoon rains in southeastern Arizona, my friend Rob Romero and I have driven the Dry Canyon road in the Whetstone Mountains to check on **Peniocereus greggii**. While doing so we have found several plumped-up examples of *Mammillaria heyderi* scattered throughout the grasslands. When we have traveled along Arizona State Route 289 to look for *Agave parviflora* and **Coryphantha recurvata**, we always check on *Mammillaria heyderi* plants growing under the shade of oak trees along the side of the road. The species is widespread from southeastern Arizona across to the panhandle of Texas and south into eastern Mexico. They grow in a variety of soil types from silty-clay to rocky limestone based at elevations from about 30–8,000 feet.

Description Plants have a flat-globular to nearly globose body to 2–5 inches tall and 2–6 inches across. Body height varies according to moisture levels; they will swell and become more noticeable during the rainy season and shrink back closer to ground level in the dry season. Bodies are dark green and clearly visible through the sparse **spines** that are clustered at the tips

Cool Cacti and Succulents for Hot Gardens

of prominently elongated **tubercles**. There are 1–2 **central spines** and 10–22 **radial spines**, that are just short of ½-inch-long. White or yellowish flowers are about 1-inch-diameter and appear in spring to summer.

Culture Plants are hardy to at least 15° F and can be grown without threat of damage in USDA zones 8b–11. These can be grown as potted specimens, but they are great hidden gems in a cactus and succulent garden. They typically need mid-day shade in summer in the very hot cities of the southwest such as Las Vegas, Palm Springs, Phoenix, and Tucson, but prefer full sun in mild summer cities like San Diego and Santa Barbara. They are low-water-using, but will benefit from receiving supplemental water in summer. Keep the soil on the dry side through winter to prevent roots from rotting. These are no speed demons when it comes to growth rate and will take a few years to become a sizable plant.

Identification *Mammillaria heyderi* is distinguished by the combination of low growing dark green body, very long **tubercles** topped by sparse **spine** clusters, and white or yellowish flowers.

Landscape Application These are relatively small plants that prefer filtered sunlight, so are best used as either a potted plant or in the shade of perennials, shrubs, or small trees. Use colorful shrubs and perennials such as *Berlandiera lyrata*, *Calliandra eriophylla*, *Dalea frutescens*, *Hibiscus martianus*, *Menodora longiflora*, and *Zinnia acerosa*, or underneath small trees such as *Acacia constricta* or *Eysenhardtia orthocarpa*. Plant with other cacti and succulents such as ***Agave schidigera***, ***Dasylirion wheeleri***, ***Echinocereus engelmannii***, and ***Euphorbia antisyphilitica***.

Precautions Protect newly planted plants from rabbits and packrats, and watch for any **mealybug** infestation that may appear between the **tubercles**; scrape off any **spine mealies** that show up on the **spines**.

Mammillaria heyderi

Mammillaria mystax
Moustache Mammillaria
SMALL CACTUS

SIZE (H x W)	4–6 inches x 5–10 inches
FLOWER COLOR	Rose-purple or pink-purple
FLOWER SEASON	Spring
EXPOSURE	Filtered light
WATER	Low
GROWTH RATE	Moderate
PRUNING	None
HARDINESS	25° F, zones 9b–11

Etymology   Karl Martius used the Greek *myst-* for the upper lip or moustache, a reference to the axillary bristles.

Field Notes   There are some spectacular specimens with exceptionally long **spines** to be seen growing in the Tehuacán-Cuicatlán Biosphere Reserve in northern Oaxaca. Some plants have fewer shorter spines while others have more numerous spines and frequently super long centrals, but they all have the ring of showy rose-purple to pink-purple flowers. These occur on flats and rocky hills in Oaxaca, Puebla, Morelos, and Veracruz from about 3,200–8,500 feet elevation.

Description   These small single-bodied plants grow to about 4–6 inches tall and 5–10 inches in diameter. **Spine** length can be quite variable, with 1–7 **central spines** that are ½–3 inches long and 3–10 shorter **radial spines** less than ½-inch-long. White axillary bristles are present and the inspiration for the species name. A profusion of 1-inch-wide rose-purple flowers ring the top of the plant in spring.

Culture   If acclimated and kept dry when the weather turns cold, plants should be able to withstand a winter low temperature of about 25° F and can be used in landscapes in USDA zones 9b–11. They do best when given some shade, especially in the really hot southwestern U.S. cities of Palm Springs, Phoenix, Tucson, and Yuma. These can be grown in decorative pots in a gritty soil mix that has great drainage and aeration. For plants established in the ground, provide supplemental water every 10–14 days in spring and summer and stop watering altogether in fall and winter. For potted plants, allow the soil to dry out between water applications.

Identification *Mammillaria mystax* is readily identified by the solitary body, long **central spines**, and deep rose-purple flowers.

Landscape Application These are easily grown either in a landscape or in decorative containers. Plant several of them around large boulders and mix with other cacti and succulents while interspersing some flowering perennials and small grasses. Try combining with *Agave schidigera*, *Coryphantha poselgeriana*, *Ferocactus acanthodes*, and *Yucca pallida* along with flowering plants like *Dalea capitata*, *Glandularia gooddingii*, *Tetraneuris acaulis*, and *Thymophila pentachaeta*. Accumulate several with variation in **central spines** and grow them in decorative pots alongside other potted cacti.

Precautions Be on the lookout for **spine mealies** and be prepared to pick them off the **spines** as soon as any show up.

Mammillaria mystax

Mammillaria petterssonii
Pettersson's Mammillaria
CLUSTERING CACTUS

SIZE (H x W)	4–6 inches x 6–8 inches, clusters to 18–20 inches
FLOWER COLOR	Pinkish red or magenta
FLOWER SEASON	Spring to summer
EXPOSURE	Filtered sun
WATER	Low to moderate
GROWTH RATE	Moderate
PRUNING	None
HARDINESS	25° F, zones 9b–11

Etymology Plantsman Heinrich Hildmann named this species in honor of German cactus collector Mr. Pettersson.

Field Notes Brian Kemble and I saw these plants on our way to El Salto Falls in Zacatecas. There were a couple large clusters that were spilling over rocks and growing through crevices in the rock. Plants can be found growing in rock crevices and rocky soil in central Mexico from about 4,000–8,500 feet elevation.

Description Plants have been described as having a single body to about 4–6 inches tall and 6–8 inches wide, but they will produce multiple heads and can become large clusters to 18–20 inches across. Bodies are medium to dark green and readily visible beneath the **spine** clusters. There are 6–7 white, light orange-yellow, or orange-brown **central spines** about 1-inch-long or slightly longer and 10 or more similarly colored **radial spines**. Dense white wool is present between the **tubercles** near the apex of the plants.

Culture My plants in Tucson have come through winter lows of about 25° F without damage and can be considered good

Cool Cacti and Succulents for Hot Gardens

candidates for USDA zones 9b–11. They make spectacular potted plants in just about any southwestern U.S. city if protected when winter low temperatures dip below 25° F. Plants prefer a bit of mid-day shade in hot summer cities such as Phoenix and Tucson, but should be able to take full sun where summer temperatures do not top triple digits F. These prefer a fast draining soil with little or no organic matter added whether in the ground or in decorative pots. They are low water using, but should be given some supplemental water in summer and kept dry in winter.

Identification *Mammillaria petterssonii* is easily identified by the combination of yellowish to orangish **spines**, white wool between the **tubercles**, and the pinkish red flowers.

Landscape Application These make great potted specimens and are very attractive when they fill out a large decorative pot. They can be planted in a low-water-use landscape complete with small grasses, flowering perennials, small shrubs, and small trees. Try mixing in grasses like *Bouteloua curtipendula* and *Bouteloua gracilis*; perennials such as *Dalea capitata*, *Glandularia gooddingii*, *Hibiscus coulteri*, and *Tetraneuris acaulis*; and small trees like *Acacia constricta* and *Acacia willardiana*. Place these so they receive some mid-day shade from the trees or afternoon shade from the grasses, perennials, or shrubs. Spine color is variable so amass several for your collection.

Precautions Watch for **mealybugs** and **spine mealies**, and remove them by hand before an infestation breaks out. Protect from javelina and rabbits when planted in the ground. Plant in an elevated area with fast draining soil.

Mammillaria rhodantha
Lemon Ball Mammillaria
CLUSTERING CACTUS

SIZE (H x W)	4–6 inches x 4–6 inches, clusters to 12–18 inches
FLOWER COLOR	Rose-red to rose-purple
FLOWER SEASON	Spring to fall
EXPOSURE	Filtered sun
WATER	Low to moderate
GROWTH RATE	Moderately slow
PRUNING	None
HARDINESS	25° F, zones 9b–11

Etymology Johann Link and Christoph Otto used the Greek *rhodos-* meaning rose-red, and the Greek *anthos-* meaning flower, to highlight the rose-red flowers.

Field Notes In 2014, Jeff Chemnick, Brian Kemble, and I went to Hidalgo, Mexico looking for cacti and succulents in preparation for a trip Jeff was to lead the next year. We saw these as solitary plants and as large clusters with many of them growing on lichen- and moss-covered rocks and boulders. We were there in mid-May, and the plants were in the midst of flowering, showing off their small, yet beautiful, flowers. This species is known to occur in the states of Jalisco, Guanajuato, Querétaro, and Hidalgo in central Mexico from 4,000–7,500 feet elevation.

Description Plants are solitary with bodies reaching 4–6 inches tall and 4–6 inches across or branching dichotomously to make clusters to 12–18 inches wide. The bright green bodies are adorned with 18–22 thin needle-like bright yellow radial spines and 6–8, 1-inch-long dark yellow central spines. Rose-red to rose-purple flowers are just over ½-inch-long and do attract hummingbirds.

Culture Larger plants are hardy to about 25° F and are good candidates for USDA zones 9b–11, while young ones will need some protection when

Cool Cacti and Succulents for Hot Gardens

the winter lows drop to the high 20's F. These benefit from having mid-day shade throughout the year in really hot southwestern U.S. cities. Plants grow best in a soil with some organic matter and excellent drainage whether in the ground or in a pot. Give them supplemental water from spring through summer, always allowing the soil to dry a little before watering again, but keep them dry through winter. These make beautiful specimens when grown in large pots.

Identification There are at least six recognized subspecies of *Mammillaria rhodantha* of which subsp. *pringlei* (sometimes sold as *Mammillaria pringlei*) is very popular owing to its long yellow **spines**.

Landscape Application Given time, plants can make sizable clusters and be a force in nearly any southwestern **xeriscape** where winter lows are mild enough. Plant these in raised beds and let them grow over rocks and fill in cracks between boulders. Put them under the shade of deciduous trees with sparse crowns so they get summer shade and dappled light in winter. Use companion plants such as *Calylophus hartwegii*, *Conoclinium dissectum*, *Dalea capitata*, *Justicia longii*, or *Zinnia grandiflora* to soften the form of the *Mammillaria* and provide extra humidity when the leafy plants get watered. Mix with *Agave schidigera*, *Dasylirion acrotrichum*, *Ferocactus histrix*, and other clustering *Mammillaria* species.

Precautions Protect from the usual suspects of javelina, packrats, and rabbits. Be on the lookout for **spine mealies,** and manually remove them with tweezers.

Mammillaria rhodantha

Mammillaria standleyi
Standley's Mammillaria
SMALL CLUSTERING CACTUS

SIZE (H x W)	3–5 inches x 3–4 inches, clusters to 12–24 inches
FLOWER COLOR	Purplish-red
FLOWER SEASON	Spring
EXPOSURE	Filtered sun
WATER	Drought tolerant to low
GROWTH RATE	Moderately slow
PRUNING	None
HARDINESS	20° F, zones 9a–11

Etymology Joseph Rose and Nathaniel Britton named this species for American botanist Paul C. Standley, who compiled the massive Trees and Shrubs of Mexico published from 1920–1924.

Field Notes One of my very first trips to Mexico was to Alamos in southern Sonora. A group of us hiked up the Canyon de las Piedras to look for interesting plants and came upon *Mammillaria standleyi* growing on rocks in the oak zone along with ***Agave bovicornuta*** and several subtropical shrubs. These are found growing in rocky soil in thorn scrub and among oaks from about 1,600–5,800 feet elevation. They occur on slopes and in mountains in the states of Chihuahua, Sonora, and Sinaloa.

Description Plants are solitary when young eventually producing several heads and forming large clusters to 8–10 inches tall by 12–24 inches across. Individual heads are dark green, 3–5 inches tall by 3–4 inches across, and

Photo by Scott Calhoun

have dense white wool in the axils of the **tubercles**. **Spine** clusters consist of 4 **central spines** each just under ½-inch-long and 14–16 **radial spines** that are slightly shorter. Pinkish-red flowers appear primarily in spring.

Culture Plants are hardy to about 20° F and are good landscape candidates for USDA zones 9a–11. They are moderately slow growing and will take several years to grow into large clusters. Plants prefer filtered sun in most all cities throughout the desert southwestern U.S., but could be acclimated to full sun in coastal California cities like San Diego, Santa Barbara, or San Francisco. Plants established in a landscape are drought tolerant, while those growing in pots relish some supplemental water in summer, but all prefer to be dry in winter.

Identification *Mammillaria standleyi* has 4 **central spines** and 14–16 **radial spines** that are thin, which sets it apart from *Mammillaria sonorensis* with 1–4 **central spines** and 9–15 **radial spines** that are short and thick.

Landscape Application Although large clusters will take several years to develop, these can be superb landscape specimens given time. Plant them in raised beds alongside other clustering *Mammillaria* species such as *Mammillaria geminispina* and *Mammillaria petterssonii*. Use cacti such as *Cleistocactus strausii*, *Espostoa lanata*, and *Oreocereus celsianus* to provide some height and succulents like *Agave schidigera* and *Agave victoriae-reginae* for a change in form and texture. To get seasonal color, use low growing flowering annuals and perennials such as *Dalea capitata*, *Eschscholzia mexicana*, *Tetraneuris acaulis*, and *Thymophylla pentachaeta*.

Precautions Watch for **mealybugs** that live in between the **tubercles** and scrap off **spine mealies** with sharp tweezers. Packrats might nibble on the **tubercles**.

Mammillaria standleyi

Myrtillocactus geometrizans
Blue Candle Cactus
COLUMNAR CACTUS

SIZE (H x W)	8–12 feet x 6–10 feet
FLOWER COLOR	Greenish-white
FLOWER SEASON	Spring to summer
EXPOSURE	Full sun
WATER	Drought tolerant to low
GROWTH RATE	Moderate
PRUNING	Remove dead stems
HARDINESS	20° F, zones 9a–11

Etymology Early 19th Century German botanist Carl Martius used the Latin for geometric to describe the curved patterning on the stems.

Field Notes There are fine stands of these in the states of Guanajuato, Hidalgo, Querétaro, and San Luis Potosí in east-central Mexico. I was with my friends Brian Kemble, Chad Davis, and Rob Nixon when we were all munching the small purple fruits like they were candy. In April 2010, Brian Kemble and I found plants in bloom in Hidalgo after looking at *Yucca queretaroensis* on the steep slopes of Barranca de Tolimán. Plants have a widespread distribution being found from Tamaulipas to Puebla and Oaxaca. They inhabit wide-open spaces on slopes, hills, and mountains from about 2,600–8,500 feet elevation.

Description These are shrub-like to tree-like plants with numerous branches from a main trunk and growing to 8–12 feet tall with a spread of 6–10 feet. Blue-green stems have 5–6 ribs frequently with curving v-shaped patterning on them. One black **central spine** is about 2 inches long surrounded by 5–9 shorter **radial spines**. Small greenish-white and pink flowers appear in spring to early summer and are followed by small edible purplish fruits.

Culture Mature established plants will tolerate winter low temperatures of about 20° F, although growing tips should be protected from extreme cold. These can be used as landscape plants in USDA zones 9a-11. Plants grow best in full sun and even with some reflected heat off a south or west-facing wall. They are not too particular about soil if drainage is adequate, as they do not like to have wet feet, especially in winter. Provide supplemental water for new plantings for the first couple summers until they become established. After establishment, plants are quite drought tolerant. They have a moderate growth rate, and no pruning is needed unless a stem dies and needs removal.

Identification The blue-green stems with few **spines** and small greenish-white and pink flowers make this easily recognized.

Landscape Application Because these can get large, it is best to plant only one of them in a landscape and surround it with smaller cacti or various succulent plants. Some suggestions would include *Echinocactus grusonii*, *Ferocactus acanthodes*, *Hesperaloe funifera*, *Jatropha dioica*, or *Yucca torreyi*. Use small and medium-sized shrubs for color and to offset the vertical lines of the *Myrtillocactus*. A few compatible plants would include *Anisacanthus quadrifidus*, *Buddleja marrubiifolia*, *Calliandra californica*, *Eremophila hygrophana*, and *Leucophyllum candidum*. These make excellent specimens in large wide-open landscapes like freeway on/off ramps.

Precautions Protect young plants and stem tips from frost damage. Screen newly planted ones to prevent rabbits and javelina from destroying them.

Myrtillocactus geometrizans

Neolloydia conoidea
Chihuahuan Beehive, Texas Cone Cactus
SMALL CACTUS

Etymology Augustin de Candolle, an early 19th Century Swiss botanist, based the species name on the Greek *cono-* meaning cone, which describes the cone-shaped body.

SIZE (H x W)	3–10 inches x 2–3 inches
FLOWER COLOR	Magenta or purplish
FLOWER SEASON	Spring to summer
EXPOSURE	Filtered light
WATER	Low to moderate
GROWTH RATE	Moderate
PRUNING	None
HARDINESS	15° F, zones 8b–11

Field Notes I spotted these in flower in central Nuevo León while on a trip in June 2006 and am now always on the lookout for them anytime I travel to the Chihuahuan Desert Region. In July 2008, there were beautiful flowering plants in the hills east of the town of General Cepeda, a name that is high on my list of all-time great city names. Plants grow on hills, slopes, and rocky shelves in limestone soil. The species is widespread from Big Bend south to Hidalgo, Mexico from 2,600–8,200 feet elevation.

Description Plants are relatively small with one to several green bodies, each 3–10 inches tall and about 2–3 inches in diameter with clusters up to 10–12 inches across. There are four black or dark brown **central spines** and 15–28 white **radial spines**. Magenta to purplish flowers are 2–3 inches across and can appear from late spring through summer.

Culture These plants are hardy to at least 15° F and can be grown in USDA zones 8b–11. They can be grown as potted plants throughout the U.S. if they are brought indoor and allowed to go dormant for the winter. They could also be grown under full spectrum grow lights while inside. Give them a fast draining soil, and add limestone pellets or powder if available. Plants have a moderate growth rate and are low-water-using even in pots.

Identification   The solid magenta to purplish flowers separate *Neolloydia conoidea* from any similar looking species of **Coryphantha** and from **Thelocactus bicolor** that has larger magenta flowers with red at the base of the **tepals**.

Landscape Application   These make excellent container plants and can be incorporated into a cactus and succulent collection. They are not common in cultivation, but should be grown more frequently. Plants are easily cultivated in pots that can then be planted in the ground once they get large enough so they are not lost or demolished by rabbits or packrats. When planting in the ground, put them in an elevated spot, whether a formal raised bed or artificial mound, to get the plants up closer to eye level. Plant with other small cacti such as **Ariocarpus trigonus**, **Astrophytum myriostigma**, **Echinocereus bonkerae**, **Mammillaria candida**, or **Stenocactus multicostatus**. Combine with rosette forming plants like **Agave schidigera**, **Agave victoriae-reginae**, or **Dasylirion acrotrichum**. Add seasonal color by using flowering annuals or perennials like *Baileya multiradiata*, *Hibiscus coulteri*, or *Zinnia grandiflora*.

Precautions   **Mealybugs** will sometimes inhabit spaces between the **tubercles**. Packrats or woodrats may nibble on the plants.

Neolloydia conoidea

Nolina matapensis
Sonoran Tree Beargrass
TREE-LIKE SUCCULENT

Etymology American botanist and Sonoran Desert researcher Ira Wiggins first collected a specimen near Mátape, Sonora and used the town name as inspiration for the species name.

SIZE (H x W)	8–20 feet x 4–6 feet
FLOWER COLOR	Tan
FLOWER SEASON	Late spring
EXPOSURE	Full sun
WATER	Low to moderate
GROWTH RATE	Slow
PRUNING	None
HARDINESS	Low 20's° F, zones 9a–11

Field Notes There are some tall plants of *Nolina matapensis* poking their droopy leaved heads above the dense vegetation along Mexico Federal Highway 16 between Hermosillo and Yécora in Sonora. One year, while exploring eastern Sonora with succulent master Gene Joseph, we saw the occasional plant in the hills east of Mazatán along the narrow two-lane Sonora Highway 20. The species has a relatively narrow distribution being found in eastern Sonora and adjacent Chihuahua. They grow in short tree forest, oak forest, and pine-oak forest from about 3,500–6,000 feet elevation.

Description A full grown Sonoran Tree Beargrass is an unforgettable sight as these behemoths can grow to 8–20 feet tall and have few or several branches with a width of 4–6 feet. The trunks grow slowly, so a realistic size for landscape plants would be closer to 6-10 feet tall. They can have 3 or more branches and get about 6 feet across. Dark green strap-shaped leaves are 3–5 feet long and about 1-inch wide. Leaf edges are finely **serrulate** and can slice into fingers giving a "paper cut" if mishandled.

Cool Cacti and Succulents for Hot Gardens

Culture Plants are hardy to the low 20's F and can be grown reliably in USDA zones 9a–11, and possibly in zone 8b if located in a warm microclimate and given some winter protection on the coldest nights. These can be grown as large potted specimens if kept warm in winter. They prefer full sun or reflected heat situations in mild summer cities but relish mid-day shade in summer in the very hot cities such as Las Vegas, Palm Springs, Phoenix, and Yuma. They are low- to moderate-water-using and will respond to supplemental water in summer, but they should be kept dry during winter. The growth rate is slow, about 2–4 inches each year, so plants will take several years to achieve dominating size. No pruning is required and it is best to leave the dead leaves covering the trunk to prevent sunburn.S

Identification *Nolina matapensis* has green leaves that droop down over the trunk, while **Nolina nelsonii** has stiff blue leaves.

Landscape Application Use these either singly as a focal point in the landscape or group several to create a small forest under which you can intersperse perennials and small or medium sized shrubs to provide a field of color. Use plants like *Acourtia wrightii, Dalea frutescens, Galphimia glauca, Menodora longiflora,* and *Telosiphonia brachysiphon*. Plant these with large cacti and succulents such as **Agave gentryi, Dasylirion acrotrichum, Cephalocereus senilis,** or **Lophocereus schottii**.

Precautions Protect plants from winter temperatures in the low 20's F and keep dry in the winter.

Nolina matapensis

Nolina microcarpa
Sacahuista, Beargrass
SHRUB-LIKE SUCCULENT

SIZE (H x W)	3–6 feet x 4–8 feet
FLOWER COLOR	Tan
FLOWER SEASON	Summer
EXPOSURE	Full sun to reflected heat
WATER	Low to moderate
GROWTH RATE	Moderately slow
PRUNING	None
HARDINESS	0° F, zones 7a–11

Etymology Sereno Watson was a 19th century American botanist who worked at the Gray Herbarium of Harvard when he named this species using the Greek *micro-* for small and the Greek *carp-* for fruit.

Field Notes There are many large clumps of these growing on the open rocky slopes along Arizona State Route 289 west of Peña Blanca Lake, and fellow cactus nut Rob Romero and I always stop for them when traveling along that road. I have come upon large specimens on the grass-covered hills south and east of Sonoita, Arizona while hunting for ***Agave parryi*** and along Middlemarch road going to the Dragoon Mountains in southeastern Arizona. These are widespread from northwestern Arizona, to New Mexico, and into Sonora and Chihuahua Mexico. They grow on grassy slopes in oak woodland and pine forest from about 3,000–8,000 feet elevation.

Description Plants form large clumps of tightly packed **rosettes**, each attaining a height of 3–6 feet with clusters growing to 4–8 feet across. Green leaves are about 3 feet long by ½-inch-wide and have decorative brushy tips and

finely **serrulate** edges that will inflict "paper cuts" if not handled with care. The 3–6-foot-tall highly branched flower stalk appears in summer and is covered with many small tan flowers.

Culture Hardy to at least 0° F, these can be grown reliably in USDA zones 7a–11. They look their best when grown in full sun or even reflected heat situations in nearly all cities of the desert southwest, and even cities above the limits of the desert such as Sierra Vista, Arizona and Las Cruces or Albuquerque, New Mexico. They are low- to moderate-water-using, responding to supplemental water in summer, but do not need extra water in winter. The growth rate is moderately slow, and plants will take several years to form large masses of leaves. Given ample room; there is no need to prune the leaves, and I highly recommend leaving the old stalks as a perch for small birds.

Identification *Nolina microcarpa* is a larger plant and has wider leaves with noticeable **serrated** margins than the smaller *Nolina texana* with its narrower smoother-edged leaves.

Landscape Application These can be used singly as a focal point in the landscape or several grouped together with *Eysenhardtia orthocarpa* and *Muhlenbergia lindheimeri* to simulate a grassland environment. Use them as an alternative to true grasses eliminating the need to shear back any dead foliage in winter. Intersperse small shrubs and perennials like *Acourtia wrightii*, *Anisacanthus thurberi*, *Dalea pulchra*, *Glandularia gooddingii*, and *Telosiphonia brachysiphon*. Plant with small trees like *Acacia constricta*, or with cacti and succulents such as ***Agave palmeri***, ***Carnegiea gigantea***, or ***Dasylirion wheeleri***.

Precautions Protect young plants from being damaged by javelina, rabbits, or packrats.

Nolina microcarpa

Nolina nelsonii
Blue-leaf Nolina
TREE-LIKE SUCCULENT

SIZE (H x W)	8–12 feet x 3–6 feet
FLOWER COLOR	Tan
FLOWER SEASON	Summer
EXPOSURE	Full sun to reflected heat
WATER	Low to moderate
GROWTH RATE	Moderately slow
PRUNING	None
HARDINESS	10° F, zones 8a–11

Etymology American botanist Joseph Nelson Rose named this species for Edward W. Nelson, an American naturalist who first collected the plant near Miquihuana, Tamaulipas.

Field Notes In September 1987, Ron Gass and I were driving on a dirt road from Palmillas to Miquihuana in southern Tamaulipas when we saw these tall blue leaved plants we thought might be a *Yucca* species. A little farther up the road we saw one with an inflorescence and immediately realized it was not a *Yucca* but a species of *Nolina*. It was not until we returned home and got out my well-worn copy of Trees and Shrubs of Mexico by Paul Standley that I was able to identify it as *Nolina nelsonii*. Plants grow on flat rocky ground and lower mountain slopes in southern Nuevo León and southern Tamaulipas between 4,600–9,000 feet elevation.

Description Over time, these tall, few-branched, trunk-forming plants can grow 8–12 feet tall and 3–6 feet in across depending on number of heads that

Photo by Janet Rademacher taken at San Antonio Botanical Garden

develop. Juvenile leaves are green to gray-green and flexible, while older mature leaves are powder blue and more rigid but still with some give to them. Individual leaves are about 2–3 feet long by 1-inch-wide and have razor sharp edges that freely slash careless handlers. The 6–9-foot-tall, thick, and highly branched **inflorescences** hold numerous small tan flowers and appear mainly summer.

Culture These are cold hardy to at least 10° F and make great landscape plants in USDA zones 8a–11. They develop their best form when grown in full sun or reflected heat situations in nearly all cities of the desert southwest and even higher elevation cities, such as Sierra Vista and Las Cruces. They are low- to moderate-water-using and will respond to supplemental water in summer but stop watering in winter. The growth rate is moderately slow, so watch patiently as the trunk develops. Do not remove the old leaves as they protect the trunk.

Identification *Nolina nelsonii* has relatively stiff bluish leaves that distinguish it from the drooping green leaves of **Nolina matapensis**, the other trunk forming species covered here.

Landscape Application The combination of size, powder blue leaves, and striking inflorescence make this an outstanding accent plant whether used singly or in groups. Surround them with a variety of other xeric plants for a complete **xeriscape**. Some suggested companion plants include **Agave gentryi**, *Dalea versicolor*, **Ferocactus pilosus**, *Leucophyllum laevigatum*, *Menodora longiflora*, and *Telosiphonia brachysiphon*.

Precautions Protect young plants from damage by javelina, rabbits, deer, or packrats.

Nolina nelsonii

Opuntia basilaris
Beavertail Cactus
SHRUB-LIKE CACTUS

SIZE (H x W)	1–2 feet x 3–6 feet
FLOWER COLOR	Pink, magenta
FLOWER SEASON	Late spring to early summer
EXPOSURE	Full sun to reflected heat
WATER	Drought tolerant to low
GROWTH RATE	Moderately slow
PRUNING	None
HARDINESS	0° F, zones 7a–11

Etymology George Engelmann and John Bigelow used the Latin *basil-* meaning from the base, to illustrate the nature of the pads originating from a common base.

Field Notes In April 2010, I went to see flowering plants of *Agave deserti* in Anza-Borrego Desert State Park in southern California and saw these plants in flower as a bonus. The species has a wide-ranging distribution and can be found in much of western Arizona, southeastern California, and southern Nevada. Plants occur on sandy, gravelly, or rocky soil on flats and mountain slopes along the Colorado River basin from near sea level to about 6,000 feet elevation.

Description This low-growing wide-spreading species will reach 1–2 feet tall and eventually spread 3–6 feet across. Bluish, blue-green, or gray-green pads will sometimes turn purplish red in cold weather. Individual pads are **obovate** or **elliptic** 3–10 inches long by 2–8 inches wide and lack large **spines** but do have numerous **glochids** at each **areole**. Pink or magenta flowers are about 3 inches wide and appear in late spring and early summer.

Culture Some forms of these are cold hardy to 0° F, and those will make great landscape plants in USDA zones 7a–11. Other forms are less hardy and might be damaged at temperatures below 20° F. These are best grown in full sun or reflected heat in the low elevation cities of the desert southwest. I suspect significant summer rain and high humidity rather than winter cold would be the limiting factors in determining where they could be used successfully.

These are drought tolerant once established, but will be fine if they receive minimal supplemental water in late spring and summer. The growth rate is moderately slow and plants will take a few years to reach a substantial size. There is no need to prune the plants unless there are dead pads.

Identification *Opuntia basilaris* plants are easily identified by their beavertail-shaped pads and pink or magenta flowers.

Landscape Application Use Beavertail Cactus plants for their electric pink or magenta flowers that make the landscape come alive in spring. Use singly or in groups as a subtle accent plant among low growing flowering perennials. Choose companion plants carefully because the flower color can be hard to work with. Try using plants with purple or white flowers such as *Glandularia gooddingii*, *Melampodium leucanthum*, *Telosiphonia brachysiphon*, or *Zinnia acerosa*. Plant with other cacti and succulents such as **Dasylirion wheeleri**, **Ferocactus acanthodes**, and **Fouquieria splendens**.

Precautions Protect young plants from javelina and rabbit damage and keep packrat nests cleaned up. Check for **cochineal scale** and wash them off with a strong stream of water or remove whole pads when necessary.

Opuntia engelmannii
Engelmann's Prickly Pear
SHRUB-LIKE CACTUS

SIZE (H x W)	3–6 feet by 4–8 feet
FLOWER COLOR	Yellow
FLOWER SEASON	Late spring
EXPOSURE	Full sun
WATER	Drought tolerant to low
GROWTH RATE	Moderately fast
PRUNING	Remove dead pads
HARDINESS	10° F, zones 8a–11

Etymology This species was named in honor of George Engelmann by Joseph Salm-Dyck.

Field Notes I see plants of Engelmann's Prickly Pear while walking in my neighborhood on the west side of Tucson and nearly anywhere I go out plant hunting in southeastern Arizona. The plants are common and easily overlooked while searching for other cacti. They have a wide-ranging distribution in the southwestern U.S. and northern Mexico, and grow in valleys, canyons, and on slopes from desert to montane habitat between 1,000–8,000 feet elevation.

Description These large shrub-like plants can be low and sprawling or upright and spreading growing to 3–6 feet tall and 4–8 feet across. Dull green to yellow-green pads are rounded to **obovate** and 6–12 inches long by 5–10 inches across. White or yellowish **spines** are darker at the base and measure ½–2 inches long. Pure yellow flowers are 2½–3½ inches long and open for one day. Flowers that open a second day are usually orange. Prime flowering season is in April and May.

Culture Plants are hardy to 10° F and can be used in USDA zones 8a–11. They are perfect for use in full sun in the desert southwest cities such as Palm Springs, Phoenix, Sierra Vista, Tucson, and Yuma. They are drought tolerant once established, but would appreciate some supplemental water if the summer is extremely hot and dry. The growth rate is moderately fast, and plants started from one or two pads will take a few years to become sizable in the landscape, so look for plants with several pads. If space is a limiting factor, try keeping them at a manageable size by periodically removing pads and giving them to neighbors.

Identification The pure yellow flowers, potentially taller size, and white **spines** separate this from the lower growing *Opuntia phaeacantha* with its dark **spines** and yellow flowers that have red or orange at the base of the petals.

Landscape Application These can be used as a centerpiece in a **xeriscape** filled with other xeric plants. Mix in a variety of perennials and small shrubs to give seasonal color with the Engelmann's Prickly Pear being a constant. Some nice options would include *Encelia farinosa*, *Ericameria laricifolia*, or *Glandularia gooddingii*. Some suggested cacti and succulents to include in your low-water-use landscape are *Agave simplex*, **Ferocactus wislizeni**, **Fouquieria splendens**, and **Hesperaloe funifera**.

Precautions Protect young plants from javelina, rabbits, and packrats. Check for **cochineal scale** or **mealybugs** and wash them off with a strong stream of water or remove whole pads when necessary. Flightless black beetles in the genus *Moneilema* are known to feed on Prickly Pear pads.

Moneilema sp. feeding on Prickly Pear

Opuntia engelmannii

Opuntia macrocentra
Long-spined Prickly Pear
SHRUB-LIKE CACTUS

Etymology German-born, American-trained George Engelmann used the Greek *macro-* meaning large, and the Greek *centro-* for center, in reference to either the large central spine, or the conspicuous red center in the flower.

SIZE (H x W)	2–3 feet x 5–6 feet
FLOWER COLOR	Yellow with red center
FLOWER SEASON	Late spring to early summer
EXPOSURE	Full sun to reflected heat
WATER	Drought tolerant to low
GROWTH RATE	Moderate
PRUNING	None
HARDINESS	10° F, zones 8a–11

Field Notes Taking photos of Prickly Pears in habitat has never been high on my list, but this is one I have seen in the desert around Tucson and have managed to pull the trigger a couple times while out hiking. *Opuntia macrocentra* is native to southeastern Arizona, southern New Mexico, western Texas, and adjacent Sonora and Chihuahua, Mexico. Plants grow in sandy desert flats, rocky hills, desert grasslands, and in oak woodlands from about 1,700–5,500 feet elevation.

Description These are low-growing wide-spreading shrub-like plants that grow to 2–3 feet tall and spread 5–6 feet across. Blue-green pads are usually tinged with purple especially near the edges and frequently turn reddish-purple

or even dark red in times of stress. Individual pads are rounded to **orbicular** or **obovate** 4–8 inches long by 4–8 inches wide. The 1–4 dark brown, reddish brown, or black and white **spines** are 2–5 inches long. Small dark yellow or reddish **glochids** should be avoided at all costs. Yellow flowers are 2–3½ inches wide with a bright red center and appear in late spring to early summer.

Culture Plants are cold hardy to at least 10° F and are nice landscape plants in USDA zones 8a–11. They grow best when placed in full sun or reflected heat situations even in the low elevation cities of the desert southwest such as Palm Springs, Phoenix, Tucson, and Yuma. These are drought tolerant once established, but would appreciate some supplemental water if the summer is extremely hot and dry. The growth rate is moderate, and they will take their sweet time to reach a substantial size. No pruning is required unless there are dead pads.

Identification *Opuntia macrocentra* plants are characterized by the blue-gray pads flushed with purplish-red and the extra-long **spine**.

Landscape Application Plants are perfect for use in a cactus and succulent landscape alongside other low-water-using plants. Try using one plant for its purplish-red pad color and the eye-catching spines. Use perennials and small shrubs to give seasonal color against the backdrop of permanence provided by the cactus and other succulents. Some good choices would include *Baileya multiradiata*, *Calliandra eriophylla*, *Dalea pulchra*, *Eremophila hygrophana*, or *Penstemon parryi*. Some suggested cacti and succulents could include *Agave simplex*, ***Dasylirion acrotrichum***, ***Ferocactus acanthodes***, ***Fouquieria splendens***, ***Hesperaloe funifera***, and ***Yucca elata***.

Precautions Protect young plants from javelina, rabbits, and packrats. Check for **cochineal scale** or **mealybugs** and wash them off with a strong stream of water or remove whole pads when necessary.

Opuntia santa-rita
Santa Rita Prickly Pear
SHRUB-LIKE CACTUS

SIZE (H x W)	3–4 (6) feet x 4–6 (8) feet
FLOWER COLOR	Lemon yellow
FLOWER SEASON	Spring
EXPOSURE	Full sun to reflected heat
WATER	Drought tolerant to low
GROWTH RATE	Moderate
PRUNING	None
HARDINESS	10° F, zones 8a–11

Etymology Two American botanists, David Griffiths and Raleigh Frederick Hare, used the occurrence of these plants in the Santa Rita Mountains in southern Arizona as the basis for the species name.

Field Notes I used to see a couple handsome specimens of this species while taking my constant four-legged companion on an early morning walk around the neighborhood. Unfortunately, they seem to have succumbed to effects of the mega-drought in the southwest and are now being turned into compost. I would watch the plants undergo their fairy-tale transformation as the pad color turned from blue-green to intense purplish-red in winter. *Opuntia santa-rita* is native to southeastern Arizona and northern Sonora and likes to inhabit rocky hills, canyons, bajadas, desert grasslands, and even juniper-oak woodland from about 2,000–5,300 feet elevation.

Description Plants are upright to wide-spreading and shrub-like eventually reaching about 3–4 feet tall and spreading 4–6 feet across, occasionally up to 6 feet by 8 feet. Blue-green pads are sometimes tinged with purple and frequently

turn reddish-purple in times of cold or stress. Individual pads are rounded to **ovate** 6–10 inches long by 4–8 inches wide. Some plants lack the long **spines** yet still have numerous yellow **glochids**, while other plants have one nearly 2-inch-long brown to black **spine**. Lemon-yellow flowers are 3–3½ inches wide and appear in late spring.

Culture Plants are cold hardy to at least 10° F and can be used in landscapes in USDA zones 8a–11. Use them in full sun or reflected heat situations even in the low elevation cities of the desert southwest such as Palm Springs, Phoenix, Tucson, and Yuma. They are drought tolerant once established, but would appreciate some supplemental water if the summer is extremely hot and dry. They have a moderate growth rate and will take a few years to become moderately sized, so start with plants that have several pads for instant impact. If space is a limiting factor, try keeping the plants at a manageable size by periodically removing some pads.

Identification *Opuntia santa-rita* plants have pure lemon-yellow flowers that distinguish them from ***Opuntia macrocentra*** and their yellow flowers with red centers.

Landscape Application Use these as a centerpiece in a cactus and succulent landscape filled with other low-water-using plants. Mix in a variety of perennials and small shrubs to give seasonal color while the Santa Rita Prickly Pear provides year-round stability. Some nice options would include *Encelia farinosa, Ericameria laricifolia*, or *Glandularia gooddingii*. Some suggested cacti and succulents to include in your low-water-use landscape are *Agave simplex,* ***Ferocactus wislizeni***, and ***Fouquieria splendens***.

Precautions Protect young plants from javelina, rabbits, and packrats. Check for **cochineal scale** or **mealybugs** and wash them off with a strong stream of water or remove whole pads when necessary.

Oreocereus celsianus
Old Man of the Andes
SHRUB-LIKE CACTUS

Etymology French botanist Charles Lemaire named this species for Jean-François Cels.

SIZE (H x W)	4–6 feet x 1–3 feet
FLOWER COLOR	Pale purplish pink
FLOWER SEASON	Spring to early summer
EXPOSURE	Filtered sun
WATER	Low to moderate
GROWTH RATE	Slow
PRUNING	None
HARDINESS	20° F, zones 9a–11

Field Notes In November 2022, I went on a trip to Argentina and Chile led by Guillermo Rivera. I was hoping to see these in their natural habitat, but unfortunately, we did not get far enough north. However, we did get to see *Oreocereus trollii*, and for more information, turn the page! *Oreocereus celsianus* occurs in far northern Argentina and southern Bolivia and plants are found on sparsely to densely vegetated rocky slopes and flats from about 10,000–12,000 feet elevation.

Description Plants branch from the base and have several upright columnar stems 4–6 feet tall and 3–5 inches in diameter. They are open shrub-like plants to 4–6 feet tall and 1–4 feet across. Individual stems have 10–25 ribs and 8–13 yellowish or red-brown **spines** sparsely surrounded by 2-inch-long white wool. Purplish-pink to reddish flowers are narrowly tubular, about 3 inches long, and appear in spring or early summer.

Culture Plants are cold hardy to about 20° F, and are perfect for use in USDA zones 9a–11. They ought to be tried in zones 8a and 8b. Even though these high elevation plants grow in full sun in habitat, they prefer to have a bit of filtered sunlight in the hot summer cities of Palm Springs, Phoenix, and Tucson. If acclimated slowly, they might be able to tolerate more sun in cities with slightly cooler summer temperatures. Be prepared to shade your plants if they start to show any sunburn. They are low-water-using, but will benefit from receiving supplemental water from late spring until fall. The growth rate is slow, so look for the largest plants you can afford. Plants do not need to be pruned so keep the loppers on the shelf.

Identification *Oreocereus celsianus* is taller with more upright stems and fewer white woolly hairs than **Oreocereus trollii**.

Landscape Application Group several of these together in a low-water-use garden along with other cacti and succulents, and then surround them with spring or summer flowering perennials and small shrubs. Some ideal companion plants would include *Baileya multiradiata*, *Ericameria laricifolia*, *Glandularia gooddingii*, *Gutierrizia microcephala*, *Hymenoxys acaulis*, and *Penstemon eatonii*. Other cacti and succulents that would do well in your low-water-use landscape alongside *Oreocereus celsianus* are **Agave ocahui**, **Dasylirion quadrangulatum**, **Echinocereus enneacanthus**, **Ferocactus gracilis**, **Hesperaloe campanulata**, and **Yucca rostrata**.

Precautions Protect young plants from javelina, rabbits, and possibly packrats, and be sure to give them a bit of shade in summer.

Oreocereus trollii
Old Man of the Andes
SHRUB-LIKE CACTUS

SIZE (H x W)	1½–2 feet x 1½–2 feet
FLOWER COLOR	Pink, carmine
FLOWER SEASON	Spring to summer
EXPOSURE	Filtered sun
WATER	Low to moderate
GROWTH RATE	Slow
PRUNING	None
HARDINESS	20° F, zones 9a–11

Etymology Swiss botanist Walter Kupper named this species for Dr. Carl Troll, a German geographer/botanist who found this in southern Bolivia in 1927.

Field Notes While on a November 2022 trip to Argentina and Chile led by Guillermo Rivera, we went to a couple spots where we got to see these in their natural habitat. We first saw them among large rocks on flat to sloping ground with a number of other interesting plants. The next spot was at higher elevation and density of the *Oreocereus* diminished drastically. Plants occur in northern Argentina and southern Bolivia. They are found on sparsely to densely vegetated rocky slopes at elevations from about 10,000–12,300 feet.

Description These shrub-like plants have several columnar stems arising from near the base. Individual stems are short columns growing to about 1½–2 feet tall and 3–4 inches in diameter. Stems are adorned with 3–5 central and 10–15 radial, yellow, brown, or reddish **spines** to about 1–2 inches long that poke out beyond the dense white woolly hairs. Tubular pink to carmine colored flowers are about 2 inches long and visible beyond

Cool Cacti and Succulents for Hot Gardens

the white wool. The flowers will attract hummingbirds during the bloom season of spring and summer.

Culture Plants are cold hardy to about 20° F and can be used in USDA zones 9a–11. Even though these high elevation plants grow in full sun in habitat, they prefer to have a bit of filtered sunlight in summer in the hot summer cities of the desert southwest such as Palm Springs, Phoenix, and Tucson. If acclimated slowly, they might be able to tolerate more sun in cities with slightly cooler summer temperatures, but be prepared to shade your plants if they start to show any sunburn.

They are low-water-using, but will benefit from receiving supplemental water from late spring until daytime temperatures begin to cool in the fall. The growth rate is slow, so look for the largest plants you can afford.

Identification *Oreocereus trollii* is shorter with shorter **central spines** and denser white woolly hairs than *Oreocereus celsianus*.

Landscape Application These look great when several are used together in a **xeriscape** alongside other cacti and succulents and with spring or summer flowering perennials and small shrubs. Other cacti and succulents that would do well in your low-water-use landscape alongside *Oreocereus trollii* are *Agave ocahui*, *Ferocactus gracilis*, and *Yucca rostrata*. Some leafy plants that would look good include *Baileya multiradiata*, *Chrysactinia mexicana*, *Glandularia gooddingii*, *Penstemon eatonii*, *Telosiphonia brachysiphon*, and *Zinnia grandiflora*.

Precautions Protect young plants from javelina, rabbits, and possibly packrats, and be sure to give them a bit of shade in summer.

Pachycormus discolor
Elephant Tree
SHRUB-LIKE SUCCULENT, TREE-LIKE SUCCULENT

Etymology Botanist George Bentham used the Greek *dis-* meaning separate or two and the Latin *color-* for color, but it is unclear exactly to what he was referring.

SIZE (H x W)	2–5 (–15) feet x 2–4 (–10) feet
FLOWER COLOR	Pink or cream
FLOWER SEASON	Late spring to summer
EXPOSURE	Full sun, reflected heat
WATER	Low
GROWTH RATE	Slow
PRUNING	To shape as a tree
HARDINESS	High 20's F, zones 10a–11

Field Notes Travel along Mexico Highway 5 south from San Felipe toward San Luis Gonzaga, and these plants start popping up among the large granitic boulders in the desert. My friend Scott Calhoun and I camped out near Santa Ynés just north of Mexico Highway 1 in Baja California and woke up to these majestic plants scattered about between the granite boulders. There are stunning specimens to be

seen on the bouldery lava flows around Volcán Tres Virgenes in Baja California Sur. Plants growing near the coast on the Pacific Ocean side are frequently windswept, and low growing but very wide-spreading. The species occurs on the Baja California peninsula and adjacent islands from near sea level to 3,000 feet.

Description In their frost-free habitat, plants are mostly tree-like, growing to 6–15 feet tall and 5–10 feet across, and have 1–3 very thick main trunks that can reach 1–2 feet in diameter. However, in cultivation they are more often shrubs reaching about 2–5 feet tall with a trunk diameter of 6–8 inches. The **pinnate** leaves have 3–11 green slightly hairy **leaflets** that drop in summer and in times of drought. Clusters of pink or cream flowers appear in late spring to summer.

Culture Plants are winter growers and probably hardy to the high 20's F. They can be used as landscape plants in frost-free USDA zones 10a–11, but best grown in large pots in cities that experience colder winters. Place the pots against a south or west facing wall for the reflected heat provided during winter, or move potted plants under a covered patio for extra protection. Plants prefer a rocky or gritty soil that has excellent drainage. Water them when they have leaves, usually from fall through spring, and keep the soil from becoming too wet when the plants drop their leaves in spring and summer.

Identification The winter growing habit, slightly hairy **leaflets**, and thickened trunks with peeling bark all make for easy identification.

Landscape Application These are great landscape plants for frost-free cities or those that experience the occasional light frost such as parts of southern California and the Bay area, and are excellent container plants throughout most of the desert southwest if given protection from killing frost. Go full Sonoran Desert and plant with *Agave cerulata*, *Calliandra californica*, *Encelia californica*, *Ferocactus gracilis*, and *Fouquieria columnaris*.

Precautions These winter growers go dormant in summer so they should be given supplemental water when in leaf, usually winter, and kept dry when leafless, usually summer.

Pachycormus discolor **275**

Parodia leninghausii

Synonym: *Notocactus leninghausii*
Yellow Tower Cactus
CLUSTERING CACTUS

SIZE (H x W)	12–24 inches x 3–4 inches stem diameter, clusters to 12–24 inches
FLOWER COLOR	Yellow
FLOWER SEASON	Summer
EXPOSURE	Filtered sun, part shade
WATER	Low to moderate
GROWTH RATE	Moderate
PRUNING	None
HARDINESS	25° F, zones 9b–11

Etymology German botanist Karl Schumann named this species in honor of Guillermo Leninghaus when he named this in the genus *Echinocactus* in 1895. It was later moved to *Notocactus* and then finally to *Parodia*.

Field Notes I have yet to travel to Brazil where these are native, so do not have first-hand knowledge about their habitat and distribution. I searched iNaturalist and found that plants have been spotted and photographed among rocks and on cliffs in the mountains of southern Brazil from 650–2,000 feet elevation.

Description Plants grow as clusters of short narrow columns, with individual stems 12–24 inches tall and 3–4 inches in diameter, and clusters attaining a diameter of 12–24 inches. Green bodies turn gray at the base as the stems age. They have 30–35 straight ribs and clusters of 15–25 pale to deep yellow thin and hair-like **spines**. Numerous wide-open pale yellow or lemon-yellow flowers are 2–2½ inches in diameter and appear at the top of the plant primarily in summer.

Culture I have a potted specimen that has not been outside of my unheated greenhouse for winter, but plants are reportedly hardy to 25° F and can be used as a landscape plant in USDA zones 9b–11. They prefer filtered light and the winter protection of a desert tree in the very hot desert cities of Palm Springs, Phoenix, and Yuma. Provide some frost protection on the coldest nights and they can then be grown in large decorative pots in cities such as Sierra Vista, Tucson, Las Cruces, or Albuquerque. They are low- to moderate-water-using and will respond to supplemental water in summer, but watering frequency should be reduced in winter. They have a moderate growth rate and require several years to develop multiple stems if grown in small pots and not pampered.

Identification The taller narrower stems set *Parodia leninghausii* apart from the lower growing *Parodia magnifica* and *Parodia mammulosa* with their wider globose to short cylindric stems.

Landscape Application These can be used in a landscape in mild winter cities like Los Angeles, San Diego, Santa Barbara, and parts of the Bay area. Group several plants in a cactus and succulent garden in these mild winter areas and watch them grow. For a South American flavor, plant with cacti from the southern hemisphere that make either low clustering mounds or moderately tall columnar plants. Some ideas would include **Cleistocactus strausii**, **Gymnocalycium spegazzini**, and **Mammillaria geminispina**. These will benefit from having "leafy" plants nearby. Use *Berlandiera lyrata*, *Chrysactinia mexicana*, and *Dalea capitata*. Small trees like *Acacia constricta* or *Eysenhardtia orthocarpa* can provide a little shade in summer.

Precautions Protect young plants from sunburn and from the ravages of javelina, rabbits, or packrats. **Mealybugs** will hide between the ribs or on old flowers, and **spine mealies** can be manually removed from any **spines**.

Parodia leninghausii

Pedilanthus macrocarpus

Synonym: *Euphorbia lomelii*
Slipper Flower
SUCCULENT, SHRUB-LIKE SUCCULENT

Etymology English-born, American-trained botanist George Bentham used the Greek *macro-* for large and the Greek *carp-* for fruit to emphasize the large fruit on these plants.

SIZE (H x W)	3–6 feet x 3–6 feet
FLOWER COLOR	Orange-red
FLOWER SEASON	Spring to fall
EXPOSURE	Full sun, reflected heat
WATER	Drought tolerant to low
GROWTH RATE	Stems are moderately fast, but slow to fill in
PRUNING	None
HARDINESS	20° F, zones 9a–11

Field Notes There are basically two distinct forms; those with more blue-gray to gray-green stems and horned fruits are found primarily in Baja California, while those with greener stems and lacking the horns on the fruit are more common along the Gulf of California coast in Sonora and Sinaloa. Brian Kemble and I camped out in the Sierra San Francisco and saw several exquisite examples of these tucked into gaps between the rounded boulders. Plants are prevalent on the Baja California peninsula and near the coast in Sonora and Sinaloa, from near sea level to 2,700 feet elevation.

Description As these plants age, they produce many narrow wand-like branching stems that are 3–6 feet long and about ¼–½-inch in diameter. They become large and shrub-like growing 3–6 feet tall and 3–6 feet across. Individual stems vary from light to medium green and being curvy and snake-like to glaucous or grayish green and nearly completely straight and upright. Orange-red slipper-shaped flowers are about 1-inch-long and appear mainly from late spring through summer. Red rounded fruit with or without horn-like projections follow the flowers.

Culture   Plants are hardy to about 20° F and are ideal for use in USDA zones 9a–11. They are quite content growing in full sun or reflected heat even in the very hot desert cities of Palm Springs, Phoenix, Tucson, and Yuma. If provided some frost protection on the coldest nights, they can be grown in mid-elevation cities such as Sierra Vista and Las Cruces. Plants are drought tolerant to low-water-using, and once established, need no supplemental water. Individual stems grow at a moderately fast clip, but new stems are produced more slowly, and plants take a few years to fill in. If you do need to prune any stems, be sure to wear gloves without any holes in them because the stems are filled with milky latex that acts like a numbing agent that should be thoroughly washed off exposed skin.

Identification   *Pedilanthus macrocarpus* has red flowers and is a larger plant than the superficially similar ***Euphorbia antisyphilitica***.

Landscape Application   Use Slipper Flower either singly or in groups in a low-water-use landscape along with a mix of groundcovers, perennials, and small shrubs such *Chrysactinia mexicana*, *Dalea capitata*, *Menodora scabra*, and *Telosiphonia brachysiphon*. Plant alongside cacti and other succulents having contrasting forms and color such as ***Agave schidigera***, ***Astrophytum ornatum***, ***Echinocactus grusonii***, and ***Ferocactus gracilis***.

Precautions   These low-care plants have no obvious pest or disease problems. The milky latex tends to repel most browsing animals.

Peniocereus greggii
Queen of the Night
CACTUS

Etymology German-born, American-trained botanist George Engelmann named this for 19th Century American explorer Josiah Gregg.

Field Notes It is always a treat to see the splash of bright red fruits on these plants that are normally hidden in shrubs and low trees. I've seen them near Laguna Viesca in northern Coahuila while poking around the desert looking for interesting plants. My friend Rob Romero and I have found them hidden among mesquite trees and in open grasslands in southeastern Arizona. Plants are native from western Arizona to southern New Mexico and north-central Mexico. They are normally found under a nurse plant and frequently on flats in deeper soils or on gravelly benches, and degraded grassland, from about 600–5,000 feet elevation.

SIZE (H x W)	2–6 feet x ½–¾ inch wide stems
FLOWER COLOR	White
FLOWER SEASON	Summer
EXPOSURE	Filtered light
WATER	Drought tolerant to low
GROWTH RATE	Slow
PRUNING	None
HARDINESS	Stems to 15° F; roots to 10° F, zones 8a–11

Description Plants have few narrow stems arising from a small to large carrot-like or turnip-like underground tuber. Stems are grayish-green to purplish, single or sparingly branched, frequently supported by a nurse plant, and 1–6 feet long and about ½–¾-inch in diameter. There are 10–13 small **spines** at each areole. Large fragrant white flowers are 6–8 inches long and 2–4 inches in diameter, open for one night, and are visited by hawkmoths. Bright red 3-inch-long fruits follow the flowers.

Culture Stems are hardy to at least 15° F while roots are protected underground and can tolerate 10° F, so plants are fine in USDA zones 8a–11. These can tolerate full sun, but prefer being tucked under the shade and support of a dense shrub or low branched tree. They are drought tolerant to low-water-using once established. Stems grow at a moderate rate and the tubers enlarge slowly over time. No pruning is necessary, and any stems cut or removed will slow down the development of the plant.

Identification *Peniocereus greggii* has 4–6 ribs which distinguishes it from *Peniocereus striatus* with its skinny cylindrical stems.

Landscape Application Tuck several of these under spiny shrubs or trees with low growing branches so the stems get some shade and support. *Celtis pallida*, *Condalia* species, *Lycium* species, and shrub-like trees such as *Acacia constricta* and *Parkinsonia microphylla* make great nurse plants for this cactus. Plant them where they will be easy to see on a summer night when the plants flower. Add other shade tolerant cacti and succulents to provide some "eye-candy" while waiting for the Queen of the Night plants to bloom. Try using *Agave schidigera*, *Ferocactus glaucescens*, or *Mammillaria standleyi*. These make wonderful potted specimens which allows for easier viewing of the flowers.

Precautions Protect plants from rabbits, deer, and javelina because they find the stems to be tasty.

Peniocereus striatus
Synonym: *Wilcoxia striata*
Dahlia-rooted Cactus, Sacamatraca, Pitayita
CACTUS

SIZE (H x W)	1–8 feet x ¼–½-inch-wide stems
FLOWER COLOR	White
FLOWER SEASON	Summer
EXPOSURE	Filtered light
WATER	Low to moderate
GROWTH RATE	Moderate
PRUNING	None
HARDINESS	Stems to 30° F; roots to 25° F, zones 9b–11

Etymology Townshend Stith Brandegee was an American botanist who used the Latin *striat-* to emphasize the thin parallel lines on the stems.

Field Notes In October 2013, Bob Webb and I were looking for populations of *Agave sobria* in hills along Bahia Concepcion in Baja California Sur. I climbed up one particular rocky hill to check on the agaves there and spotted a *Peniocereus striatus* in fruit, so I worked my way across the rocks to snap a few digital images. Plants grow in sandy soil, alluvial plains, or low rocky hills throughout much of Baja California Sur, western Sonora, Sinaloa, and southwestern Arizona from near sea level to about 2,000 feet elevation.

Description Plants have one or more slender stems growing from tuberous roots. Individual stems are grayish and upright or scrambling up into shrubs eventually reaching 5–8 feet long but only about ¼–½-inch in diameter.

There are 8–9 low flat ribs separated by narrow grooves giving stems their striate appearance. The 5–12 small needle-like **spines** are light brown or gray and frequently fall off with age. Narrowly funnelform white flowers are about 4 inches long and 3 inches in diameter and open at night. Scarlet red 2-inch-long fruits follow.

Culture Stems are hardy to about 30° F while roots are protected underground and hardy to about 25° F. Plants can be grown in the landscape in USDA zones 9b–11 and in pots in colder zones if they are protected from frost. These are best grown in some shade under a nurse plant. They are low-water-using once established but flower production may increase if plants are given periodic supplemental water as the weather heats up. Growth rate is moderate with new stems appearing slowly with age. Only prune back damaged stems.

Identification Growth habit and thin stems are similar to *Echinocereus poselgeri*, but *Peniocereus striatus* has large white flowers that open at night, while the *Echinocereus* has large rose-pink or magenta flowers that open during the day.

Landscape Application These can be used for their surprise value when the flowers appear in summer. When planted under a nurse plant, they are inconspicuous until the large white flowers open on a warm summer night. Some great nurse plants include spiny shrubs such as *Celtis pallida* and *Zizyphus obtusifolia* or shrub-like trees such as *Acacia constricta* and *Parkinsonia microphylla*. Plant them where they will be easy to spot on a warm summer night as you wait for the flowers to appear. Use other shade tolerant cacti and succulents as "eye-candy" to fill the space. Try using **Agave bovicornuta** or **Echinocereus viereckii subsp. morricalii**. These make wonderful potted specimens that allow them to be grown closer to the house and make it more convenient to see the flowers.

Precautions Protect your plants from being eaten or damaged by rabbits, packrats, javelina, or deer.

Peniocereus striatus

Stenocactus multicostatus

Synonym: *Echinofossulocactus multicostatus*
Brain Cactus
SMALL CACTUS, CLUSTERING CACTUS

SIZE (H x W)	2–2½ inches x 3–4 inches
FLOWER COLOR	White with purplish-violet midstripe
FLOWER SEASON	Summer
EXPOSURE	Filtered light
WATER	Drought tolerant to low
GROWTH RATE	Moderate
PRUNING	None
HARDINESS	15° F, zones 8b–11

Etymology   Plantsman Heinrich Hildmann used the Latin *multi-* for many and the Latin *costa-* for ribs to accentuate the numerous ribs on these plants.

Field Notes   In July 2008, Chad Davis and I were west of General Cepeda in southern Coahuila looking at cool cacti when we came across *Stenocactus multicostatus* plants growing on a rocky hillside. Eight years later, I was back in the same general area with three other plant nerds, and we saw more of these cool little plants growing on another rocky hillside among a variety of shrubs and grasses alongside **Thelocactus bicolor**. The four of us also saw plants growing in pine needle-covered soil in the Sierra Madre Oriental south of Galeana in Nuevo León. *Stenocactus multicostatus* is found growing on rocky hills in southern Coahuila and in the Sierra Madre Oriental of Nuevo León and Tamaulipas from about 5,200–8,200 feet elevation.

Description In habitat, plants are usually solitary with a depressed globose body about 2–2½ inches tall and 3–4 inches across. While under cultivation they may get slightly larger and grow more than one body to form small clusters to 12–15 inches across. At maturity, these have about 100 thin sharply angled wavy ribs evoking the common name of Brain Cactus. There are 3 **central spines** and 4 **radial spines** at each **areole**. Flowers are 1-inch-long, and white with a purplish-violet midstripe.

Culture These are hardy to at least 15° F and can be used in the landscape in USDA zones 8b–11. Plants grow best in filtered light whether in a pot or the landscape. They are drought tolerant to low-water-using, but will show signs of stress if kept too dry in the heat of summer. The growth rate is moderate and can be sped up slightly by giving the plants some supplemental water from spring through summer.

Identification With its 100+ thin wavy ribs, Stenocactus multicostatus is easily distinguished from all other species. Other species in the genus to look for include: Stenocactus coptogonus is mostly solitary with few ribs and short **spines**; Stenocactus ochoterananus is solitary with many thin **radial spines**, long **central spines**, and pink flowers; and Stenocactus vaupelianus which is solitary with long **central spines**, densely woolly, and with yellow flowers.

Landscape Application These small plants are perfect for growing in decorative containers or planting in the ground if you have a clustering specimen. Plant in a small cactus and succulent garden with similar size plants such as **Ariocarpus fissuratus**, **Mammillaria grusonii**, **Obregonia denegrii**, and **Thelocactus bicolor**. Plant under the shade of small trees like Acacia constricta or Eysenhardtia orthocarpa.

Precautions Plants will likely be nibbled on by packrats and virtually destroyed by hungry javelina, so protect them from predation.

Stenocereus alamosensis
Octopus Cactus
SHRUB-LIKE CACTUS

Etymology John Merle Coulter named this species for its occurrence near Alamos, Sonora.

SIZE (H x W)	6–10 feet x 6–10 feet
FLOWER COLOR	Red
FLOWER SEASON	Summer
EXPOSURE	Full sun, filtered sun, part shade
WATER	Low to moderate
GROWTH RATE	Moderate
PRUNING	None or remove frozen growth
HARDINESS	Mid-20's F, zones 9b–11

Field Notes The material used for the original description was collected near Alamos, Sonora, but these plants have a wide-spread distribution. I encountered them while hiking in the Sierra de Alamos. They are found from near the coast and into the foothills of the Sierra Madre Occidental in central Sonora and Sinaloa. Plants occur from near sea level to about 2,000 feet elevation.

Description These plants have several narrow dark green stems that grow to 6–10 feet tall and arch out reaching 6–10 feet or more across. Individual stems are about 2 inches in diameter and covered with clusters of stout **spines**. The 4 **central spines** are ¾–1-inch-long, and are longer than the 15–18 **radial spine**s. Red flowers are tubular to funnel-shaped, about 1½ inches long, and attract hummingbirds when they appear in summer.

Cool Cacti and Succulents for Hot Gardens

Culture Gene Joseph at Plants for the Southwest in Tucson had plants come through winter low temperatures in the mid-20's F with no damage. These should be great landscape plants for shady areas in USDA zones 9b–11 and possibly in zone 9a although they might suffer minor damage when winter overnight lows dip to 20° F. Plants are low- to moderate-water-using when the temperatures heat up, but the soil should be kept dry in winter. These do best when placed in full sun, or some shade in cities with very hot summers such as Phoenix, Tucson, and Yuma.

Identification Narrowly cylindric arching stems and red funnel-shaped flowers are distinctive features of *Stenocereus alamosensis*.

Landscape Application Find a spot under the canopy of a deciduous or semi-deciduous desert tree such as *Acacia constricta*, or *Eysenhardtia orthocarpa*, and allow ample room for the plants to spread. Use these with other shade-loving accent plants, perennials, and small shrubs including **Agave bovicornuta**, **Agave ovatifolia**, *Ageratum corymbosum*, *Aquilegia chrysantha*, *Conoclinium dissectum*, *Dioon edule*, **Gymnocalycium spegazzini**, *Heuchera sanguinea*, and *Poliomintha maderensis*.

Precautions Although these are generally easy to care for, protect them from rabbits and packrats for the first couple years in the landscape.

Stenocereus eruca
Creeping Devil
SPRAWLING CACTUS

SIZE (H x W)	2–5 feet x 2–5 inch stem diameter
FLOWER COLOR	White at the base, rose-pink to lavender at tip
FLOWER SEASON	Summer
EXPOSURE	Full sun
WATER	Drought tolerant to low
GROWTH RATE	Moderate
PRUNING	None
HARDINESS	25° F, zones 9b–11

Etymology Townsend Stith Brandegee used the Latin *eruc-*, which means caterpillar, for the species name because he stated that the uplifted heads and reflexed spines give the plants a resemblance to huge caterpillars.

Field Notes The first time I saw these plants in Baja California, we were camped among them and awoke to a foggy morning. Looking out of my tent, I could see the tips of the plants poking above the sand and barely visible through the fog. I saw them again in 2018 while driving on the Ciudad Insurgentes-La Purisima highway in Baja California Sur. These have a limited distribution in Baja California Sur along the Pacific coast from about sea-level to 200 feet elevation.

Description Stems are **prostrate** with the tip slightly **ascending**. Individual branches can root as they grow and can reach 2–10 feet long by about 3–5 inches in diameter. **Spines** are strongly reflexed and about 2–3 inches long. Flowers are white at the base, grading into rose-pink, and slightly lavender at the tips, about 5 inches long, and open at night.

Culture   Plants are hardy to about 25° F and can be grown in USDA zones 9b–11.   Grow in full sun and a sandy fast-draining soil for best growth. The growth rate is moderate, but plants flourish in the ground with minimal care. They are drought tolerant to low-water-using, and will tolerate supplemental water in spring and summer if the soil has perfect drainage. No need for any pruning, although new plants can be started by stem cuttings.

Identification   These are such unusual and distinctive plants that they cannot be confused other cacti.

Landscape Application   Plants can be grown in a **xeriscape** or cactus and succulent garden in many cities in the desert southwest. They have thrived in Los Angeles, Phoenix, and Tucson if the soil has good drainage. They are eye-catching because of their unusual growth habit. Go full on Baja California and plant with non-cactus succulents such as ***Agave sobria***, ***Fouquieria splendens***, and *Yucca valida*. Mix in spring or summer flowering perennials and small shrubs for a spectacular color display. Try using *Anisacanthus thurberi*, *Ambrosia bryantii*, *Calliandra californica*, *Encelia californica*, *Ruellia peninsularis*, and *Zinnia acerosa*.

Precautions   Plants are relatively carefree in most situations, but the soil needs to have excellent drainage.

Stenocereus eruca

Stenocereus marginatus

Synonym: *Pachycereus marginatus*
Mexican Fence Post
COLUMNAR CACTUS

Etymology Augustin de Candolle used the Latin *margin-* for the appearance of a continuous margin formed by the seemingly connected areoles.

SIZE (H x W)	5–10 feet x 3–5 feet
FLOWER COLOR	Pinkish-red to red
FLOWER SEASON	Spring to summer
EXPOSURE	Full sun
WATER	Drought tolerant to low
GROWTH RATE	Moderate
PRUNING	None
HARDINESS	Mid-20's F, zones 9b–11

Field Notes Stems of these are frequently planted as an informal fencing to keep in animals, but to see them growing wild is special. Frequent traveling companion Brian Kemble and I stopped for these growing without cultivation in the state of Hidalgo, Mexico while returning from the spectacular Barranca de Toliman. In the wild, these are found mostly in central and southern Mexico from about 4,600–8,500 feet elevation.

Description This cactus has several narrow upright stems to 5–10 feet tall and 5–8 inches in diameter, and clustering to 3–5 feet or more across. There can be 4–7 ribs, usually 5, with numerous **areoles** that are nearly connected and give the appearance of a continuous line or "margin." There are 1–3 **central spines** and 5–9 **radial spines**, all less than ½-inch-long. Flowers are tubular, less than 2 inches long, pinkish-red to reddish on the outside and pinkish or white inside. Flowering is primarily in late spring and summer.

Culture Plants are hardy to about the mid-20's F and are suitable for the landscape in USDA zones 9b–11, and even 9a with some winter protection. Use these in full sun or even against a south or west facing wall for extra warmth in winter. Plants are low-water-using or even drought tolerant once established, but they will respond to periodic supplemental water in summer. However, they should be kept dry in winter. No pruning is necessary unless stems get frozen. Wait until spring to cut dead stems.

Identification *Stenocereus marginatus* plants are easily recognized by the close-set **areoles** that appear to form a continuous line.

Landscape Application Mexican Fence Post plants can be used singly as a strong vertical focal point in a cactus and succulent garden or in a mixed **xeriscape** with colorful perennials and small to medium-sized shrubs. Use them with succulents and other cacti such as ***Agave gentryi***, ***Dasylirion acrotrichum***, ***Echinocactus grusonii***, ***Hesperaloe funifera***, ***Opuntia santa-rita***, and ***Yucca torreyi***. Plant several spring flowering perennials such as *Baileya multiradiata, Glandularia gooddingii, Penstemon parryi, Tetraneuris acaulis,* and *Thymophylla pentachaeta*. These tall plants will eventually stand above shrubs like *Anisacanthus quadrifidus, Buddleja marrubiifolia, Calliandra californica,* and *Leucophyllum candidum*. They work well in wide-open spaces seen on highway on/off ramps and industrial parks.

Precautions Protect young plants and growing tips from frost and sun, and keep rabbits and javelina away for the first two or three years after planting.

Stenocereus thurberi
Synonym: *Lemaireocereus thurberi*
Organ Pipe Cactus
COLUMNAR CACTUS

SIZE (H x W)	6–20 feet x 4–8 feet
FLOWER COLOR	Pale pink to lavender
FLOWER SEASON	Spring to summer
EXPOSURE	Full sun, reflected heat
WATER	Drought tolerant to low
GROWTH RATE	Slow
PRUNING	None
HARDINESS	Mid-20's F, zones 9b–11

Etymology   German-born, American-trained botanist George Engelmann honored American botanist George Thurber who first collected this in Sonora, Mexico.

Field Notes   While hiking through Organ Pipe Cactus National Monument, be on the lookout for these multi-stemmed wonders that reach the northern end of their distribution there. Take a drive from Tucson south of the border to Hermosillo, Sonora and you will see classic examples of this cactus among the desert vegetation. In the heart of their range, plants are locally common on slopes and plains where they grow in sandy or gravelly desert soil. These are found in southern Arizona, throughout much of Sonora, northern Sinaloa, and Baja California Sur from near sea level to 3,600 feet elevation.

Description   These are columnar cacti with multiple upright stems arising from the base or a short trunk. Each stem is about 6–8 inches in diameter and can grow to 6–20 feet tall with ancient plants achieving a spread of 4–8 feet. Narrow stems have 12–19 ribs and **spine** clusters have 1–3 **central spines** and about 12 **radial spines**, all being straight, gray to black, and 1–2 inches long. White or pink to lavender funnel-shape flowers are night-blooming, about 3–4 inches long, and appear in spring and summer. Variety *littoralis* has flowers that are deep pink and open during the day. (photo below).

Culture   Plants are hardy to about the mid-20's F and make great landscape subjects for USDA zones 9b–11 and possibly 9a if planted in a reflected heat situation or given some winter protection. Plants are drought tolerant once established but will benefit from receiving supplemental water in summer, especially in the very hot southwestern U.S. cities of Palm Springs, Phoenix, and Yuma, but keep soil dry in winter. Plants are slow growing, so start with large plants. In hot summer cities, *Stenocereus thurberi* subsp. *littoralis* prefers some shade in summer.

Identification   *Stenocereus thurberi* is not easily confused with any other *Stenocereus* species. *Stenocereus thurberi* subsp. *littoralis* is a smaller plant with thinner stems.

Landscape Application   Plan your garden around this centerpiece and use masses of smaller cacti, succulents, perennials, and small or medium size shrubs to complete the landscape. Some other cacti and succulents that work well with Organ Pipe are **Agave deserti**, **Echinocactus grusonii**, **Ferocactus gracilis**, and **Fouquieria splendens**. For seasonal color, try using *Calliandra californica*, *Justicia californica*, and *Penstemon parryi*. These are great for wide-open spaces like freeway on/off ramps and large landscapes around big buildings.

Precautions   Protect young plants and tips of stems from frost, and screen them from rabbits and javelina until they are established.

Stenocereus thurberi

Thelocactus bicolor
Glory of Texas
SMALL CACTUS, CLUSTERING CACTUS

SIZE (H x W)	4–15 inches x 1–7 inches
FLOWER COLOR	Magenta with red in center
FLOWER SEASON	Spring and summer
EXPOSURE	Full sun
WATER	Drought tolerant to low
GROWTH RATE	Moderate
PRUNING	None
HARDINESS	10° F, zones 8a–11

Etymology Frenchman Henri Galeotti used the Latin *bicolor*, a reference to the two colors in the flower.

Field Notes A stop at Cerro Bola in 2006 resulted in my first exporsure to *Thelocactus bicolor*. In 2016, Jeff Chemnick, Brian Kemble, Walker Young, and I were driving along a dirt side road to the south of Coahuila Highway 105 looking for cool cacti and stopped for plants of *Thelocactus bicolor* growing tucked next to limestone rock on a low grassy hill. Plants grow on limestone or among limestone rocks. The species is native from west Texas south into the Chihuahuan Desert from 250–7,900 feet.

Description Plants have small cylindrical bodies that are 4–15 inches tall and 1–7 inches in diameter. They are mostly single-stemmed but sometimes clustering as in subsp. *bolaensis*. Colorful **spines** are yellowish white to reddish purple, and ½–1¾-inch-long. Magenta flowers are darker red in the center, 2–3 inches in diameter, and can attract both bees and hummingbirds. Plants bloom several times in spring and summer. There are several subspecies, each with their own interesting traits. Collect them all, including: *bolaensis*, *flavidispinus*, *schottii*, and *schwarzii*.

Culture Plants are hardy to 10° F without sustaining frost damage and are perfect for USDA zones 8a–11. Young or newly planted plants will need some protection from the full sun, but established ones can tolerate full sun even in hot summer cities of Palm Springs, Phoenix, and Tucson.

They are drought tolerant to low-water-using once established, but plants may produce more flowers when watered every 2–3 weeks as the weather heats up. Plants have a moderate growth rate and can add an inch or more of growth every year when grown in the ground and given extra water in summer.

Identification The darker red at the base of the flowers is quite distinctive among the genus.

Landscape Application As small plants, these work well in smaller yards so frequently seen in new housing developments. Plant several of them in a cactus and succulent garden where boulders are used to provide backdrops for plants. Use small flowering perennials to help shade and cool the soil, and give seasonal color in the landscape. Some great plants to include are *Glandularia gooddingii*, *Hymenoxys acaulis*, and *Thymophylla pentachaeta*. These can also be grown in decorative pots and featured in a collection along with other smaller cacti and succulents.

Precautions Protect the plants from rabbits, packrats, and javelina for the first couple years in the landscape.

Dense white spines seen on *Thelocactus bicolor* var. *bolaensis*

Thelocactus buekii
Buek's Thelocactus
SMALL CACTUS

SIZE (H x W)	1–5 inches x 3–7 inches
FLOWER COLOR	Magenta
FLOWER SEASON	Spring to summer
EXPOSURE	Filtered sun
WATER	Drought tolerant to low
GROWTH RATE	Moderate
PRUNING	None
HARDINESS	15° F, zones 8b–11

Etymology This plant was named by Jacob Klein in 1859 for German botanist Heinrich Buek.

Field Notes In 2016, I was with three other cactus and succulent fanatics scouting out locations for a tour the next year. While driving along an unnumbered road in Nuevo León, we stopped at a limestone hill that looked to have potential for interesting plants, and one of the first ones we saw was *Thelocactus buekii* with a flower advertising its location. We found more plants further up the hill tucked among limestone rocks and hidden by low-growing grasses. Three years later, Tristan Davis and I stopped at the same hill to see these and all the other very cool cacti. Plants prefer limestone soil, rarely gypsum, in xeric vegetation only in Nuevo León from about 3,000–6,900 feet elevation.

Description These have a single depressed to globose body 1–5 inches tall and 3–7 inches in diameter. Bodies are dark olive-green to reddish brown with conical **tubercles** topped by 1–7 straight or slightly curved grayish **central spines** that are up to 3 inches long and 4–12 grayish **radial spines** that are about

1-inch-long. Magenta flowers are 1½–3 inches in diameter and bloom several times throughout summer.

Culture Plants have tolerated winter low temperatures in the range of 15°–20° F and can be considered hardy in USDA zones 8b–11. Established plants prefer filtered sun in hot summer cities of Palm Springs, Phoenix, Tucson, and Yuma, but can tolerate more sun in cooler summer cities of Las Cruces and Sierra Vista. They are low-water-using once established, but should flower more often when watered every 2–3 weeks as the weather heats up. Plants have a moderate growth rate and can add an inch or more of growth every year when grown in the ground and given extra water in summer. Do not even think about pruning these plants!

Identification *Thelocactus buekii* has magenta flowers and a flat body with **tubercles** not aligned as ribs, while *Thelocactus tulensis* has taller bodies with **tubercles** aligned as ribs and white to light pink flowers.

Landscape Application These smaller plants fit well in postage stamp sized yards frequently seen in new housing developments. Use them singly or in groups with other cacti such as ***Coryphantha poselgeriana***, ***Echinocereus parkeri***, and ***Mammillaria grusonii***, and place near boulders that can be used as backdrops for plants. Plant small flowering perennials to help shade and cool soil and to give seasonal color in the landscape. Some great choices would be *Baileya multiradiata*, *Glandularia gooddingii*, *Justicia longii*, *Tetraneuris acaulis*, *Thymophylla pentachaeta*, and *Zinnia acerosa*. Small grasses like *Bouteloua barbata* and bulbs like *Cooperia drummondii* and *Zephyranthes citrina* are perfect for providing some cover for *Thelocactus buekii*. Plants can also be grown in decorative pots and featured in a collection along with other smaller cacti and succulents.

Precautions It would be a good idea to protect the plants from rabbits, packrats, and javelina for the first couple years in the landscape.

Thelocactus conothelos
Cone-like Thelocactus
SMALL CACTUS

Etymology Jacob Klein and Eduard August von Regel used the Greek *konos-* for cone and the Greek *thele-* for **tubercle** to describe the cone-shaped **tubercles** on this species.

SIZE (H x W)	2–10 inches x 3–7 inches
FLOWER COLOR	White, magenta, yellow, orange
FLOWER SEASON	Late winter to late spring
EXPOSURE	Filtered sun
WATER	Low
GROWTH RATE	Moderate
PRUNING	None
HARDINESS	15° F, zones 8b–11

Field Notes There is a wide variety of intriguing plants along the logging road that goes from La Peña in southern Tamaulipas up into the high elevation of Cerro Peña Nevada. In 2014, I was on this road with Jeff Chemnick and Brian Kemble when we stopped to look at **Nolina nelsonii** and found plants of *Thelocactus conothelos*. Plants occur in xeric vegetation on limestone hills in Nuevo León, San Luis Potosí, and Tamaulipas from about 4,000–7,200 feet elevation.

Description These have a single globose body 2–10 inches tall and 3–7 inches in diameter. Bodies are dark olive-green to reddish brown with conical **tubercles** topped by 4 grayish **central spines** that are up to 3 inches long and 7–20 grayish ½-inch-long **radial spines**. White, yellow, orange, or magenta flowers are 2–2½ inches in diameter and bloom several times throughout summer. In addition to subspecies *conothelos*, there are three others: *aurantiacus*, *saussieri*, and **argenteus**, which is quite distinct and treated on the following pages.

Culture Plants in Tucson have tolerated winter low temperatures of 15° F and can be considered hardy in USDA zones 8b–11. They prefer filtered sun in hot summer cities of Palm Springs, Phoenix, Tucson, and Yuma, but can tolerate more sun in cooler summer cities of Las Cruces, San Diego, and Sierra Vista. They are drought tolerant to low-water-using once established but should flower more often when watered every 2–3 weeks as the weather heats up. Plants have a moderate growth rate and can add an inch or more of growth every year when in the ground and given extra water in summer.

Identification *Thelocactus conothelos*, ***Thelocactus buekii***, and *Thelocactus tulensis* can all have dark olive-green bodies. *Thelocactus conothelos* tends to have more green in the body with conical **tubercles** pointing up, while ***Thelocactus buekii*** tends to have a flatter body with fewer **spines**, and *Thelocactus tulensis* tends to have wispier **spines**. The yellow and orange flowered varieties are very easy to identify.

Landscape Application This cactus works well in the smaller yards often seen in new housing developments. Use them singly or in groups and mixed with small flowering perennials in a **xeriscape** or a cactus and succulent garden. Some great perennials to include are *Baileya multiradiata, Justicia longii, Tetraneuris acaulis,* and *Thymophylla pentachaeta*. A small grass such as *Bouteloua barbata* could also be used to provide some shade. Try planting alongside succulents and other cacti such as ***Agave victoriae-reginae***, ***Astrophytum coahuilense***, ***Coryphantha poselgeriana***, ***Hesperaloe campanulata***, and ***Mammillaria grusonii***. Grow these in decorative pots and keep in a collection along with other smaller cacti and succulents.

Precautions It would be a good idea to protect the plants from rabbits, packrats, and javelina for the first couple years in the landscape.

Thelocactus conothelos subsp. *argenteus*
Silver-spine Thelocactus
SMALL CACTUS

SIZE (H x W)	3–7 inches x 5–6 inches
FLOWER COLOR	Magenta
FLOWER SEASON	Late winter to summer
EXPOSURE	Filtered sun
WATER	Low
GROWTH RATE	Moderate
PRUNING	None
HARDINESS	15° F, zones 8b–11

Etymology Charles Glass and Robert Foster used the Latin *argent-* meaning silver for the silvery white spines on this subspecies of *Thelocactus conothelos*.

Field Notes Arguably, this is the most attractive subspecies of ***Thelocactus conothelos***. It is restricted to the Valley of La Ascención in Nuevo León. In June 2016, Jeff Chemnick, Brian Kemble, and I stopped at a limestone hill and found plants of *Thelocactus conothelos* subsp. *argenteus* growing in crevices and pockets of soil at the base of large limestone rocks. I returned to the same area in May 2019 with my friend Tristan Davis to get more photos of these spectacular plants. Plants occur in xeric vegetation on limestone hills in Nuevo León from about 5,500–6,900 feet elevation.

Description Plants have a single globose to elongate body 3–7 inches tall and 5–6 inches across. The conical **tubercles** are not aligned into ribs and are topped by 4–6 straight needle-like 1–2-inch-long silvery white **central spines** and 20–25 silvery white needle-like **radial spines**. Magenta flowers are about 2 inches wide and bloom several times from late winter to summer and might occasionally be visited by hummingbirds.

Culture Botanist Matt Johnson has plants that have been through winter lows of 15° F without incurring damage, so consider these hardy in USDA zones 8b–11. These are best grown in filtered sun in hot summer cities of Palm Springs, Phoenix, Tucson, and Yuma, but should be able to tolerate more sun in cooler summer cities of Las Cruces, San Diego, and Sierra Vista. They are low-water-using once established doing well when watered every 10–14 days as the weather heats up. Plants have a moderate growth rate, taking several years to achieve baseball size. No pruning is ever needed, so just sit around enjoying them.

Identification *Thelocactus conothelos* subsp. *argenteus* tends to have slightly more pronounced **tubercles** than does *Thelocactus macdowellii*.

Landscape Application With showy snow-white spines when mature, these are best used in a spot where they can be seen every day. They fit well in smaller yards that have become the norm in many new housing developments. Plants really stand out when used in front of large dark colored rocks in a xeric garden. Intersperse showy perennials and similar sized cacti. Some suggested perennials are *Tetraneuris acaulis*, and *Zinnia grandiflora*, while compatible cacti and succulents include **Agave victoriae-reginae**, **Astrophytum myriostigma**, and **Mammillaria chionocephala**. These look great in decorative pots and displayed alongside other smaller cacti and succulents.

Precautions Keep plants lightly shaded in cities where summer temperatures routinely climb into triple digits. Inspect the plants closely for **mealybugs** as they can hide beneath the dense spination.

Thelocactus conothelos subsp. argenteus

Thelocactus heterochromus

Synonym: *Thelocactus bicolor* subsp. *heterochromus*
Showy Thelocactus
SMALL CACTUS

SIZE (H x W)	2–4 inches x 4–6 inches
FLOWER COLOR	Magenta with red throat
FLOWER SEASON	Summer to fall
EXPOSURE	Minimal shade, full sun
WATER	Low
GROWTH RATE	Moderately slow
PRUNING	None
HARDINESS	15° F, zones 8b–11

Etymology Frédéric A. C. Weber was a French botanist who chose to use the Greek *hetero-* for different and the Greek *chrom-* for color when describing this species.

Field Notes In July 2008, My friend Chad Davis and I were driving along a nearly deserted two-lane highway in the state of Durango, Mexico on our way back to Arizona when we saw a white flowered form of *Leucophyllum laevigatum*. I hit the brakes while looking for a safe place to pull off the road. While poking around the area, I spied the bright magenta flower of *Thelocactus heterochromus* partially hidden among rocks and low grasses. Plants grow in pebbly limestone soil on flats and hills in Chihuahua and Durango from about 4,300–7,200 feet elevation.

Description These have a single slightly flattened or globose body 2–4 inches tall and 4–6 inches across. Bodies are green with rounded **tubercles** that are aligned to form ribs. Each **tubercle** has 1–4 straight or slightly curved 1–2-inch-long **central spines** and 6–10 straight or slightly curved 1½-inch-long **radial spines**. Flowers are magenta with a red throat 1–3 inches wide and will bloom several times in summer and into fall. Bees and the occasional hummingbird will visit the flowers.

Culture Cultivated plants in Tucson have been through a winter low of 15° F without sustaining damage and can be used in USDA zones 8b–11. These are best grown in minimal shade in hot summer cities of Palm Springs, Phoenix, Yuma, and Tucson, but should

be able to tolerate more sun in cooler summer cities of Las Cruces, San Diego, and Sierra Vista. If these are grown in too much shade, the plants become **etiolated**. They are low-water-using once established doing well when watered every 10–14 days in summer. Plants have a moderately slow growth rate, taking several years to achieve baseball size, so start with a large plant.

Identification *Thelocactus heterochromus* has a darker green body, rounded **tubercles**, and 1–4 **central spines** that are white with red bands while *Thelocactus hexaedrophorus* has a grayish green body, **tubercles** that are subtly pointed, and 0–1 **central spines**, and fewer **radial spines** that are generally mostly all white or grayish white.

Landscape Application These attractive plants are on the small side and should be placed where they can be seen every day. Use large rocks as a backdrop in a xeric garden, and plant small perennials, similar sized cacti, and the occasional large accent plant. Some suggested plants are *Amoreuxia palmatifida*, *Hibiscus coulteri*, *Tetraneuris acaulis*, and *Thymophylla pentachaeta*. These are perfect for growing in decorative pots and showing off in a collection along with other smaller cacti and succulents.

Precautions Mealybugs like to hide under **spine** clusters and between the ribs.

Thelocactus heterochromus

Thelocactus hexaedrophorus
Six-sided Nipple Cactus
SMALL CACTUS

SIZE (H x W)	2–4 inches x 4–6 inches
FLOWER COLOR	White or pink
FLOWER SEASON	Spring to fall
EXPOSURE	Filtered sun
WATER	Low
GROWTH RATE	Moderate
PRUNING	None
HARDINESS	15° F, zones 8b–11

Etymology Frenchman Charles Antoine Lemaire used the Greek *hexa-* meaning six and the Greek *phoros-* meaning carrying, a reference to the 6-angled **tubercles** on the plant body.

Field Notes One summer, my friend Chad Davis and I spotted *Thelocactus hexaedrophorus* on a low hill between Matehuala and Doctor Arroyo while looking for *Pelecyphora strobiliformis*. Years later, in May 2019, my friend Tristan Davis (no relation to Chad) and I were stomping around on a hill in Nuevo León when we came across more small plants, several of which had a very attractive orange-red blush on the body. These can be found growing with desert scrub and in grasslands on gentle slopes and plains in limestone soil in north-central Mexico from 3,200–7,500 feet elevation.

Description These have a single body that is slightly flattened or globose to 2–4 inches tall and 4–6 inches across. In cultivation, the body is typically more rounded and either blue-green or gray-green. **Tubercles** are rounded and topped by 0–1 white **central spines** that are up to 1-inch-long, and 4–8 straight or slightly curved **radial spines** that are white and up to 2 inches long. Flowers are white or pink, 2–4 inches wide, and will bloom several times in spring, summer, and fall.

Culture Cultivated plants in Tucson have been through low temperatures of 15° F without suffering any frost damage and are considered hardy in USDA zones 8b–11. They can tolerate full sun even in hot summer cities of Palm Springs,  Phoenix, Tucson, and Yuma but need to be acclimated slowly. These can be grown in very light shade, but too much shade will cause the plants to become **etiolated**. They are low-water-using once established doing well when watered every 10–14 days in summer. Plants have a moderate growth rate.

Identification *Thelocactus hexaedrophorus* has a gray-green or blue-green body and 0–1 **central spines** and **radial spines** that are generally mostly all white or grayish white while *Thelocactus heterochromus* has a darker green body and 1–4 **central spines** that are white with red bands. Variety *lloydii* has more rounded tubercles and lacks the central spine.

Landscape Application Because of their smaller size, group several together for a more impressive impact, especially when flowering. Use these near large rocks in a xeric garden along with other cacti and succulents such as *Agave parrasana*, *Astrophytum myriostigma*, *Fouquieria splendens*, *Mammillaria candida*, and *Yucca rostrata*. Mix in some small perennials such as *Amoreuxia palmatifida*, *Dalea wrightii*, *Hibiscus martianus*, *Justicia longii*, *Tetraneuris acaulis*, and *Zinnia acerosa*. These look great in decorative pots in a collection with other smaller cacti.

Precautions Inspect the plants closely for **mealybugs** as they can hide under **spine** clusters, between the **tubercles**, and more prominently on **spines**.

Thelocactus macdowellii
MacDowell's Thelocactus
SMALL CACTUS

SIZE (H x W)	2–5 inches x 3–5 inches
FLOWER COLOR	Magenta to pinkish
FLOWER SEASON	Late winter to summer
EXPOSURE	Full sun, filtered sun
WATER	Low
GROWTH RATE	Moderately fast
PRUNING	None
HARDINESS	15° F, zones 8b–11

Etymology Leopold Quehl was a German amateur botanist who named this in honor of plant collector J.A. MacDowell.

Field Notes While helping Jeff Chemnick lead a cactus expedition in northeastern Mexico the group went to a canyon outside of Saltillo, Coahuila in hopes of finding *Thelocactus macdowellii*. Alas, none of the eagle-eyed plant geeks were able to find a single plant and I must wonder if we were in the wrong side canyon. Looks like a trip back to the mountains northeast of Saltillo is in order. These typically grow in Chihuahuan Desert scrub on limestone slopes and hills in Coahuila and Nuevo León from about 3,100–5,200 feet elevation with one locality recorded at close to 7,900 feet.

Description Plants have a single green globose body 2–5 inches tall and 3–5 inches across. Bodies are obscured by the dense covering of silver-white **spines** giving the plant the look of a snowball. There are 2–4 straight silver-white to pure white central spines up to 2 inches long, and 15–25 straight **radial spines** that are pure white and about 1-inch-long. Magenta to pinkish flowers are

Cool Cacti and Succulents for Hot Gardens

1½–3 inches wide and will bloom several times from late winter through spring and even summer, with the occasional hummingbird looking for nourishment.

Culture Cultivated plants have survived overnight low temperatures of 15° F without sustaining any frost damage, so these can be considered hardy in USDA zones 8b–11. Plants will tolerate full sun in cities where summer temperatures stay below triple digits if they have been acclimated slowly over the course of 2–3 years. If grown in too much shade, the plants will stretch and become **etiolated**. If they are put in full sun without being acclimated, the plants will sunburn severely. Whether in pots or in the ground, they are low-water-using. Plants have a moderate growth rate, so be patient and enjoy watching them grow.

Identification *Thelocactus macdowellii* and ***Thelocactus conothelos* subsp. *argenteus*** are very difficult to tell apart, and I cannot offer any real tips other than the latter tends to have more pronounced **tubercles**.

Landscape Application These small plants are perfect for use in a scaled down cactus and succulent garden or in a decorative pot in a cactus collection. Group several together among a jumble of large rocks along with other smaller cacti and succulents such as ***Agave victoriae-reginae***, ***Astrophytum myriostigma***, ***Echinocereus reichenbachii***, and ***Mammillaria candida***. Mix in some small perennials for seasonal flowers but not so many as to cover up the smaller cacti. Try using *Amoreuxia palmatifida*, *Hibiscus denudatus*, *Tetraneuris acaulis*, and *Zinnia grandiflora*.

Precautions Whether in the ground or in pots keep them away from places accessible to javelina. Inspect the plants closely for **mealybugs** as they will hide between **tubercles** and on **spines**. Slowly acclimate the plants to full sun situations in the landscape to keep them healthy and thriving.

Thelocactus rinconensis
Nipple Cactus
SMALL CACTUS

SIZE (H x W)	2–6 inches x 4–8 inches
FLOWER COLOR	White, yellowish, or pink
FLOWER SEASON	Spring to fall
EXPOSURE	Full sun
WATER	Low
GROWTH RATE	Moderate
PRUNING	None
HARDINESS	15° F, zones 8b–11

Etymology 19th Century German botanist Heinrich Poselger named this species for its occurrence near La Rinconada in Nuevo León.

Field Notes In July 2009, my friend Scott Calhoun and I were driving along a dirt road northeast of Saltillo, Coahuila and stopped to photograph a flowering plant of *Anisacanthus quadrifidus*. While walking among the desert vegetation, we saw plants of *Thelocactus rinconensis* scattered about both in the open and nestled among a low growing *Calliandra* species. I have also seen really nice plants while traveling from Miquihuana in southern Tamaulipas to Dr. Arroyo in Coahuila. Plants are found in open desert scrub and occasionally mountain slopes on limestone soil in the Chihuahuan Desert of Coahuila and Nuevo León from about 2,000–6,500 feet elevation.

Description Plants usualy have a single globose to flattened globose blue-green body 2–6 inches tall and 4–8 inches across, rarely will they cluster with multiple bodies. Distinct nipple-like **tubercles** are elongated, conical, and angled, measuring ½–1-inch-long and topped with up to 5 **radial spines**

and 3–4 **central spines** that are 2–3 inches long and can be thin and flexible or thick and stiff. White, yellowish, or pink flowers are 2–3 inches wide and will bloom several times from spring until fall.

Culture These have been in the trade for many years, are reliably hardy to winter lows of 15° F, and are perfect for landscape use in USDA zones 8b–11. Plants can tolerate full sun even in hot summer cities of Palm Springs, Phoenix, and Tucson if they have been acclimated slowly. They are low-water-using once established and have a moderate growth rate, so be patient with them.

Identification *Thelocactus rinconensis* is readily distinguished from other species by the combination of blue-green body, elongated **tubercles**, relatively heavy erect **spines**, and white to pink flowers. *Thelocactus hexaedrophorus* has more rounded **tubercles** and spreading **spines**.

Landscape Application These make great landscape subjects when used in a smaller cactus and succulent garden. Plant multiples of them among a jumble of large rocks along with other cacti and succulents such as *Agave parrasana*, *Astrophytum capricorne*, and *Echinocereus stramineus*. Mix in smaller plants such as *Dalea capitata*, *Hibiscus martianus*, and *Zinnia acerosa*. These look great in decorative pots also.

Precautions Inspect the plants closely for mealybugs as they can hide between the **tubercles** while **spine mealies** will hang out on the spines themselves.

Thelocactus rinconensis

Trichocereus candicans

Synonym: *Echinopsis candicans*
Argentine Giant, White-flower Trichocereus
CLUSTERING CACTUS

Etymology John Gillies was an 18th Century Scottish surgeon turned botanist who described this species using the Latin *candi-* for the white flowers.

SIZE (H x W)	2–3 feet x 4–7 inches stem diameter, clusters to 4–6 feet wide
FLOWER COLOR	White
FLOWER SEASON	Spring to summer
EXPOSURE	Full sun, filtered sun
WATER	Drought tolerant to low
GROWTH RATE	Moderate
PRUNING	None
HARDINESS	20° F, zones 9a–11

Field Notes In November-December 2022, I went on a trip to Argentina and Chile led by tour guide extraordinaire, Guillermo Rivera. He assured me we would get to see plants of *Trichocereus candicans*, and he was true to his word. Our first day out we made a stop near the city of Capilla del Monte and saw these along with several other cacti I did not know, but now want to grow. These are mostly found growing in rocky soil in the mountains and hills of northern Argentina from about 3,000–6,000 feet elevation.

Description Plants tend to be more shrubby with upright to sprawling stems arising from near the base and spreading to form clusters 4–6 feet across. Individual stems are light to medium green about 4–7 inches in diameter

with 9–11 ribs harboring clusters of 10–12 brownish-yellow or gray 1½-inch-long **radial spines** and 1 or more 1–4-inch-long **central spines**. Large funnel-shaped flowers are white, fragrant, and up to 10 inches long by 7–8 inches across at the tip. Prime flowering time is late spring to early summer with flowers opening at night.

Culture Plants are hardy to at least 20° F and are reliable landscape plants in USDA zones 9a–11. Although plants will tolerate filtered sun and still produce their showy flowers, they are best grown in full sun to keep them dense and promote maximum flowering. They have a moderate growth rate and are low-water-using to drought tolerant once established, but will grow a little faster with supplemental water in summer, especially in the very hot southwestern U.S. cities of Palm Springs, Phoenix, Tucson, and Yuma. Soil should be kept dry in winter. These do not need any pruning.

Identification *Trichocereus candicans* is readily recognized by its sprawling stems and large white flowers. There are many hybrid *Trichocereus* cultivars with flower colors in various shades of red, pink, orange, and yellow.

Landscape Application These shrubby cacti should be placed so they can be seen from a patio where you would be sitting on a pleasant spring or early summer evening as the large showy flowers would begin to open. Plant with other cacti and succulents such as **Agave ocahui**, **Echinocactus grusonii**, **Euphorbia antisyphilitica**, **Fouquieria splendens**, **Opuntia macrocentra**, and **Yucca rostrata**. Use low-growing small shrubs and perennials such as *Calliandra eriophylla*, *Chrysactinia mexicana*, *Dalea frutescens*, *Glandularia gooddingii*, and *Zinnia acerosa*. Owing to their low growth and showy flowers these are a natural for street medians.

Precautions Young plants might be the target of hungry packrats, rabbits, or javelina, so be sure to protect them for the first couple years or even longer.

Trichocereus terscheckii

Synonym: *Echinopsis terscheckii*
Cardon Grande, Argentine Saguaro
COLUMNAR CACTUS

Etymology Frenchman Antoine Parmentier named this plant in honor of German gardener Carl Terscheck.

Field Notes I have yet to see these magnificent plants in their natural habitat and have put them on my bucket list. My friend Jan Emming is growing these at his Destination Forever Ranch in northwestern Arizona, so much of the information here is gathered from his blog and other sources having direct experience with them. These are native to northern Argentina and southern Bolivia from about 2,500–6,500 feet elevation.

SIZE (H x W)	25–30 feet x 1–1½ feet stem diameter, 4–6 feet wide
FLOWER COLOR	White
FLOWER SEASON	Mid-spring to mid-fall
EXPOSURE	Full sun, reflected heat
WATER	Drought tolerant to low
GROWTH RATE	Slow
PRUNING	None
HARDINESS	10° F, zones 8a–11

Description These have been dubbed the Argentine Saguaro because of their resemblance to the Sonoran Desert icon ***Carnegiea gigantea*** (Saguaro). *Trichocereus terscheckii* can grow quite large, reaching 25–30 feet or more tall by 4–6 feet or more wide with an individual stem diameter of 1–1½ feet. The plants are columnar and grow multiple stems as they age. Stems have 8–15 ribs and a bright green epidermis. There are 10–16 golden yellow **spines** measuring up to 4 inches long. White flowers are 6–8 inches long by about 6 inches across, open at night, and are usually visited by bats. Flowers can appear anytime from mid-spring until mid-fall.

Culture Plants are hardy to about 10° F and ideal for USDA zones 8a–11. They are best grown in full sun or reflected heat situations in the desert southwest. Plants are slow growing even with supplemental water in summer. They are drought tolerant once established, so do not water excessively, especially in winter. Because of the slow growth rate, start with large plants.

Identification Compared to *Carnegiea gigantea*, *Trichocereus terscheckii* is greener with golden yellow **spines**, tends to branch lower down, and has longer flowers that appear lower on the stem.

Landscape Application These can be used in much the same manner as *Carnegiea gigantea* in that they make spectacular focal points in a **xeriscape**. Use them singly or group several together if there is sufficient space. Plants fit nicely in any cactus and succulent garden or when mixed with a variety of medium-sized shrubs and perennials. Some companionable cacti and succulents include *Agave deserti*, *Echinocactus grusonii*, *Fouquieria splendens*, and *Yucca rostrata*. A few compatible shrubs and perennials include *Buddleja marrubiifolia, Eremophila hygrophana, Justicia californica, Leucophyllum candidum,* and *Simmondsia chinensis*. These are ideal for the wide-open spaces and desert landscapes around big buildings.

Precautions Protect young plants from packrats, rabbits, or javelina.

Yucca carnerosana

Synonym: *Yucca faxoniana*
Spanish Bayonet
TREE-LIKE SUCCULENT

SIZE (H x W)	6–12 feet x 4–5 feet
FLOWER COLOR	White
FLOWER SEASON	Spring to early summer
EXPOSURE	Full sun
WATER	Low to moderate
GROWTH RATE	Slow
PRUNING	None
HARDINESS	10° F, zones 8a–11

Etymology Susan McKelvey was an American botanist who named this species for its occurrence at Carneros Pass in Coahuila.

Field Notes It is always great to see the incredible stand of *Yucca carnerosana* while driving along Nuevo León Highway 58 east of San Roberto. When traveling south along Mexico Federal Highway 57 between Saltillo and Matehuala, you crest one particular low hill and a large valley opens before you. Look out over this valley to be greeted by a view of thousands of these plants standing watch over the terrain protecting their homeland. Plants are widespread in eastern Mexico and are found growing on bajadas, gentle to steep slopes, and rocky ridges in desert-scrub, grassland, and oak-juniper woodland from about 5,500–8,500 feet elevation.

Description This impressive arborescent species typically has a single trunk that is rarely branched and grows 6–12 feet tall with a leaf crown about 4–5 feet across. Stout dark green leaves are about 1–3 feet long and 2–3 inches

wide clothed with curling white marginal fibers along the edge and ending with a vicious terminal spine. Old dry leaves hang on the stem all the way to the ground and protect the trunk from sun and cold. The upright flower stalk is 3–6 feet tall with numerous 4-inch-long white flowers held completely above the leaf crown in spring and early summer.

Culture Plants are hardy to 10° F and are ideal for use in USDA zones 8a–11. They will tolerate full sun in all major cities throughout the desert southwest. These are low-water-using once established but will grow slightly faster and be less stressed when the root zone is soaked periodically from spring until fall. Plants grow well in rocky desert soil and do not need added amendments. They are slow growing and will require several years to begin towering over the other plants in your landscape.

Identification *Yucca carnerosana* has shorter narrower leaves, a taller **inflorescence**, and slightly narrower trunk compared to *Yucca faxoniana*.

Landscape Application *Yucca carnerosana* is used as a bold focal point in any low-water-use landscape and can be used as a solitary specimen or, if there is ample room, several can be grouped together to create a small forest. Choose companion plants with a variety of shapes, sizes, and flower colors to paint a picture with this yucca as a centerpiece. Add shrubs with blue-gray, gray, or whitish leaves such as *Buddleja marrubiifolia*, *Encelia farinosa*, or *Leucophyllum candidum* to contrast the green of the *Yucca* and those with a showy flower display such as *Anisacanthus quadrifidus*, *Dalea frutescens*, and *Tecoma stans*. Make it a complete landscape by using other succulents such as **Agave ovatifolia**, **Ferocactus pilosus**, and **Fouquieria splendens**.

Precautions Small plants ought to be protected from hungry animals for the first couple years. Spray with an insecticide if you see damage caused by running bugs.

Yucca elata
Soaptree Yucca
TREE-LIKE SUCCULENT

SIZE (H x W)	6–15 feet x 4–10 feet
FLOWER COLOR	White
FLOWER SEASON	Summer
EXPOSURE	Full sun
WATER	Low
GROWTH RATE	Slow
PRUNING	None
HARDINESS	0° F, zones 7a–11

Etymology German-born botanist George Engelmann named this species using the Latin *elat-* meaning high, a reference to the tall stem when compared to look-alike species with a short stem.

Field Notes *Yucca elata* plants grow naturally in the grasslands around my hometown of Tucson, and I have passed by so many that they go unnoticed until they are in full glorious bloom. These are easily spotted along Interstate 10 in southeastern Arizona and on the eastern side of the Whetstone Mountains near Kartchner Caverns. There is a particularly robust population along Interstate 10 between Deming and Lordsburg in southern New Mexico. The species is widespread in the southwestern U.S. and parts of adjacent Mexico and are found on flats, plains, and hills from about 1,500–6,000 feet elevation.

Description The striking form adds dramatic flair to any low-water-use landscape in the desert southwest. Full grown plants are tree-like reaching 6–15 feet tall with one main trunk when young but multiple trunks on older plants. They can have 1–5 short branches with a spread of 4–10 feet. Narrowly **linear** grayish-green to yellow-green leaves are 1–2 feet long and about ½-inch-wide with a white margin that peels off into thin curly fibers. Old dry leaves are persistent for many years resulting in a characteristic "shaggy" appearance that protects the trunk from sun and cold. The upright **inflorescence** appears in summer and is 3–15 feet tall with many 2–3-inch-long white flowers held high above the leaves.

Culture Plants can survive 0° F with no damage and are ideal for use in USDA zones 7a–11. They can be grown in full sun in all major cities throughout the desert southwest. Once established, they are low-water-using, but will benefit from having the root zone thoroughly soaked infrequently from spring until fall. They grow well in rocky desert soil and do not need added amendments. These are slow growing so look for plants in large containers that will rise above shrubs and perennials in your landscape.

Identification *Yucca elata* has narrow leaves with fibers along the margin while *Yucca linearifolia* plants lack marginal fibers.

Landscape Application Use these singly as an accent or group several together if the space allows. Mix with a variety of other plants including cacti, succulents, perennials, and shrubs. Compatible cacti and succulents could include *Agave palmeri*, *Echinocereus engelmannii*, *Ferocactus wislizeni*, and *Fouquieria splendens*, while some good shrubs and trees would be *Acacia constricta, Anisacanthus thurberi, Calliandra eriophylla, Parkinsonia microphylla,* and *Viguiera stenoloba*.

Precautions Leaves of young plants might be taste tested by desert animals or chewed off and taken away for nest building, so screen the plants until they get some height to them.

Yucca elata

Yucca filifera
Palma China
TREE-LIKE SUCCULENT

Etymology Benjamin Chabaud was a French botanist who used the Latin *filum-* for thread and the Latin *fer-* for carrying to denote the threads along the leaf margins.

SIZE (H x W)	10–20 feet x 3–15 feet
FLOWER COLOR	White
FLOWER SEASON	Spring
EXPOSURE	Full sun, filtered sun
WATER	Low to moderate
GROWTH RATE	Slow
PRUNING	None
HARDINESS	5° F, zones 7b–11

Field Notes In September 1986, Ron Gass and I set up camp on a dirt road leading to the town of Miquihuana in southern Tamaulipas. We awoke in the morning to these plants towering over our tents after having kept watch through the night. Immense stands of these can be seen along Mexico Highway 57 in central Nuevo León. Plants inhabit Chihuahuan Desert scrub, grassland, thorn-scrub, and pinyon-oak-juniper vegetation in central and eastern Mexico. They grow in deeper soils derived from limestone and various volcanic soils from about 1,400–7,900 feet elevation.

Description Full grown plants are massive and have a single trunk that flares at the base to 6 feet across. In habitat, some of the largest plants can grow 30–40 feet tall with a spread of 15–25 feet. However, in cultivation one could expect a size of 10–20 feet tall with a canopy 3–15 feet across. Very stiff dark green leaves are 1–2 feet long, about 1-inch-wide, have a dark brown margin with curling fibers, and a stout terminal **spine**. The 5–6-foot-long flower stalk is pendant and filled with showy white flowers in spring.

Culture Plants can withstand winter low temperatures to at least 5° F and are considered hardy in USDA zones 7b–11. They grow well in full sun or reflected heat even in the hot summer cities of Palm Springs, Phoenix, and Yuma. These are low- to moderate-water users needing supplemental water in the heat of summer. They grow well in rocky desert soil and do not need added amendments. They are slow growing and will require several years to begin towering over the other plants in your landscape.

Identification Yucca filifera has pendant **inflorescences** that separate it from Yucca decipiens with its upright **inflorescences**.

Landscape Application These may be hard to come by in the nursery trade, but if you can find a source for them, use the plants as a centerpiece in any low-water-use landscape. Plants grow large enough that they can be used to tower above a landscape filled with native or near-native desert shrubs and perennials. Some suggestions would include shrubs such as Acacia angustissima, Buddleja marrubiifolia, Dalea bicolor, and Leucophyllum candidum. Add cacti and other succulents such as **Agave gentryi** and **Echinocactus platyacanthus**.

Precautions Small or newly planted plants might need protection from hungry bunnies. Treat for **running bugs** if damage is spotted on the leaves.

Yucca filifera

Yucca linearifolia
Linear-leaf Yucca
TREE-LIKE SUCCULENT

Etymology Karen Clary is an American botanist who named this plant using the Latin *linear-* meaning line and the Latin *folius-* meaning leaf to emphasize the very narrow leaves.

SIZE (H x W)	6–10 feet x 3–10 feet
FLOWER COLOR	White
FLOWER SEASON	Spring
EXPOSURE	Full sun, filtered sun
WATER	Low to moderate
GROWTH RATE	Slow
PRUNING	None
HARDINESS	10° F, zones 8a–11

Field Notes While driving along the bumpy dirt road from Galeana to Rayones with Carl and Wade of YuccaDo Nursery fame, we spotted a few of these plants in a small side canyon just off the road. Fellow plant nerd, Scott Calhoun and I drove along another bumpy dirt road in Nuevo León and spotted more plants off in a distant valley. I have seen another population growing on a north-facing hillside east of General Cepeda. Plants are found in shady slot canyons, broad open valleys, and open north facing slopes in Coahuila and Nuevo León from about 2,600–6,500 feet elevation.

Description Young plants have a single unbranched trunk 6–10 feet tall and a rosette of leaves about 3–4 feet across, while ancient ones can have 2–4 branches and an overall crown diameter of up to 8–10 feet. Narrowly **linear** green or grayish-green leaves are about 1–2 feet long by ⅛-inch-wide and can shimmer in a breeze. The 2–4-foot-tall flower stalk has many 2-inch-wide creamy-white flowers in late spring.

Culture The San Marcos Growers website indicates plants are hardy to 12° F, so these should be hardy in USDA zones 8a–11. Plants will tolerate full sun in mild summer cities of the southwest, but filtered sun is best when grown in the hot summer cities of Palm Springs, Phoenix, and Tucson. Plants grow well in rocky desert soil, and are low- to moderate-water-using once established, but will respond to periodic supplemental water from spring until fall. They are slow growing and will require several years to begin towering over the other plants in your landscape.

Identification *Yucca linearifolia* can be difficult to distinguish from *Yucca queretaroensis*. However, *Yucca linearifolia* leaves are slightly flatter and with a shorter terminal spine.

Landscape Application *Yucca linearifolia* is a new plant to the nursery industry, so if you can find them, amass several for use in your low-water-use landscape. Mature plants are tall enough that they can be used as a show piece surrounded by native or near-native desert shrubs and perennials. Some great companion plants would be *Anisacanthus quadrifidus*, *Buddleja marrubiifolia*, *Dalea frutescens*, *Galphimia glauca*, *Glandularia gooddingii*, and *Viguiera stenoloba*. Mix in cacti and other succulents like **Agave ovatifolia**, **Echinocereus enneacanthus**, and **Echinocactus platyacanthus**.

Precautions Protect young plants from hungry bunnies, javelina, and possibly deer. Treat for **running bugs** if damage is spotted on leaves.

Yucca linearifolia

Yucca rigida
Blue Yucca
TREE-LIKE SUCCULENT

Etymology German-born, American-trained botanist George Engelmann used the Latin *rigid-* for the stiff leaves.

Field Notes My good friend Ron Gass and I saw these spectacular plants in September 1986 while driving from Torreón to Cuatrociénegas in central Coahuila. We camped out in the vast Bolsón de Mapimí and awoke to these outstanding plants poking their powder blue leaves above thick stands of *Larrea divaricata*. In July 2009, my friend Scott Calhoun and I were returning to Tucson from Oaxaca, Mexico and stopped at an enormous stand of these marvelous plants along Mexico Federal Highway 49 north of the Zacatecas-Durango border. Plants grow on flats and slopes, in northcentral Mexico from about 1,200–5,900 feet.

SIZE (H x W)	6–15 feet x 4–8 feet
FLOWER COLOR	White
FLOWER SEASON	Late spring
EXPOSURE	Full sun, reflected heat
WATER	Drought tolerant to low
GROWTH RATE	Moderate
PRUNING	None or remove old flower stalks
HARDINESS	10° F, zones 8a–11

Description Plants have a single trunk with 3–7 (or more) branches and grow to 6–15 feet tall with a spread of 4–8 feet. Rigid powder-blue leaves have a thin yellow border, are about 2–3 feet long by 1-inch-wide, have a very sharp tip, and should be given a wide berth in the landscape. Old leaves hang on and protect the trunk from sun and cold. The 3–5-foot flower stalk has white 3-inch flowers in late spring.

Culture Plants can tolerate winter low temperatures to at least 10° F and are considered hardy in USDA zones 8a–11. They grow well in full sun or reflected heat even in the hot summer cities of Palm Springs, Phoenix, and Yuma. These are drought tolerant once established and grow fine in most desert soils if supplemental watering is adjusted accordingly. They have a moderate growth rate but still need several years to get large, so look for plants in larger containers.

Identification With its wider and stiffer leaves, *Yucca rigida* is easily separated from *Yucca rostrata* with narrower and more flexible leaves.

Landscape Application Large plants make a bold statement in any low-water-use landscape especially when planted among native or near-native desert shrubs and perennials. Ideal companion plants include shrubs and perennials like *Acacia angustissima*, *Buddleja marrubiifolia*, *Encelia farinosa*, *Eremophila hygrophana*, and *Glandularia gooddingii*. Round out your landscape by adding cacti and other succulents such as *Echinocereus enneacanthus*, *Echinocactus grusonii*, and *Fouquieria splendens*. These do well in tough situations like street sides and medians, just keep away from high traffic areas because of the sharp tipped leaves.

Precautions Mature well-established plants are bullet-proof, but young ones should be protected from deer, rabbits, javelina, and packrats.

Yucca rostrata
Beaked Yucca
TREE-LIKE SUCCULENT

SIZE (H x W)	5–12 feet x 3–6 feet
FLOWER COLOR	White
FLOWER SEASON	Late spring to summer
EXPOSURE	Full sun, reflected heat
WATER	Drought tolerant to low
GROWTH RATE	Moderate
PRUNING	None or remove old flower stalks
HARDINESS	5° F, zones 7b–11

Etymology German-born botanist George Engelmann used the Latin *rostr-*, meaning beak, to describe the long beak on the fruit.

Field Notes Ron Gass and I saw these while driving up the old cobblestone road on the Mamulique **micro-ondas** hill in central Nuevo León. More recently Jeff Chemnick, Brian Kemble, Walker Young, and I were looking for cool cacti along Mexico Federal Highway 30 south of Cuatrociénegas and stopped to look at these plants standing head and shoulders above the surrounding shrubs. *Yucca rostrata* is found in the Big Bend region of Texas, south and east into Coahuila and Nuevo León. Plants grow on rocky limestone hills, slopes, and bajadas from about 1,000–4,600 feet elevation.

Description Plants have a single trunk and are unbranched when young, but sometimes older ones develop 2–5 branches near the top. Individual plants will grow to 5–12 feet tall, and spread 3–6 feet across. Thin flexible powder-blue leaves are narrowly linear, about 24 inches long and ½-inch-wide with a narrow yellow margin. The flower stalk is 3–5 feet tall, filled with white 2–3-inch-wide flowers, and appears in late spring and early summer.

Culture These are care-free plants that tolerate winter low temperatures to the 5–10° F range and are hardy in USDA zones 7b–11. They grow well in full sun or reflected heat even in the hot summer cities of Palm Springs, Phoenix, and Tucson. They are drought tolerant to low-water-using once established but will benefit from occasional supplemental water in the heat of summer. They grow well in most desert soil types if the supplemental watering is adjusted for the speed at which excess water drains. They are slow growing, so start with large plants for an immediate impact. Only prune off the old flower stalks.

Identification *Yucca rostrata* has narrower more flexible leaves that can be described as user-friendly, which sets it apart from the stiffer leaved **Yucca rigida**. *Yucca rostrata* is a taller plant with fewer branches and longer leaves than **Yucca thompsoniana**.

Landscape Application Group several of these to serve as a dramatic centerpiece in a low-water-use landscape surrounded by several native or near-native desert shrubs and perennials. Ideal companion plants include shrubs and perennials like *Anisacanthus quadrifidus*, *Chrysactinia mexicana*, *Encelia farinosa*, and *Leucophyllum candidum*. Add cacti and other succulents such as **Agave gentryi**, **Echinocactus ingens**, **Echinocereus stramineus**, **Ferocactus pilosus**, and **Hesperaloe funifera**.

Precautions Protect newly planted specimens from rabbits, javelina, and deer until they are established.

Yucca rostrata

Yucca schottii

Sometimes placed with *Yucca madrensis*
Hoary Yucca, Schott's Yucca
TREE-LIKE SUCCULENT

SIZE (H x W)	6–12 feet x 3–5 feet
FLOWER COLOR	White
FLOWER SEASON	Summer
EXPOSURE	Partial shade, full sun
WATER	Low to moderate
GROWTH RATE	Slow
PRUNING	None
HARDINESS	0° F, zones 7a–11

Etymology Arthur Schott first collected material that botanist George Engelmann used when naming this plant in Schott's honor. Sometimes included with Yucca madrensis, but the two are quite different.

Field Notes I am always looking for these plants whenever I travel to the mountains of southeastern Arizona. They are a favorite to see in the Huachuca Mountains while looking at the spectacular *Agave parryi* var. *huachucensis* plants that grow there. Plants grow on open grassy slopes or the shade of oaks and pines in southeastern Arizona, southwestern New Mexico, and northern Mexico from about 4,000–7,000 feet.

Description These yuccas have a single trunk that can grow to 6–12 feet tall with a leaf crown about 3–5 feet across. The single trunk may have one or two branches. Stout blue-green to dark green leaves are upright to spreading, straight to slightly curved, about 1½–3 feet long and 1–2½ inches wide, with a sharp terminal spine. Old dry leaves

Cool Cacti and Succulents for Hot Gardens

drape down over the stem protecting the trunk from sun and cold. The upright flower stalk is 1–3 feet tall, only half exposed above the leaves, and with numerous 1–2-inch-long white flowers. Flowering is mostly in summer.

Culture Plants are hardy to at least 0° F and are ideal for use in USDA zones 7a–11. They prefer partial shade in hot summer cities and full sun in cities with summer highs mostly below 100° F. They are low-water-using once established but those growing in full sun will need supplemental water applied periodically from spring until fall. Plants grow well in a soil with excellent drainage and some organic matter. They are slow growing and will require several years to begin towering over the other plants in your landscape.

Identification The leaves on *Yucca schottii* are slightly narrower and lighter green or blue-green than the darker green leaves of **Yucca carnerosana**.

Landscape Application *Yucca schottii* functions as a bold focal point in any low-water-use landscape and can be used as a solitary specimen or with several grouped together. They can be placed in full sun or on the north side of buildings where they will receive shade in the winter and sun in the summer. Add shrubs with blue-gray, gray, or whitish leaves such as *Encelia farinosa*, *Eremophila hygrophana*, or *Leucophyllum candidum* to contrast the green of the Yucca and those with showy flowers such as *Anisacanthus quadrifidus* and *Justicia californica*. Make it a complete landscape by using cacti and other succulents such as **Agave ovatifolia**, **Echinocereus stramineus**, and **Ferocactus pilosus**.

Precautions Protect small plants from hungry animals for the first couple years, and treat if you see damage caused by **running bugs**.

Yucca schottii

Yucca thompsoniana
Thompson's Yucca
TREE-LIKE SUCCULENT

SIZE (H x W)	5–8 feet x 4–8 feet
FLOWER COLOR	White
FLOWER SEASON	Late spring to summer
EXPOSURE	Full sun, reflected heat
WATER	Drought tolerant to low
GROWTH RATE	Slow
PRUNING	None or remove old flower stalks
HARDINESS	0° F, zones 7a–11

Etymology William Trelease named this species in honor of Charles Henry Thompson of the Missouri Botanical Garden.

Field Notes I have seen these in western Texas on state route 285 while driving through the limestone hills not far north of Sanderson. I have also seen plants in northern Coahuila as they start to grade into the taller single-trunked *Yucca rostrata* with their more flexible leaves. These plants are found in western Texas and adjacent northern Mexico growing on rocky limestone hills, slopes, and ridges in grasslands from about 2,000–4,400 feet elevation.

Description These plants have a short single trunk with few to many branches. They will grow to about 5–8 feet tall and spread 4–8 feet across. Stiff blue leaves are narrowly linear, about 6–12 inches long and ½-inch-wide, and have a distinctive thin yellow margin. The flower stalk is 5–6 feet tall rising high above the leaf crown and is covered with 3-inch-long by 3-inch-wide white bell-shaped flowers. Peak flowering time is in late spring and early summer.

Culture Plants are native to areas where winter lows drop to 10° F, but have survived 0° F and can be considered hardy in USDA zones 7a–11. Plants grow well in full sun and reflected

Cool Cacti and Succulents for Hot Gardens

heat even in the hot summer cities of Palm Springs, Phoenix, and Yuma. They are drought tolerant to low-water-using once established but will benefit from occasional supplemental water in the heat of summer. They are slow growing so look for large plants that will make an immediate impact in the landscape. No pruning is necessary except to remove old flower stalks.

Identification These have a single short trunk with several branches, shorter stiffer leaves, and a flower stalk held well above the leaf crown, while **Yucca rostrata** has longer more flexible leaves and a flower stalk that rises moderately above the leaf crown.

Landscape Application Use singly as a focal point or centerpiece in a low-water-use **xeriscape** amid a plethora of native or near-native desert shrubs and perennials. These spiky plants complement the softer forms of plants such as *Buddleja marrubiifolia*, *Chrysactinia mexicana*, *Dalea frutescens*, *Encelia farinosa*, *Eremophila hygrophana*, *Larrea divaricata*, *Leucophyllum candidum*, and *Viguiera stenoloba*. Round out your landscape by adding cacti and other succulents such as **Agave colorata**, **Echinocactus grusonii**, **Ferocactus pilosus**, and **Opuntia santa-rita**.

Precautions Protect newly planted specimens for the first couple years until they are established and left alone by voracious desert critters such as rabbits, packrats, javelina, or deer.

Yucca thompsoniana

Yucca treculeana
Trecul's Yucca
TREE-LIKE SUCCULENT

SIZE (H x W)	10–15 feet x 4–6 feet
FLOWER COLOR	White
FLOWER SEASON	Late spring to summer
EXPOSURE	Full sun, reflected heat
WATER	Drought tolerant to low
GROWTH RATE	Slow
PRUNING	None or remove old flower stalks
HARDINESS	15° F, zones 8b–11

Etymology Frenchman Élie-Abel Carrière honored fellow French botanist August A. Trécul with the naming of this species.

Field Notes In March 2015, I was in western Texas looking at wildflowers with Ron Gass and Dave Palzkill when we spotted flowering plants of *Yucca treculeana*. Plants are widespread from southern New Mexico through the southern half of Texas and into adjacent northern Mexico. They grow in a variety of soil types and are found on slopes, bajadas, valleys, and plains in Chihuahuan desert scrub, grasslands, oak savanna, and woodland from near sea level to 5,600 feet elevation.

Description Plants have either a single trunk or multiple trunks and each can be unbranched or sparingly branched. They can eventually grow to about 10–15 feet tall with the crown spreading to 4–6 feet across. Dark green, yellowish-green, or gray-green leaves are linear, about 8–48 inches long and 1–2 inches wide, with a brown margin typically without curly fibers. The flower stalk is 4–5 feet tall and partially contained within the leaf crown. Flowers are white, often tinged with reddish-purple, and measure about 3 inches wide. Peak flowering time is in late spring and early summer.

Cool Cacti and Succulents for Hot Gardens

Culture Plants are found in areas ranging from humid coastal habitats to arid deserts and hardiness probably varies with provenance but are generally hardy to 15° F and are safe to use in USDA zones 8b–11. They grow well in full sun and reflected heat even in the hot summer cities of Palm Springs, Phoenix, and Yuma. Plants are drought tolerant to low-water-using once established but will benefit from occasional supplemental water in the heat of summer. The growth rate is slow, so look for large plants that will make an immediate impact in the landscape. No pruning is necessary except to remove old flower stalks.

Identification *Yucca treculeana* has relatively smooth leaves that typically lack fibers along the margins while *Yucca torreyi* has scabrous leaves and prominent fibers along the margins.

Landscape Application These plants can be used singly as a focal point in a low-water-use landscape amid a plethora of native or near-native desert shrubs and perennials. Their spiky appearance complements the softer forms of shrubs such as *Buddleja marrubiifolia*, *Larrea divaricata*, *Leucophyllum candidum*, and *Viguiera stenoloba*. Round out your landscape by adding in some cacti and other succulents such as **Agave havardiana**, **Echinocactus grusonii**, **Ferocactus pilosus**, and **Opuntia macrocentra**.

Precautions Protect newly planted specimens for the first couple years until they are established. After establishment, they should be left alone by rabbits, packrats, javelina, or deer.

GLOSSARY

Accent Plant: Plant used as a focal point in the landscape.
Acuminate: Tapering gradually to a sharp tip, commonly used for leaf shape.
Areole: Region on a cactus that bears spines or flowers.
Ascending: Sloping or leading upward.
Cactus: Any plant belonging to the family of Cactaceae. Compare to **succulent**.
Caliche: Hardened layer of calcium carbonate like cement that is impervious to water and roots. It occurs worldwide in arid and semiarid regions.
Caudex: Stem of a plant, but in the cactus and succulent world, the term is generally used for a trunk that is squat and abnormally thickened.
Central spine(s): The inner **spine(s)** in a **spine** cluster.
Cephalia(um): Section of a cactus with flowers. This area is not capable of photosynthesis. Compare to **pseudocephalium**.
Cladistics: A system of classification based on presumed phylogenetic relationships.
Cochineal scale: Soft bodied insect that feeds on *Opuntia*; juveniles secrete the white waxy substance over their bodies for protection.
Crenate: Having large rounded teeth along the leaf edge.
Cuneate: Wedge-shaped triangular and tapering to a point at the base.
Deciduous: Refers to leaves that fall from the plant usually in winter or in times of drought.
Decumbent: Reclining on the ground with the tips turned up.
Dioecious: Male and female flowers are on separate plants.
Elliptic: In the shape of an ellipse, about 1½ times longer than wide and rounded at both ends.
Etiolated: When deprived of sufficient light, plants become pale, and growth stretches abnormally.

Fasciculate: Arranged in a tight bundle or clustered tightly together.
Fissure: A natural split, crack, groove, or narrow opening which makes the tubercle look wrinkled.
Glaucous: Covered with a whitish or bluish coating that is frequently composed of wax.
Glochids: A barbed hair or bristle, mostly seen on species of *Opuntia*.
Inflorescence: Grouping of flowers.
Keeled: A narrow ridge usually associated with the sharp bottom of a boat.
Lanceolate: Frequently used to describe leaves that are rounded at the base with a long taper to the tip.
Leaflet: The ultimate division of a compound leaf.
Linear: Leaf shape that is long and narrow with parallel sides.
Linear-lanceolate: Leaf shape that overall is narrow and the same width from the base to the middle or above and then tapering to the tip.
Mammillate: Describes a leaf margin with breast-shaped or nipple-like protrusions.
Mealybug: An insect that pierces into the plant and feeds on juices, they will secrete a powdery wax layer for protection.
Micro-ondas: Microwave towers in Mexico used for broadcasting and radar.
Monophyletic: A group of organisms (plants or animals) derived from a common ancestor.
Oblanceolate: The reverse of **lanceolate**, with the narrowed end at the base and expanding to a rounded tip.
Obovate: The reverse of **ovate**, with the narrowed end closer to the base.
Odd pinnate: A leaf that has an odd number of leaflets.
Offset: A young plant produced at the end of a **rhizome** or **stolon**.
Offsetting: Producing offsets.
Orbicular: Approximately circular in outline.
Ovate: Egg shaped in outline.
Panicle: A compound **inflorescence** in which the main axis is branched, and the side branches are composed of loose flower clusters.
Pinnate: A compound leaf with **leaflets** arranged along a central axis like a bird's feather.
Prickle: Sharp projections derived from the epidermis; for example, rose prickles. Compare to **spines** and **thorns**.
Prostrate: Lying flat on the ground or trailing on the ground.
Pseudocephalium: Section of a cactus where flowers originate. This section is still capable of photosynthesis. Compare to **cephalium**.
Raceme: An **inflorescence** where the flowers are attached to the main axis with a **pedicel**.

Radial spine(s): Outer **spines** in a **spine** cluster.
Rhizome: An underground horizontal stem that can produce a new plant.
Rosette: A circular cluster, usually leaves or flower petals.
Running bug: An insect called *Agaveocoris barberi* (formerly *Caulotops barberi*) that pierces the leaves and sucks out juices resulting in stipling on the leaves.
Serrate: Leaf margins with small teeth resembling those seen on a saw.
Serrulate: Diminutive of **serrate**, leaf margins with very fine teeth.
Spatulate: Leaf blade that is elongate and rounded at the apex with a long taper to the base.
Spider mite: Tiny arachnids with piercing mouth parts allowing them to feed on plants by sucking out juices. Usually noticeable by webbing produced.
Spike: An **inflorescence** where the flowers are attached directly to the main axis without a pedicel.
Spike-like: Term used for an *Agave* **inflorescence** with flowers attached to the stalk by a short pedicels, technically a **raceme**. Compare to **panicle**.
Spine: Modified leaf or leaf parts; *Acacia* spines are modified leaf stipules.
Spine mealies: Egg cases of mealybugs attached to cactus spines.
Stolon: A stem that grows along the ground and produces new roots.
Succulent: A loosely defined category generally used for plants that have some type of succulence whether in the leaves, roots, or trunks. Cacti are succulents, but not all succulents are cacti.
Teats: Fleshy protuberances under the teeth on leaf margins of *Agave*.
Teeth: Spine-like projections along leaf margins of *Agave* and *Aloe*.
Tepal(s): Term used when sepals and petals are similar and indistinguishable from each other, or when sepals grade into petals.
Trichome(s): A small hair or other outgrowth from the plant epidermis.
Tubercle: An enlarged modified leaf base manifesting as a protuberance on the body of a cactus.
Xeriscape: Low-water-use landscape using drought tolerant plants.

PLANT DATABASE

Reference Table

This table provides a summary of each species in this book, organized by category and name. Plants that cross multiple categories are listed for each category.

Size	Name	🐦	🐝	🦇	Water Use	Page #
Small Cactus	Ariocarpus fissuratus	●	●		●	66
	Ariocarpus retusus	●	●		●	68
	Ariocarpus trigonus		●		●	70
	Astrophytum asterias		●		●	72
	Astrophytum capricorne		●		●	74
	Astrophytum coahuilense		●		●	76
	Astrophytum myriostigma		●		●	78
	Astrophytum ornatum		●		●	80
	Coryphantha poselgeriana	●	●		●	110
	Echinocereus dasyacanthus	●	●		●	138
	Echinocereus reichenbachii	●	●		●	152
	Echinocereus viridiflorus var. canus		●		●	158
	Escobaria vivipara	●	●		●	162
	Gymnocalycium monvillei	●	●		●●	216
	Gymnocalycium spegazzinii	●	●		●●	218

Plant Database   337

Size	Name	🐦	🐝	🦇	Water Use	Page #
Small Cactus	Leuchtenbergia principis		●		●	228
	Mammillaria candida		●		●●	232
	Mammillaria chionocephala		●		●●	234
	Mammillaria grahamii	●	●		●	238
	Mammillaria grusonii		●		●	240
	Mammillaria heyderi		●		●	242
	Mammillaria mystax	●	●		●	244
	Neolloydia conoidea	●	●		●●	254
	Stenocactus multicostatus		●		●	284
	Thelocactus bicolor	●	●		●	294
	Thelocactus buekii	●	●		●	296
	Thelocactus conothelos	●	●		●	298
	Thelocactus conothelos subsp. argenteus	●	●		●	300
	Thelocactus heterochromus	●	●		●	302
	Thelocactus hexaedrophorus		●		●	304
	Thelocactus macdowellii	●	●		●	306
	Thelocactus rinconensis		●		●	308
Clustering Cactus	Coryphantha erecta		●		●●	106
	Coryphantha macromeris	●	●		●	108
	Coryphantha recurvata		●		●	112
	Echinocereus bonkerae	●	●		●	136
	Echinocereus engelmannii	●	●		●	140
	Echinocereus enneacanthus	●	●		●	142
	Echinocereus fasciculatus	●	●		●	144
	Echinocereus nicholii	●	●		●	146
	Echinocereus parkeri	●	●		●	148
	Echinocereus pentalophus	●	●		●●	150
	Echinocereus stramineus	●	●		●	154
	Echinocereus viereckii	●	●		●	156

Cool Cacti and Succulents for Hot Gardens

Size	Name	🐦	🐝	🦇	Water Use	Page #
Clustering Cactus	*Ferocactus robustus*		●		●	196
	Grusonia bradtiana		●		●	214
	Mammillaria geminispina		●		●●	236
	Mammillaria grahamii	●	●		●	238
	Mammillaria petterssonii		●		●●	246
	Mammillaria rhodantha	●	●		●●	248
	Mammillaria standleyi	●	●		●	250
	Parodia leninghausii		●		●●	276
	Stenocactus multicostatus		●		●	284
	Thelocactus bicolor	●	●		●	294
Sprawling Cactus	*Echinocereus pentalophus*	●	●		●●	150
	Echinocereus viereckii	●	●		●	156
	Grusonia bradtiana		●		●	214
	Stenocereus eruca		●		●	288
	Trichocereus candicans		●	●	●	310
Small Barrel-like Cactus	*Denmoza rhodacantha*	●	●		●	126
	Echinocactus horizonthalonius	●	●		●	130
	Echinocactus parryi	●	●		●	132
	Ferocactus fordii	●	●		●●	180
	Ferocactus glaucescens		●		●	182
	Ferocactus latispinus	●	●		●●	190
Barrel Cactus	*Denmoza rhodacantha*	●	●		●●	126
	Echinocactus grusonii		●		●	128
	Echinocactus platyacanthus		●		●	134
	Ferocactus acanthodes		●		●	174
	Ferocactus chrysacanthus		●		●	176
	Ferocactus emoryi	●	●		●	178
	Ferocactus gracilis	●	●		●	184
	Ferocactus hamatacanthus		●		●	186

Plant Database

Size	Name	🐦	🐝	🦇	Water Use	Page #
Barrel Cactus	Ferocactus histrix		●		●	188
	Ferocactus latispinus	●	●		●●	190
	Ferocactus pilosus	●	●		●	192
	Ferocactus rectispinus	●	●		●	194
	Ferocactus wislizeni	●	●		●	198
Shrub-like Cactus	Corryocactus erectus	●	●		●●	104
	Opuntia basilaris	●	●		●	262
	Opuntia engelmannii		●		●	264
	Opuntia macrocentra	●	●		●	266
	Opuntia santa-rita		●		●	268
	Oreocereus celsianus	●	●		●●	270
	Oreocereus trollii	●	●		●●	272
	Stenocereus alamosensis	●	●		●●	286
Short Columnar Cactus	Astrophytum ornatum		●		●	80
Columnar Cactus	Carnegiea gigantea	●	●	●	●	96
	Cephalocereus senilis		●		●●	98
	Cleistocactus hyalacanthus	●			●●	100
	Cleistocactus strausii	●			●●	102
	Corryocactus erectus	●	●		●●	104
	Espostoa blossfeldiorum			●	●	164
	Espostoa lanata		●		●	166
	Espostoa melanostele		●		●	168
	Lophocereus schottii		●		●	230
	Myrtillocactus geometrzans		●		●	252
	Stenocereus marginatus	●	●		●	290
	Stenocereus thurberi		●	●	●	292
	Trichocereus terscheckii		●	●	●	312
Cactus	Peniocereus greggii		●		●	280
	Peniocereus striatus		●		●●	282

Cool Cacti and Succulents for Hot Gardens

Size	Name	🐦	🐝	🦇	Water Use	Page #
Succulent Rosette	Agave bovicornuta	●	●		●●	22
	Agave bracteosa		●		●●	24
	Agave cerulata	●	●		●	26
	Agave colorata	●	●		●	28
	Agave deserti	●	●		●	30
	Agave geminiflora	●	●		●●	32
	Agave gentryi	●	●		●●	34
	Agave nickelsiae		●		●	36
	Agave ocahui		●		●	38
	Agave ovatifolia	●	●		●●	40
	Agave palmeri	●	●	●	●●	42
	Agave parrasana	●	●		●●	44
	Agave parryi	●	●		●●	46
	Agave schidigera	●	●		●●	48
	Agave striata	●	●		●●	50
	Agave victoriae-reginae	●	●		●●	52
	Aloe comosa	●	●		●●	54
	Aloe ferox	●	●		●●	56
	Aloe marlothii	●	●		●●	58
	Aloe striata	●	●		●●	60
	Aloe variegata	●	●		●●	64
	Dasylirion acrotrichum		●		●●	114
	Dasylirion gentryi		●		●●	116
	Dasylirion leiophyllum		●		●●	118
	Dasylirion miquihuanense		●		●●	120
	Dasylirion quadrangultum		●		●●	122
	Dasylirion wheeleri		●		●●	124
Succulent	Hesperaloe campanulata	●	●	●	●	220
	Hesperaloe funifera		●	●	●	222
	Hesperaloe parviflora	●	●		●	224
	Pedilanthus macrocarpus	●			●	278

Plant Database **341**

Size	Name	🐦	🐝	🦇	Water Use	Page #
Shrub-like Succulent	Aloe striatula		●	●	●●	62
	Beaucarnea gracilis			●	●●	82
	Beaucarnea recurvata			●	●●	84
	Bulbine frutescens			●	●●	86
	Bursera fagaroides			●	●	88
	Bursera hindsiana			●	●	90
	Bursera microphylla			●	●	92
	Calibanus hookeri			●	●●	94
	Erythrina flabelliformis	●			●	160
	Euphorbia antisyphilitica			●	●	170
	Euphorbia resinifera			●	●	172
	Fouquieria diguetii	●		●	●	202
	Fouquieria fasciculata			●	●	204
	Fouquieria macdougalii	●		●	●	206
	Fouquieria purpusii			●	●	208
	Fouquieria shrevei			●	●	210
	Fouquieria splendens	●		●	●	212
	Jatropha dioica			●	●	226
	Nolina microcarpa			●	●●	258
	Pachycormus discolor			●	●	274
	Pedilanthus macrocarpus	●			●	278
Tree-like Succulent	Beaucarnea gracilis			●	●●	82
	Beaucarnea recurvata			●	●●	84
	Bursera fagaroides			●	●	88
	Bursera hindsiana			●	●	90
	Bursera microphylla			●	●	92
	Fouquieria diguetii	●		●	●	202
	Fouquieria fasciculata			●	●	204
	Fouquieria macdougalii	●		●	●	206
	Nolina matapensis			●	●●	256
	Nolina nelsonii			●	●●	260
	Pachycormus discolor			●	●	274

Size	Name	🐦	🐝	🦇	Water Use	Page #
Tree-like Succulent	Yucca carnerosana				●●	314
	Yucca elata				●	316
	Yucca filifera				●●	318
	Yucca linearifolia				●●	320
	Yucca rigida				●	322
	Yucca rostrata				●	324
	Yucca schottii				●●	326
	Yucca thompsoniana				●	328
	Yucca treculeana				●	330
Columnar Succulent	Fouquieria columnaris		●		●	200

Ferocactus acanthodes

Plant Index **343**

PLANT INDEX

By Common Name

Agave Cactus, 228
Arbol de Barril, 204
Argentine Giant, 310
Argentine Saguaro, 312
Baja Fire Barrel, 184
Baja Wax Agave, 26
Beaked Yucca, 324
Beargrass, 258
Beavertail Cactus, 262
Beehive Cactus, 162
Bell-flower Hesperaloe, 220
Bishop's Cap, 78
Black Lace Cactus, 152
Blossfeld's Espostoa, 164
Blue Barrel, 182
Blue Barrel Cactus, 130
Blue Candle Cactus, 252
Blue Yucca, 322
Blue-leaf Nolina, 260
Bonker's Hedgehog, 136
Boojum, 200
Brain Cactus, 284
Brushy-tip Green Desert Spoon, 114
Buek's Thelocactus, 296
Cabbage Head Agave, 44
California Barrel, 174
Candelilla, 170
Cardon Grande, 312
Chihuahuan Beehive, 254
Cirio, 200
Clanwilliam Aloe, 54
Coahuila Star Plant, 76
Compass Barrel, 198
Cone-like Thelocactus, 298
Copal, 90
Copal, 92
Coral Aloe, 60
Coral Bean, 160
Cow's Horn Agave, 22
Creeping Devil, 288
Dahlia-rooted Cactus, 282
Desert Agave, 30
Desert Spoon, 124
Durango Delight, 48
Eagle-claw Cactus, 130
Elephant Tree, 88
Elephant Tree, 92
Elephant Tree, 274
Emory's Barrel, 178
Engelmann's Hedgehog, 140
Engelmann's Prickly Pear, 264
Erect Coryphantha, 106
Espadin, 50
Fierce Aloe, 56
Fire Barrel, 174
Fire Barrel, 192
Fishhook Barrel, 198
Ford's Barrel, 180
Gentry's Agave, 34
Gentry's Desert Spoon, 116
Giant Barrel Cactus, 134

Giant Fishhook Barrel, 186
Giant Hesperaloe, 222
Glory of Texas, 294
Goat's Horn Cactus, 74
Golden Barrel, 128
Graham's Fishhook, 238
Graham's Pincushion, 238
Graybeard Cactus, 158
Green Spider Agave, 24
Gruson's Mammillaria, 240
Hardy Aloe, 62
Hedgehog Cactus, 144
Heyder's Pincushion, 242
Hoary Yucca, 326
King Ferdinand Agave, 36
Ladyfinger Cactus, 150
Leatherstem, 226
Lemon Ball Mammillaria, 248
Linear-leaf Yucca, 320
Living Rock, 66
Living Rock, 68
Living Rock, 70
Long-spine Barrel, 194
Long-spined Prickly Pear, 266
MacDowell's Thelocactus, 306
Maguey Verde, 34
Marloth's Aloe, 58
Mescal, 46
Mescal Ceniza, 28
Mexican Boulder Plant, 94
Mexican Fence Post, 290
Mexican Ponytail Palm, 82
Miquihuana Desert Spoon, 120
Monk's Hood, 80
Monville's Gymnocalycium, 216
Moroccan Mound, 172
Mounding Barrel, 196
Mountain Aloe, 58
Moustache Mammillaria, 244
Needle-leaf Agave, 50
Nichol's Hedgehog, 146
Nickels' Agave, 36
Nipple Beehive Cactus, 108
Nipple Cactus, 308
Ocahui, 38
Ocotillo, 212
Octopus Cactus, 286
Old Man Cactus, 98
Old Man of the Andes, 270
Old Man of the Andes, 272
Organ Pipe Cactus, 292
Organillo, 214
Palma China, 318
Palmer's Agave, 42
Palo Adán, 202
Parker's Hedgehog, 148
Parry's Agave, 46
Parry's Barrel Cactus, 132
Partridge Breast Aloe, 64
Peruvian Old Lady, 168
Peruvian Old Man, 166
Pettersson's Mammillaria, 246
Pitayita, 282
Ponytail Palm, 84
Porcupine Barrel, 188
Poselger's Coryphantha, 110
Purpus's Bottle Plant, 208
Queen Victoria Agave, 52
Queen of the Night, 280
Red Elephant Tree, 90
Red False Yucca, 224
Red Hesperaloe, 224
Red Hot Chili Poker Cactus, 104
Red-spine Denmoza, 126
Reichenbach's Hedgehog, 152
Sacahuista, 258
Sacamatraca, 282
Saguaro, 96
Sand Dollar Cactus, 72
Sangre de Drago, 226
Santa Cruz Beehive Cactus, 112
Santa Rita Prickly Pear, 268
Schott's Yucca, 326
Sea Urchin Cactus, 72
Senita, 230
Showy Thelocactus, 302
Shreve's Ocotillo, 210
Shrubby Bulbine, 86
Silver Torch Cactus, 100
Silver Torch Cactus, 102
Silver-spine Thelocactus, 300
Six-sided Nipple Cactus, 304
Slim-leaf Ponytail Palm, 82
Slipper Flower, 278
Smooth-leaf Desert Spoon, 118

Snowball Mammillaria, 232
Snowy-head Mammillaria, 234
Soaptree Yucca, 316
Sonoran Tree Beargrass, 256
Sotol, 118
Sotol, 124
Spanish Bayonet, 314
Spegazzini's Gymnocalycium, 218
Splinter Agave, 48
Squid Agave, 24
Standley's Mammillaria, 250
Star Cactus, 72
Star Cactus, 80
Strawberry Hedgehog, 142
Strawberry Hedgehog, 154
Striped-stemmed Aloe, 62
Texas Cone Cactus, 254
Texas Rainbow Cactus, 138
Thompson's Yucca, 328
Tiger Aloe, 64
Toothless Desert Spoon, 122
Torote, 88
Torote Blanco, 92
Torote Prieto, 90
Torote Verde, 206
Trecul's Yucca, 330
Twin-flower Agave, 32
Twin-spine Mammillaria, 236
Viejo, 98
Viejo, 214
Viereck's Hedgehog, 156
Whale's Tongue Agave, 40
White-flower Trichocereus, 310
Wide-spine Barrel, 190
Yellow Tower Cactus, 276
Yellow-spined Barrel, 176

By Botanical Name

Agave bovicornuta, 22
Agave bracteosa, 24
Agave cerulata, 26
Agave colorata, 28
Agave deserti, 30
Agave ferdinandi-regis, 36
Agave geminiflora, 32
Agave gentryi, 34
Agave nickelsiae, 36
Agave ocahui, 38
Agave ovatifolia, 40
Agave palmeri, 42
Agave parrasana, 44
Agave parryi, 46
Agave schidigera, 48
Agave striata, 50
Agave victoriae-reginae, 52
Aloe comosa, 54
Aloe ferox, 56
Aloe marlothii, 58
Aloe striata, 60
Aloe striatula, 62
Aloe variegata, 64
Aloiampelos striatula, 62
Ariocarpus fissuratus, 66
Ariocarpus retusus, 68
Ariocarpus trigonus, 70
Astrophytum asterias, 72
Astrophytum capricorne, 74
Astrophytum coahuilense, 76
Astrophytum myriostigma, 78
Astrophytum ornatum, 80
Beaucarnea gracilis, 82
Beaucarnea recurvata, 84
Bulbine frutescens, 86
Bursera fagaroides, 88
Bursera hindsiana, 90
Bursera microphylla, 92
Calibanus hookeri, 94
Carnegiea gigantea, 96

Cephalocereus senilis, 98
Cleistocactus hyalacanthus, 100
Cleistocactus strausii, 102
Corryocactus erectus, 104
Coryphantha erecta, 106
Coryphantha macromeris, 108
Coryphantha poselgeriana, 110
Coryphantha recurvata, 112
Dasylirion acrotrichum, 114
Dasylirion gentryi, 116
Dasylirion leiophyllum, 118
Dasylirion miquihuanense, 120
Dasylirion quadrangulatum, 122
Dasylirion wheeleri, 124
Denmoza rhodacantha, 126
Echinocactus grusonii, 128
Echinocactus horizonthalonius, 130
Echinocactus ingens, 134
Echinocactus parryi, 132
Echinocactus platyacanthus, 134
Echinocereus bonkerae, 136
Echinocereus dasyacanthus, 138
Echinocereus engelmannii, 140
Echinocereus enneacanthus, 142
Echinocereus fasciculatus, 144
Echinocereus nicholii, 146
Echinocereus parkeri, 148
Echinocereus pentalophus, 150
Echinocereus reichenbachii, 152
Echinocereus stramineus, 154
Echinocereus viereckii, 156
Echinocereus viridiflorus
    var. *canus*, 158
Echinofossulocactus
    multicostatus, 284
Echinopsis candicans, 310
Echinopsis terscheckii, 312
Erythrina flabelliformis, 160
Escobaria vivipara, 162
Espostoa blossfeldiorum, 164
Espostoa lanata, 166

Espostoa melanostele, 168
Euphorbia antisyphilitica, 170
Euphorbia lomelii, 278
Euphorbia resinifera, 172
Ferocactus acanthodes, 174
Ferocactus chrysacanthus, 176
Ferocactus cylindraceus, 174
Ferocactus emoryi, 178
Ferocactus fordii, 180
Ferocactus glaucescens, 182
Ferocactus gracilis, 184
Ferocactus hamatacanthus, 186
Ferocactus histrix, 188
Ferocactus latispinus, 190
Ferocactus pilosus, 192
Ferocactus rectispinus, 194
Ferocactus robustus, 196
Ferocactus wislizeni, 198
Fouquieria columnaris, 200
Fouquieria diguetii, 202
Fouquieria fasciculata, 204
Fouquieria macdougalii, 206
Fouquieria purpusii, 208
Fouquieria shrevei, 210
Fouquieria splendens, 212
Gonialoe variegata, 64
Grusonia bradtiana, 214
Gymnocalycium monvillei, 216
Gymnocalycium spegazzinii, 218
Hamatocactus hamatacanthus, 186
Hesperaloe campanulata, 220
Hesperaloe funifera, 222
Hesperaloe parviflora, 224
Idria columnaris, 200
Jatropha dioica, 226
Kroenleinia grusonii, 128
Lemaireocereus thurberi, 292
Leuchtenbergia principis, 228
Lophocereus schottii, 230
Mammillaria candida, 232
Mammillaria chionocephala, 234

Mammillaria geminispina, 236
Mammillaria grahamii, 238
Mammillaria grusonii, 240
Mammillaria heyderi, 242
Mammillaria mystax, 244
Mammillaria petterssonii, 246
Mammillaria rhodantha, 248
Mammillaria standleyi, 250
Myrtillocactus geometrizans, 252
Neolloydia conoidea, 254
Nolina matapensis, 256
Nolina microcarpa, 258
Nolina nelsonii, 260
Notocactus leninghausii, 276
Opuntia basilaris, 262
Opuntia engelmannii, 264
Opuntia macrocentra, 266
Opuntia santa-rita, 268
Oreocereus celsianus, 270
Oreocereus trollii, 272
Pachycereus marginatus, 290
Pachycormus discolor, 274
Parodia leninghausii, 276
Pedilanthus macrocarpus, 278
Peniocereus greggii, 280
Peniocereus striatus, 282
Stenocactus multicostatus, 284
Stenocereus alamosensis, 286
Stenocereus eruca, 288

Stenocereus marginatus, 290
Stenocereus thurberi, 292
Thelocactus bicolor, 294
Thelocactus bicolor subsp. *heterochromus*, 302
Thelocactus buekii, 296
Thelocactus conothelos, 298
Thelocactus conothelos subsp. *argenteus*, 300
Thelocactus heterochromus, 302
Thelocactus hexaedrophorus, 304
Thelocactus macdowellii, 306
Thelocactus rinconensis, 308
Thrixanthocereus blossfeldiorum, 164
Trichocereus candicans, 310
Trichocereus terscheckii, 312
Wilcoxia striata, 282
Yucca carnerosana, 314
Yucca elata, 316
Yucca faxoniana, 314
Yucca filifera, 318
Yucca linearifolia, 320
Yucca madrensis, 326
Yucca rigida, 322
Yucca rostrata, 324
Yucca schottii, 326
Yucca thompsoniana, 328
Yucca treculeana, 330

ACKNOWLEDGEMENTS

Putting together a book, even a revision of a previous book like this, is not a simple task and many people are needed to be thanked. First and foremost, I would like to acknowledge, thank, and recognize the two most important people in my life. My wife **Carol** who has selflessly given her love and supported my crazy notions, one of which has been this book, and my son **Brian** whose enthusiasm and steadiness has fostered, nurtured, and guided me through both Cool Plants books projects. He had to learn the intricacies of layout and design along the way while keeping me focused on the outcome.

There have been many people along the way who have fueled my interest in desert plants. I would like to acknowledge the following University of Arizona professors who all shared their passion for arid-lands plants, **Dr. Lemoyne Hogan**, **Warren Jones**, **Charles Sacamano**, **Dr. Charles Mason**, and **Dr. Tony Burgess**. A listing of influential plant people would not be complete without thanking **Dr. Richard Felger** for sharing his interest and passion for plants.

Many thanks to Mountain States Wholesale Nursery owner **Ron Gass** who took a leap of faith and ventured south of the border into the Chihuahuan Desert Region with this green neophyte. We saw a lot of very cool cacti and succulents that have since made their way into hot gardens throughout the desert southwest. There are many cactus and succulent fanatics who have been instrumental in promoting low-water-use plants for the desert southwest. Many thanks go out to **Scott Calhoun**, **Jeff Chemnick Tristan Davis**, **Tim Gregory**, **Brian Kemble**, and **Bob Webb** for braving the wilds of Mexico with me, and to **Rob Romero** for taking me along on many trips throughout Arizona. I have learned a lot from many members of the **Tucson Cactus and Succulent Society**. Editor extraordinaire **Tristan Davis** has been an important cog in the wheel of writing *Cool Cacti and Succulents for Hot Gardens*. Finally, I would be remiss in not thanking my mom, **Patti**, who helped me learn how to grow my very first Creeping Charlie.